COUNTDOWN TO WAR

Countdown to War

A Personal Memoir of Europe
1938–40

GEOFFREY COX

WILLIAM KIMBER · LONDON

First published in 1988 by
WILLIAM KIMBER & CO. LIMITED
100 Jermyn Street, London, SW1Y 6EE

© Geoffrey Cox, 1988

ISBN 0–7183–0674–0

Typeset by Grove Graphics, Tring
and printed and bound in Great Britain by
Mackays of Chatham PLC, Letchworth

3   5   7   9   10   8   6   4   2

For the Eight

Contents

List of Illustrations

Illustrations in the Text

CHAPTER ONE

Mission to a Faraway Country

Punctually at 11.15 on 3 August 1938, in the pale steamy sunshine of a Central European summer morning, the Paris–Prague express crossed the German frontier and drew into the Czechoslovak border station of Eger.

On the platform a group of customs and passport officers, German and Czech, moved towards the five cars which made up the train. In one of the first-class compartments a small, quiet man with thin grey hair, wearing a wide wing collar and a pale grey suit, glanced out at the platform, and then returned to his reading. Viscount Runciman of Doxford, millionaire British ship owner, personal friend of Mr Neville Chamberlain, had arrived in Czechoslovakia on his mission, to mediate between the Czechoslovak government and its Sudeten German minority.

In the dusty side street half a dozen Sudeten Germans pressed against the goods yard railings, staring at the train. There were no cheers, no marching throngs, no sign of the heiling battalions of Storm Troopers which the Neo-Nazi German Sudeten leader Konrad Henlein could have summoned at will. Clearly he and his followers had orders to lie low. Nor had any Czechoslovak ministers come to the border to meet Lord Runciman. Their official reception was to be in Prague – a clear sign that they had not sought, and did not welcome, this intrusion into their affairs. Only two burly Czech policemen in blue uniforms, with broad red stripes down their trouser legs, and trailing long scabbarded swords, took up their positions outside Lord Runciman's carriage window.

Frontier formalities did not take long. There were few tourists heading for Prague in this troubled summer. Passports were quickly stamped, a Czech detective nodded an all clear to the station-master, pulled a set of overalls over his tweed suit, clambered into the cab beside the engine driver, and the express departed on its final lap to the Czechoslovak capital.

11

Beyond Eger Sudetenland lay in all its beauty. Rolling hills covered with dark pines; corn fields, half cropped where cloud shadows followed one another over the gold of corn and the brown of stubble; red-roofed, white-walled villages; peasants cycling home to their midday meal. Beauty and peace. How far any crisis seemed from all this – and yet how near it was.

The Victoria Hotel, outside Eger Station, was Henlein's headquarters, from which was to be unleashed before the summer was out the insurrection in which eighty people were to be killed. Into these quiet villages by which the train passed tins marked as containing fruit, which were really camouflaged grenades, and cans marked as bicycle oil, which contained high explosive, were being stored under barn floors or in pits in the woods – as the Czech police were later to discover. Only twenty minutes' car drive to the north, in his flat in a suburb of Asch, right on the German border, Konrad Henlein awaited Hitler's next orders.

Now the train was approaching Marienbad, a favourite resort of Edward VII in those days early in the century when the rich and the great had gone to a spa each summer to starve themselves for a month, drink the medicinal waters, and prepare themselves for a further eleven months of ten-course meals. The other famed spa of these Bohemian mountains, Karlsbad, lay a little to the south. The Emperor Francis Joseph had gone there regularly. Amongst its pre-Great War guests had been a slim young Englishman named Neville Chamberlain, who had taken its waters as a cure for the gout which troubled him, and in this way paid his only visit to the faraway country of which we knew so little.

Trout streams wound through the pine and beech forests: in the hay fields peasants scythed and raked their second cut of the thick grass matted with wild flowers; children bathed in small lakes; beyond the carriage windows the Bohemian countryside steadily unrolled itself. Then suddenly we were in the outskirts of Pilzen, and Lord Runciman was over another frontier, the unseen one between Sudetenland and the truly Czech areas. Here were the hundred chimneys of the Skoda arms works, their smoke mingling with the rain clouds which had suddenly blown up, and Czech names only on the railway station, and peasant women, handkerchiefs on head, queueing at the booking office.

Prague was now only an hour away. Soon we were running

alongside the Moldau river, with thousands of brown-skinned bathers in the fields by its edge, waving to the train as it went by. Then the Hradschin Castle on the skyline, and at last the Wilson Station in Prague, named in that flush of post-war hopefulness after the American president who had been one of the main architects of this now threatened state.

On the platform waited representatives of the Czech Government, and the British Minister in Prague, Mr Basil Newton, in an Anthony Eden black Homburg hat. With him were two men, one middle-aged, stocky, with a black Hitler moustache, the other young, neat, fair. They were two of Henlein's chief lieutenants, and were presented to Lord Runciman by the British Minister.

That night Lord Runciman held a press conference – the only one he was ever to hold in Czechoslovakia. Into one end of the lounge of the Hotel Alcron, where the mission was staying, were jammed 300 Czech, German, British, American, French and Central European journalists. Cinema arc lights made the sweltering evening more infernal still. Lord Runciman, now in a black suit with a wing collar, looking like a Liberal front bencher from a Victorian sketch of the House of Commons, came quietly through the curtains and stood on a small dais. (It had been hastily moved from the other end of the room, where otherwise Lord Runciman would have been filmed against the bronze statue of a nude woman, her arms outstretched in supplication.) In a genial, low voice Runciman read a little speech. He said, 'I am the friend of all and the enemy of none. I have learned that permanent peace and tranquillity can be secured only on a basis of mutual consent. There is much to be said for the exercise of patience.'

It was generally agreed that the mission had made a good start. The Czech papers the next morning came out with welcoming headlines 'The Lord Arrives'. The French, availing themselves of the fortnight's annual holiday decreed by the Popular Front Government in 1936, swarmed in unprecedented numbers onto the Riviera beaches. The British people in their deckchairs by the seaside read optimistic messages in their newspapers. The *Observer*'s editor, the great J. L. Garvin, assured his readers that 'the nation is justified in packing up for the holidays with a free heart'. Neville Chamberlain departed to fish for salmon in Scotland and in Berlin Adolf Hitler finalised his plans, under the guise of manoeuvres for assembling one and a half million troops, and putting the nation on a war footing, by the end of August.

*

The Runciman mission was the first positive British move to try to cope with Hitler's drive to absorb into the Reich all neighbouring areas which had inhabitants of German race. Ever since he had attained power as German Chancellor in January 1933 Adolf Hitler had been engaged in overturning those clauses of the Treaty of Versailles which had been devised to clip the wings of the German Reich after World War I. The ban on conscription, and the limitation of the Reichswehr to 100,000 men had been the first to go. Controls on rearmament, and on the construction on an air force, had been the next to be disregarded. In 1935 Great Britain had condoned German naval rearmament in an Anglo-German Naval Agreement, in which Hitler agreed to keep the German fleet to one third of the size of Britain's. In 1936 came the reoccupation of the Rhineland, which had been declared a demilitarised zone not only at Versailles but in the Treaty of Locarno of 1925. Two years later, in March 1938, Hitler spread his power into an area into which not even the Kaiser's Germany had penetrated, when by the Anschluss he absorbed Austria into the Reich.

British policy in the face of those moves had been to protest – and to yield. A guilty feeling that the Treaty of Versailles had been too harsh on the Germans, coupled with a belief that the Nazi Reich was a bastion against Communist Russia, helped to shape this stance. But the main factor, particularly in the mind of Neville Chamberlain, who had become Prime Minister in 1937, was undoubtedly to avoid a renewal of the horrors of the war of 1914–18, to which had now been added the further danger of mass bombing from the air. But when, in the spring of 1938, Hitler, having absorbed Austria, turned his pressure onto Czechoslovakia, Neville Chamberlain realised that any further German expansion brought with it a very real risk of war. There were three million people of German stock within the boundaries of Czechoslovakia, mostly in the strategically important mountain ranges of Bohemia and Moravia. These Sudeten Germans, as they came to be called, had never been citizens of the Reich. Before Czechoslovakia came into being in 1919 they had been citizens of the Austro-Hungarian Empire. Some of them had long-held pan-Germanic views. Others

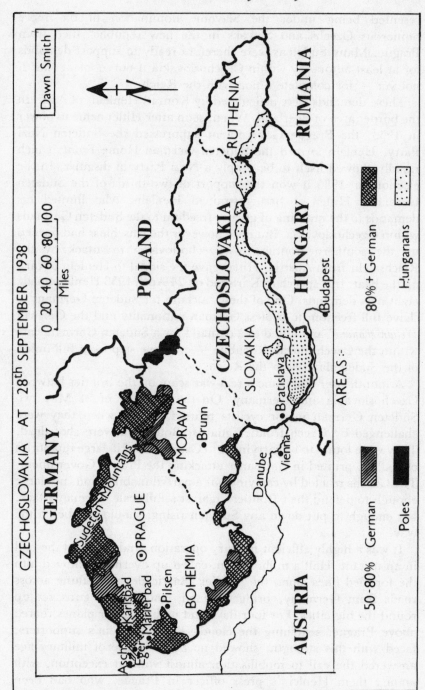

CZECHOSLOVAKIA AT 28th SEPTEMBER 1938

Dawn Smith

Miles
0 20 40 60 80 100

GERMANY

POLAND

RUTHENIA

RUMANIA

CZECHOSLOVAKIA

HUNGARY

Budapest

SLOVAKIA

Bratislava

Vienna

Danube

MORAVIA

Brunn

Sudeten Mountains

BOHEMIA

⊙PRAGUE

Pilsen

Karlsbad

MährePbad

Eger

Asch

AUSTRIA

AREAS:-

50-80% German

80%+ German

German

Poles

Hungarians

resented being under the Slavonic domination of the more
numerous Czechs and Slovaks in the new republic ruled from
Prague. Many Sudetens were therefore ready to support demands
for at least autonomy within Czechoslovakia if not – or at least if
not yet – for complete union with the Reich.

These demands were articulated by Konrad Henlein, of Asch, in
the border area of Egerland. When, soon after Hitler came to power
in 1933, the Prague Government suppressed the Sudeten Nazi
Party, Henlein formed the Sudeten German Home Front, which
rapidly showed itself to be simply a Nazi Party in disguise. In the
elections in 1935 it won the support of two-thirds of the Sudeten
Germans. Hitler at first restrained Henlein, who limited his
demands to the granting of greater freedom to the Sudeten Germans
within Czechoslovakia. But once however the Anschluss had opened
up the southern frontiers of Czechoslovakia to attack by the
Reichswehr from Austria, Hitler gave the signal to Henlein to turn
up the heat. In a speech in Karlsbad on 24 April 1938 Henlein made
eight new demands. One of these, a claim for Sudeten Germans to
'have full freedom to profess German nationality and the German
Weltanschauung' amounted to a demand for a Sudeten German state
within the Czechoslovak Republic – only one step from full union
of the Sudetenland with the Reich.

A month later had come a real war scare on the frontier between
Czechoslovakia and Germany. On the morning of 21 May two
Sudeten German motor cyclists refused to stop when they were
challenged by Czech frontier guards. Both men were shot dead.
They were found to be carrying into Czechoslovakia large quantities
of leaflets, printed in Germany, attacking the Prague Government.
The Czechs reacted by carrying out a partial mobilisation, not large
enough to defend their frontiers against a full-scale German attack,
but enough to put down any Sudeten rising, should one be on the
way.

It was a highly efficient military operation, and it lanced the boil
in an instant. Half a million men, called up overnight, moved into
the fortified lines along the frontier. Barricades were flung across
roads from Germany, bridges mined, anti-aircraft guns set up
round the big cities. For four days and nights fighter planes roared
above Prague, searching the cloudy skies. Henlein's supporters,
faced with this strength, showed no fight. Those of military age
answered the call to mobilisation almost without exception, with
among them Henlein's press officer in Prague, who had been

assuring the foreign press that in a day or two 'You see big things from us'. White stockings, that unofficial Nazi badge, disappeared overnight.

Hitler waited four days before issuing a further series of indignant denials that anything like a thrust into the Sudetenland had been contemplated. Henlein was told to re-open the negotiations with the Czech Government. He was rushed into Prague by night to meet the Czech premier, M Hodza, travelling in a fast car, with Czech motor- cycle police screening him from any over-patriotic Czechs along the route.

This May crisis alarmed Neville Chamberlain and his Foreign Secretary, Lord Halifax. They realised that it was no longer practicable just to turn a blind eye to German expansion. For the first time a country which was prepared to fight stood in Hitler's way. Though Britain had no treaty obligations to Czechoslovakia, the French did. And if France got drawn into a war over Czechoslovakia, then Britain would inevitably find herself drawn in too. Faced with this danger, the British Government fell back on a traditionally British device – that of a Committee of Inquiry. If an investigator, proclaimed as fair-minded and independent, went to Czechoslovakia, and decided that Henlein – and Hitler – had a case, at least for the autonomy of the Sudeten areas, then perhaps the Czech will to resist could be weakened, and public opinion in France and Germany could be prepared for a withdrawal of the direct French treaty guarantees – and the indirect British guarantee – of the present frontiers of Czechoslovakia.

The Chamberlain Government chose a spectacular background against which to deploy this plan – the visit of the new British monarch King George VI and Queen Elizabeth to Paris in July 1938. The visit was a brilliant success. For four days the streets of central Paris were submerged in a sea of bunting and Union Jacks. Huge crowds lined the boulevards to cry '*Vive le roi – vive la reine*', and went wild with delight when the royal couple broke with all precedent and appeared just before midnight on the balcony of their apartments in the Quai d'Orsay, to wave to the crowds below as they had done from the balcony of Buckingham Palace on their coronation a year before.

In the royal entourage had been the Foreign Secretary, Lord Halifax, who had arrived in the scarlet and gold uniform of a royal chamberlain, a bearskin helmet crooked under his arm. But he lost little time in exchanging these for the striped trousers and black jacket of the statesman and in settling down for discussions with the French Foreign Minister, the devious M Georges Bonnet. On the final day of the visit Bonnet summoned the press to his ornately gilded room in the Quai d'Orsay to announce that the French Government warmly welcomed the decision of the British Government to send Lord Runciman, a statesman with a high reputation for fairness, to Czechoslovakia. Runciman's role would be to investigate the Sudeten crisis, and to offer any appropriate mediation between the Sudeten Germans and the Prague Government. So was opened up the primrose path to Munich, to the agreement of 30 September 1938, which was to sacrifice Czechoslovakia to Germany in the hope of avoiding war – that war which was to come a year later.

CHAPTER TWO

Personal Journey

I travelled into Czechoslovakia on the same train as Lord Runciman, as a special correspondent of the London *Daily Express*, which was then at the peak of its influence as the daily newspaper with the largest circulation in the world. I had come to Europe from New Zealand six years earlier, as a Rhodes Scholar to Oriel College, Oxford. During my vacations I had set about learning as much as I could of this Europe which had been the setting for the events which had filled the newspapers and periodicals of my childhood and youth, the continent of the Great War, of the Bolshevik Revolution, and of the rise of dictators like Mussolini of Italy and Primo de Rivera of Spain, the place of the Great Slump and of Stalin's Five Year Plans.

In the summer of 1932 I had taken an Intourist trip through Russia, from Leningrad to Moscow and then down the Volga to Stalingrad, and across to the Ukraine. It had left me with some good impressions – the sense of fulfilment in the bearing of workers who had risen to manage great factories; hefty but eager young men and women athletes in a new sports stadium in Moscow; sun-tanned children, clad in red shorts, in a crèche amid pinewoods. Other impressions were less favourable – drunks lying inert in gutters along the drab, unkempt Nevsky Prospect in Leningrad; a mounted policeman breaking up a rioting queue outside a vodka shop; and in particular the massed crowds of peasants, many of them women and children, tearful and harassed, all carrying great bundles, fighting to board steamers on the Volga or trains in the Ukraine. Only later did I realise that we had witnessed the stampede of the peasantry from Stalin's man-made famine in the Ukraine. But there was no mistaking the meaning of another scene which we came upon suddenly – to the manifest embarrassment of our guides – in a dusty street in Kuybyshev on the Volga. A long column of peasants, great bearded men in bast shoes and bast leggings, were being marched off under the guard of troops with long, sword-type

19

bayonets on their rifles, and wearing peaked cloth caps with a red star on the front, exactly as had been depicted in the sketches of artists at the time of the Russian Civil War.

I carried away from the Soviet Union the belief that if – as many of the pundits of the day assured us – the future lay with communism, it was going also to be a future of harsh political authoritarianism which would bear hard on the empirical reformism that I had adopted from the pioneering background of New Zealand. I had also come up against something quite unexpected – the realisation that war might come again in my lifetime. Warnings of war, training for war, preparations for war had been everywhere apparent in Russia, under banners calling upon all citizens to be ready to defend the Soviet Union. This was in jarring contrast to the belief inculcated in us in our schools and universities that the League of Nations and the Kellogg Pact had meant that our generation could, for ever, say goodbye to all that.

Later that summer I saw something of Germany in the last few months of the Weimar Republic. I spent a month at Heidelberg, studying German, and came to know quite another aspect of those pre-Hitler days than that of the decadent Berlin which has become its hallmark, that Berlin of *Cabaret* and George Grosz and Brecht. Side by side with this was a Germany of the open air and of the cult of physical fitness, a country where lithe, sun-browned young men and women swam in the as yet unpolluted rivers, where hikers sang as they made their way in bands, a guitar player at the head, along paths through pine forests, where families crowded into new sports grounds built with the loans America had thrust on Germany in the twenties. This was a Germany tasting freedom. It was the knowledge that this freedom would be crushed under the Nazis which made me an unhesitating opponent of Hitler from the moment he became Chancellor in January 1933, before it was clear that he represented an even greater danger to freedom not only in Germany but throughout the world.

This stance, ironically, led me to gain a close acquaintance with the Third Reich. In 1934 a German Rhodes Scholar at Oxford, stung by an anti-Nazi talk I had given to a discussion club, challenged me to serve a period during my next vacation in the Arbeitsdienst, the Nazi Youth Labour Service. There, he claimed, I would discover the true nature of National Socialism. I took up the challenge, and spent three weeks in a Labour Camp outside

Hannover, wearing a khaki uniform, one of a squad drilling with spades instead of rifles, and working to drain marshland. We were told this was to provide land on which to grow more grain, but I suspect that a more likely use was for airfields from which to bomb London.

Another chance Nazi acquaintance, a school teacher from Nuremberg in England to improve his English, was equally shocked by my attitude. He was a sincere and long-time Nazi, typical of the many basically decent lower-middle class Germans who had turned to Hitler out of their fears of socialism and communism, and out of distaste for the decadence of Berlin. His family owned a bookshop on the main square in Nuremberg. He invited me to join them on seats they placed in the shop window, to watch the parade at the annual Nazi Party Rally. In the evening they would take me to hear Hitler address the Party faithful. The dais on which Hitler, flanked by the other main Nazi leaders, took the salute at a march past of the storm troopers and the SS, was only some fifty yards from the bookshop window. I found myself, as a result, with a front row seat at an occasion which found its way into the history books and – even more importantly for the later television years – into the film archives. For this was the Nuremberg Rally filmed by Leni Riefenstahl for her epic propaganda film *The Triumph of the Will*, a work which has been drawn on ever since by countless producers of documentaries about Nazism. Leni Riefenstahl was very much in evidence on that overcast September morning, a striking figure, in this most masculine of settings, in a cream-coloured suit and a close fitting hat. She stood with her camera crews at the side of the saluting stand, and on one occasion, when there was a pause in the parade, she appeared on the platform and took Hitler by the sleeve, drawing him to a point where she could get a better shot.

The old Market Square in Nuremberg, renamed only a few weeks earlier as the Adolf Hitler Platz, provided the type of historic setting beloved by Hitler and his propaganda chief, Dr Goebbels, for the opening parade of this week of marches and speeches. The reddish stone buildings, dating back to the fifteenth century, were draped with long red banners, each with a white circle within which was a huge black swastika. Other swastika flags and garlands and bunting hung above every shop and office. Only the front of Nuremberg's great church, the Frauenkirche, whose pinnacles, jagged shapes like stone pine trees, rose on either side towards the peak of its tall, triangular facade, was left unadorned.

Stands for dignitaries and for the press had been built around three sides of the square. The saluting base was in its centre: beside it a military band. As the bandmaster held up his gleaming, tas- selled staff, the drums rolled, and the band struck up one of the Nazi Party's many rousing marching tunes. From a side street, in ranks twelve abreast, came column upon column of SA men in their brown uniforms, and SS men in black, their boots crashing in unison on the pavement as they passed their leader.

The bookseller had binoculars, and through them I studied eagerly this man who was to play such a huge part in the lives – and deaths – of so many millions. I did not envisage him then as a mass murderer, or even as someone bound to make war on Britain, but chiefly as the most formidable embodiment of dictatorship, of a form of government which, in those days of the great Depression, might engulf us all, even in countries where democracy was so deeply rooted as in Britain. Dictatorship was by no means a dirty word everywhere in the Western world. Mussolini had been in power in Italy for over a decade. Kemal Attaturk was widely praised for having used authoritarian methods to bring his country into the modern world. Primo de Rivera had been dictator of Spain from 1923–30. Poland was under the absolutist rule of .Pilsudski, Portugal under that of Salazar, and Yugoslavia under that of King Alexander. Mussolini had many British admirers. Even Churchill had some good words to say of him. As late as October 1937 Churchill was to write in the *Evening Standard* of Mussolini's 'amazing qualities of courage, comprehension, self-control and perseverance'. Lloyd George was to say 'Hitler is one of the greatest men I have ever met'. D. H. Lawrence in *Kangaroo* had presented a picture of an Australian would-be dictator which had many sympathetic aspects. Written in 1922, it forecast a situation which, ten years later, seemed briefly to be a possibility, when a World War I veteran, Colonel Campbell, formed a para-military force, the New Guard, to oppose the left wing Labour Government of the New South Wales. Campbell had one brief moment of glory, when one of his sympathisers, an ADC on the Governor General's staff, galloped forward, sword raised, and slashed the ribbon across the newly built Sydney Bridge to prevent the Labour Prime Minister carrying out the opening ceremony.

In Britain itself Sir Oswald Mosley's British Union of Fascists was, literally and metaphorically, on the march. 'Hurrah for the Blackshirts' Lord Rothermere had proclaimed in the *Daily Mail*. Only a few weeks before I had come to Germany, Mosley's Black-shirts, at a mass rally at Olympia, had demonstrated a sickening brutality in dealing with hecklers and interrupters of a rally at which their leader had spoken. Even though the disruption of the speech had been clearly planned, chiefly by Communists, the violence shown by the black-uniformed stewards, women as well as men, had been so ugly and wanton that it was to do lasting damage to Fascism in Britain. No doubt, coming as I did from a young, new country, I tended to see these complex European issues too sharply in terms of black and white, not to make sufficient allowance for the durability of British parliamentary democracy. Yet right wing totalitarianism was a real threat to Britain at this time, particularly if Fascism and Nazism became dominant throughout the Continent, isolating Britain and so helping to impose at Westminster an authoritarian government which would be Fascist in everything but name, a black jacket and striped trousers Fascism, if not a Blackshirt one. That at any rate is how I saw events at that time, and why I studied these men on the platform at Nuremberg as the enemies of personal liberty not only in their own country, but everywhere.

Hitler wore the brown uniform of the SA, but with a well-cut jacket, a collar and tie, a Sam Browne belt, knee breeches and knee-high leather boots. The Iron Cross hung on his left breast pocket, and on his left sleeve was a swastika armband. But for this, and the high boots, his uniform could at first glance have been taken for that of a British army officer wearing a rather odd shade of khaki. He was hatless, and his dark hair was brushed down closely and sleekly, except for one long lock which tended to slip over his forehead.

Seen in close-up through the binoculars, Hitler looked very much as he was portrayed in the newspapers and magazines of the time – a tribute to the effectiveness of the still picture in those pre-television days. I scanned his face eagerly for signs of the mystical powers of leadership which had won him such a grip on the German people. But they were difficult to detect. His face revealed a strange blend of ordinariness and strength. The nose was somewhat more prominent, the moustache a shade larger – and to that degree less comic – and the chin more determined than I had expected. Perhaps it was the low forehead, sloping back abruptly, and the fleshy cheeks

which made it seem so ordinary, the kind of face one would not have
glanced at twice in a crowd.

Hitler's stamina was remarkable. For four hours he stood, with
only intermittent breaks, as the brown ranks of the SA and the black
ranks of the SS passed in front of him. As the chromium-plated
metal standard carried by each detachment came abreast of him,
Hitler would swing his right arm across his chest, then sweep it out
in the Nazi salute. At the same time his eyes would fix on the face
of the men in the ranks with an intent, concentrated stare. He would
then move his arm slowly to the right, following the standard,
through an arc of about fifteen degrees, and then cut it back
abruptly to his side, hooking his right thumb into his belt until the
next column approached. It was a skilfully designed movement,
military and precise, which enabled him to alternate two or three
minutes of saluting with a similar period of rest – without the rest
appearing as slack or untidy. Even though the parade was organised
to provide an occasional pause, the strength necessary for four hours
of such activity was considerable.

Hitler was flanked by the other main Nazi leaders, their brown
uniforms contrasting with the grey of Reichswehr generals and the
purple and black of two bishops, one of whom wore an Iron Cross
alongside the crucifix which dangled on a chain round his neck.
There was an unmistakable air of relaxation, almost of jollity,
amongst Goering and Goebbels and Himmler and the other Nazi
chieftains on the dais. And well there might be. For the Nazi Party
had not only survived, but emerged strengthened at the end of three
traumatic months, which had begun on 30 June with the slaughter
of Ernst Roehm, the commander of the Storm Troopers, and some
thousand of his senior officers and men. Roehm, a homosexual
thug, had been one of Hitler's earliest associates in the Nazi Party,
and he had stood at Hitler's side on this very spot a year earlier, as
his Brownshirt battalions had marched in pride past their leader at
the first Party Rally since Hitler had become Chancellor in January
1933. Now Roehm was dead, shot on Hitler's orders by an SS
execution squad. Ostensibly Roehm had been accused of preparing
a putsch, but in reality he had been sacrificed to placate the
Reichswehr, who resented and distrusted this alternative Brownshirt
army.

The killings had created a sensation abroad, stigmatising
National Socialism as a grisly creed which devoured its own leaders
even more speedily than Bolshevism had done in Russia. But within

Germany it brought Hitler a swift reward. On 1 August the aged President Hindenburg had died, and the Reichswehr commanders acquiesced in Hitler's demand that the posts of President and of Chancellor should be merged in the new post of Reichsführer. Endorsed by a plebiscite in mid-August, this change gave Hitler greater power than any previous leader of Germany, including the Kaiser, had possessed.

The full impact of these events was not clear to me that morning as I stared out from the bookseller's window. But the fact that the Nazi leaders were very pleased with themselves, and with the way events had turned out, was plain to see.

Goering, whose flesh seemed to slop over at every point within his brown shirt, was clearly in high good humour, exchanging jokes with the burly and bald-headed Julius Streicher, present in his dual capacity as party Gauleiter for Nuremberg and as editor of *Der Stürmer*, the party's virulently anti-Semitic journal. Goebbels, a small figure under a wide, flat cap with a swastika badge, his club foot disguised by long trousers – he was the only party leader not wearing jack boots – looked at first sight like a boy among adults. Only when one looked closely did one see that his sharp, wary expression was far from that of a youth. Even Himmler, his spectacles glittering in the sun, his black SS uniform standing out amongst the prevailing brown of the platform party, allowed himself an occasional smile.

Physically they were an ignoble lot, far from being the embodiment of the Master Race which they proclaimed Germany to be. Only Hess, erect and stern, like an overgrown boy scout in his brown shirt and black tie, had any physical presence, and that was marred by the deep-set, harsh fanaticism of his eyes under their heavy eyebrows. Even Baldur Schirach, leader of the Hitler Youth, was already running to fat within his calculatedly boyish uniform. Yet my bookseller host and his Nazi family and friends saw no such defects. To them these were demi-gods, the men who had protected Germany from Bolshevism and corruption by international Jewry. Any defects they might have were to be glossed away. Goering was to them a merry figure, a man who enjoyed life, to be admired now for his lustiness, '*Der Dicke*' – the Plump Fellow. Goebbels, I was assured, was a clever man, 'the kind the Führer needs to combat the many enemies threatening the Reich'. And when Hitler smiled patiently as Leni Riefenstahl posed him for yet one more shot, my hosts were almost in ecstasy at these signs of the humanity of this

Supreme Being, so understanding even with so many weighty con-
cerns on his mind.

That evening Hitler delivered his main speech of the rally, in the
vast new concrete exhibition hall on the outskirts of the city. We
were there early to secure a good place in the body of the hall. Once
again I had a better vantage point than that available to the foreign
press, for I was part of the audience in the midst of the Party
faithful, caught up in its reactions and its moods, not observing it
from a place set apart. Around me were the men and women from
whom National Socialism derived its basic support – peasants in
dark suits, clearly their Sunday best; shopkeepers; small
businessmen; clerks. Amongst them were many women. Behind the
platform a huge metal swastika was ringed with red paper flowers,
about the words '*Alles für Deutschland*' – All for Germany – painted
in blood red letters six feet high. The pillars along the walls bore the
swastikas, surmounted by the German eagle. High up in the wings
electricians were busy with batteries of arc lights. From the rostrum
in front of the platform a voice called, '*Achtung, achtung,* silence. We
are testing the loud speakers.'

Slowly the minutes passed. A man in front of me ate tomatoes
from a paper bag. A Storm Trooper walked up and down the aisle
spraying the sultry air with eau de cologne. Then a sudden blare of
trumpets, and everyone was on his feet. 'Yes, there he is, there.
Heil, heil.' Through the thicket of outstretched hands the dark head
of Hitler could be seen, as he made his way with his officers down
the central aisle, and took his place on the platform.

The trumpets sounded again. In the entrance stood a black-
uniformed standard bearer holding the 'Blood Flag', the banner
carried in the first, abortive Nazi putsch in 1923. It was borne
swiftly up the hall, in the glare of the arc lights. Behind came the
SA section standards, three abreast, sweeping up the central
gangway in a stream of gleaming metal, their storm trooper bearers
hidden by the tasselled swastika banners.

One of Dr Goebbels' most astute techniques then came into play.
Instead of the meeting launching immediately into vehement
political oratory, an orchestra played the prelude to Act II of
Lohengrin. It was mood music on a grand scale, preparing the
audience's mind for higher things and deeper thoughts, and at the
same time throwing a cloak of respectability and legitimacy in
advance over whatever outrageous assertions or claims Hitler might
make. Opponents of Nazism even argued that classical music of

this kind purged the audience of its better feelings, leaving its baser instincts open to exploitation by Hitler's oratory. Certainly an almost religious hush had spread over the whole vast audience by the time the prelude finished.

The mood then abruptly changed. Rudolf Hess, looking more than ever like a grown-up boy scout, strode to the rostrum, curtly declared the meeting open, and then cried, 'The Leader speaks.' In a tumult of cheering and heiling, Hitler's brown-uniformed figure took its place at the rostrum.

He spoke for an hour and a half. It was a speech aimed not for foreign consumption but at the German people, at emphasising that he now embodied Germany, that the Nazis had supreme power. His long, convoluted sentences, his addiction to high-sounding, abstract words and sudden bursts of slang were difficult for me to follow, so that I was not caught up in the emotions he roused. But the crowd clearly were. A mother in front of me turned to her teenage son, her eyes bright with tears. No one seemed to notice the stage management behind it all. As Hitler worked towards a climax the arc lights came on, one after another, until he rounded off his sentence, fist in air, in a blaze of purplish light. When he brought his fist down on the rostrum, and turned to his text again, every light would go out except one beside him, illuminating his face. At his feet crouched cameramen, and a film camera on a moving trolley moved up and down the aisle.

Whenever he made a deliberate pause, brushing back his thin, shining hair from his eyes, the crowd were on their feet shouting, '*Heil, heil.*' One woman broke into hysterics, and went on with a shrill '*Heil, heil*' after the others had ceased, until she was pulled down into her seat. The tense, straining, menacing voice continued. 'The world outlook of the German people, the whole character of the German race demands . . .'

The Führer finished amidst a tumult of cheering, clapping, heiling. The SS guards smiled with pride. Hess mounted the rostrum. His voice sounded deep and calm after Hitler's: 'The Party is Hitler. But Hitler is Germany. All for Germany means all for Hitler.' The band broke into '*Deutschland über Alles*' and then '*Die Fahne Hoch*'. Hitler stalked out through the cheering throngs, the standards followed in their gleaming stream, the crowd surged to the doorway. Outside it was raining. By a corrugated iron refreshment shelter a child was looking for a dropped handkerchief. The trams were crowded, and it was late in the night before I made my way to the railway station.

None of this shifted me from my belief that Hitler was both dangerous and evil, a view which had been literally further hammered into me late one night in a street in Berlin. I failed to salute the swastika banner of a platoon of Storm Troopers marching off the railway station to take the train for the Nuremberg festival. Confident of my status as a foreigner, I was showing my passport to the squad commander when others of the squad came up from behind and hit me on the head. I came to in the gutter a few minutes later, to see the squad continuing their march in the distance. I was not seriously hurt, with only a few cuts on the scalp, and a throbbing head. My wounds were cleaned and dressed in a nearby chemist's shop where I was taken by a man who assured me – whether with sincerity or sarcasm – that I would understand such actions once Mosley won power in Britain.

My Arbeitsdienst experiences brought me the unexpected bonus of an entry into journalism. I emerged from my time in the labour camp to find that I had the answer to a question which was being investigated at the time by the foreign press corps in Berlin. Were these labour camps, as the Nazis claimed, a way of rehabilitating the unemployed youth and giving a sense of service, or were they a form of disguised military service? The answer was that they were a bit of both. Since I could provide first-hand information, the *New York Times* invited me to write an article on the camp. They made it the cover story in their Sunday magazine. The weekly *Spectator* in London took a similar piece from me. They printed it in the same issue as carried an attack by their art correspondent, one Anthony Blunt, on Salvador Dali's work as 'psycho-sexual exposition, not art'. Armed with my cuttings of these articles I was able, in the spring of 1935, to secure a toehold in Fleet Street. The Liberal *News Chronicle* gave me a trial as a reporter 'on space', as a freelance. This meant that I was paid only for such of the stories as I got into the paper.

In time I won my way onto the regular reporting staff, at first in the far from glamorous role of late-night reporter, sprinting off to cover fires and crimes in the small hours. But it gave me an invaluable apprenticeship in covering hard news, and brought me a footing within Fleet Street at a time when newspapers occupied the centre of the media stage in the way in which television does today.

Eighteen months after I had joined the *News Chronicle*, the Spanish Civil War offered me a lucky break. In October 1936 Franco's forces were advancing on Madrid in a seemingly unstoppable fashion. The *News Chronicle* was an ardent opponent of the Franco regime. There seemed every chance that any *Chronicle* reporter who was in Madrid when the city fell would be arrested or held in detention – as indeed six months later Arthur Koestler, the *News Chronicle* correspondent in Malaga, was jailed when that city fell. The paper was reluctant to have one of its stars, like Vernon Bartlett or Philip Jordan, wasted in this way, so the editor, Gerald Barry, looked around the newsroom for someone more expendable, and his eyes fell on me. 'Sorry, Geoffrey, but you are for it' were the words with which the news editor told me to set off for Madrid.

I went with avidity, not only because it was a big story, but because I was passionately on the side of the Republicans. Not only was Franco an ally of Hitler and Mussolini, both now flexing their muscles in the face of what seemed the inert and frightened democracies, a Spanish dictator who had to be opposed if we were to prevent authoritarianism spreading to Britain, but there was also the prospect of a better and freer life which had opened up before the Spanish people. After the first rising of the Generals had been thwarted in Madrid and Barcelona, there emerged the hope of a new order in which the peasants could own their lands, in which schools and hospitals and freedom might be open to all. The egalitarianism in which I had been steeped since childhood in New Zealand led me perhaps to over simplify the issues, and to read too much into those early, exhilarating days of the summer and autumn of 1936 in Spain, the time which André Malraux wrote of as the Days of Hope. But I shared fully Malraux's view, expressed in the final passage of his book *Man's Hope*, that the Spanish people were hearing in those months 'the voice of that which is more inspiring even than the blood of men, more enigmatic even than their presence on earth – the infinite possibilities of their own destiny'.[1]

The immediate problems facing me in Madrid were, however, more practical. Early in November as Franco's troops reached the outskirts of the city the Republican Government fled to Valencia. Most of the foreign press went with them. I stayed, and found myself one of only two Fleet Street newspapermen in the capital. And Madrid did not fall. Instead of finding myself expelled or in prison, I found my reports leading the front page of the paper day

1 Random House, 1938. Translated by Stuart Gilbert and Alastair Macdonald.

after day, particularly when Franco turned his German and Italian bombers against the city in a foretaste of the raids which the civilian populace in every European city dreaded – and about which they wished eagerly to read.

When I went back to London in December, after the first Franco offensive had ground to a halt, I had assumed it would be for a short spell of leave before I returned to Spain again. But this was not to be. The other senior correspondents on the *News Chronicle* now claimed their share of this major story. I would have to wait my turn in the queue. In the meanwhile, in the chastening way of Fleet Street, I found myself chasing late fires once again.

To offset my frustration I wrote a short book about that first battle for Madrid. Victor Gollancz published it in the spring of 1937 – books came out speedily in those days. It sold well, and attracted the attention of Arthur Christiansen, then at the peak of his fame as editor of Lord Beaverbrook's *Daily Express*. He offered me the post of *Express* correspondent in Vienna. This was one of the plum journalistic jobs of the time, for the whole of Central Europe and the Balkans was your bailiwick.

I was reluctant to leave the *News Chronicle*, not only because I was broadly in agreement with its political stance, and in particular with its staunch opposition to Fascism, but also because it offered its journalists a remarkable degree of editorial freedom. Having selected its correspondents, it trusted them, and printed their stories unchanged. The maverick Conservatism of Beaverbrook's *Daily Express* was much less to my taste, and there was always the fear that you might find yourself being called upon to dance to the tune of its subtle and powerful proprietor. But the attractions of a senior post as a foreign correspondent were strong, and the money was good. That loomed a larger factor now, for in 1935 I had married Cecily Turner, a student at Oxford with me, and our first child was due in the autumn. So I took the gamble, and in June 1937 set off for Vienna.

Austria was a country which I had come to know in my Oxford days, having spent the long summer vacation there in 1933. At that time it had been a blend of the vestiges of Habsburg grandeur; of a widely praised Viennese municipal socialism, which had given the city modern flats and crèches and schools and sports stadia; and of the Catholic Nationalism of Chancellor Dollfuss. But since then the Socialists had been hunted from power in Vienna, and the workers' flats shelled by artillery to dislodge the Socialist militia which had resisted the change. In turn Dollfuss had been murdered by the Nazis. Now the tall, arid figure of Chancellor Kurt Schuschnigg ruled over a state grey and drab with unemployment, whose people waited with either hope or fear – depending upon whether they were Nazis or not – for the day when Adolf Hitler would move to take Austria, his original homeland, into the Reich.

That merger, the Anschluss of Austria and Germany, did not come during my time as Vienna correspondent of the *Daily Express*. I had been there only six months, just enough time to begin to get to know the marvellously varied and fascinating lands which I had to cover, and to settle into a flat in Vienna, where our son Peter was born in September 1937, when Christiansen moved me to Paris. It was promotion, for Paris was the most senior *Express* post in Europe, but I went sadly, not only because I liked Vienna but because I wanted to be on the spot when Hitler began the thrust eastwards which was clearly his next move.

I did, however, manage to persuade Christiansen to let me go back to Austria to cover what, at the time in March 1938, was seen merely as a plebiscite being held by Schuschnigg to confirm the stand he was taking for the independence of Austria against Nazi pressure.

Many leading American correspondents were on the train from Paris on the night of 11 March, among them John Whitaker of the *Chicago Daily News* and the famed H. R. Knickerbocker, of the Hearst Press. There was also a young reporter from the *New York Herald Tribune,* Walter Kerr, with whom I was to share many assignments in the next few years, and who was to become one of my closest friends. It was a moment to savour as I sat with them round a table in the *wagon-lit* dining car late into the night, as the pundits swapped reminiscences, and argued about the future of Europe.

We woke the next morning, in the brilliant light reflected from the snow-covered mountainsides, to astonishing news. Hitler had denounced the plebiscite, and was moving his troops into Austria. In the train corridor I was approached by a small, well-dressed, extremely agitated Austrian Jew, appalled at finding himself returning into the jaws of the avowed enemies of his race. Was it true, he asked me, that the great H. R. Knickerbocker was on the train? When I told him this was so, relief spread over his face. 'With the foreign press here they won't dare to do anything wrong, will they? Will they?' he kept asking. 'We will be all right with you there.'

It was an impressive reminder of the power which the press possessed in those days – or had possessed. I wished I could have shared in his confidence, even if there was more wishfulness than real hope in his words. But I knew in my bones that we were a very fragile defence indeed against the forces even then being released upon the people of Austria.

In Innsbruck Kerr and I hired a car and set off up the road towards the German border. In the hall of the hotel, the Jew who had spoken to me on the train, his face grey with fear, was frantically trying to get through on the telephone to Switzerland, whilst in the corner the radio blared out the cheers of the crowds waiting in Linz for Hitler's arrival.

It was a brilliantly clear morning, and the snow, still heavy on the mountainsides, lay in streaks across the black earth of the fields. The road wound alongside the River Inn. At one bend a peasant boy in *Lederhosen*, a tiny swastika flag in his hand, rushed to the roadside shouting, 'The German Army is coming: the German Army is coming.' We had just time to pull on to the road edge as, round the corner, came a dozen or so steel-helmeted motor cyclists, rifles slung on their backs. Behind them came a line of swiftly moving, camouflage-bedaubed military trucks filled with grey-green uniformed troops, sitting bolt upright, rifles between their knees. In some trucks a heavy machine-gun barrel pointed skywards; others hauled anti-tank guns, their barrels covered with canvas. Then came the sound of drums, and a long column of infantry marching three abreast, following along behind a regimental band. Then came a line of staff cars, some with skis piled on top.

It was a thrilling, chilling sight. Here in the bright spring sunshine were the machines of war rolling across frontiers, like the first falling rocks and shifting earth of a great landslide which could engulf us all. That morning, on that chilly mountain road, I was sure not only that war would come, but had already made its own remorseless beginning.

Scene after scene was etched into my mind as the day wore on. As the Reichswehr columns approached Innsbruck, from a side road a yellow sports car appeared and halted. A bronzed woman in an expensive coat jumped out, and flung her arms round the neck of the nearest German officer. At the Brenner Pass a German

Hitler taking the salute at Nuremberg parade, 1934.

Nazi leaders at the Nuremberg Rally, 1934. Fr[ont] row, right to left — Streiche[r,] Hitler, Hess, Lutze (Chief [of] the Storm Troopers) and Himmler.

Members of German You[th] Labour Corps in the camp [in] which the author served.

mechanised army unit and a straggling column of Austrian Nazi Storm Troops in white shirts, black trousers and swastika armbands halted a few yards from the Italian frontier post. A Reichswehr colonel, clicking the heels of his shiny, high leather boots together, saluted the Austrian customs official and assured him of the 'comradely feelings of the Germans'. The late afternoon sun glowed on the snowy slopes of the Dolomites as the swastika flag was raised on the Austrian customs post. In fields near Kitzbuhel children ploughed knee deep through snow to pick up yellow leaflets scattered from German planes, welcoming Austria into the Reich. The road behind was jammed with horse-drawn field kitchens, and horse-drawn machine guns. And in the streets of Innsbruck, as the foremost German units marched into the town, I found myself standing next to a grey-haired Jewish woman tremblingly holding out her hand in the Hitler salute whilst the crowd roared out the Horst Wessel Nazi hymn, the words of which she tried with her mouth but clearly did not know.

I got as far as Strasbourg by midnight, and got a bed in an hotel which had Reichswehr sentries on the door, and the names of twenty-seven German officers, among them a major-general, in the register. By midday on Sunday I was back in Vienna making my way through streets where units of the Reichswehr rumbled through, not halting, but moving on towards the Czech and Hungarian frontiers.

That evening the press were summoned to the Federal Chancellery, where we were informed that the new Austrian Chancellor, the Nazi lawyer Seyss-Inquart, and his cabinet had declared that Austria had become a state of the German Reich. A monocled official, Dr Mazar, read the announcement to us in a room just down the corridor from that in which Chancellor Dollfuss had been shot dead by the Nazis three and a half years before. Through the windows came the shouts of the crowds, cheering the Reichswehr as they drove along the Ringstrasse.

The next day ecstatic crowds lined the streets to see Adolf Hitler drive in triumph into the city which had rejected him as a failed artist and casual labourer twenty-five years earlier. A huge crowd packed the space in front of the Imperial Hotel. When Hitler appeared on the balcony, a triumphant, smiling figure in the same type of brown shirt uniform he had worn at Nuremberg, every arm went out in salute. I raised my own with them. To have done anything else would have been suicide, for no passport, no claim to be a foreigner could have stood against the hysteria which filled the air.

All around me the chant of 'Sieg Heil! Sieg Heil!' rose like an insistent, gigantic drumbeat. Hitler's face flushed with pleasure as he looked down on this city where he had known failure, and which he now faced as Leader of a Reich more powerful than anything the Hohenzollerns or the Habsburgs had known. Despite the dangers which my mind told me lay ahead, I felt surge through me a sense of exhilaration at witnessing this moment when a page of history was being turned, however deadly the message written on it.

Already the mass arrests of Jews and Socialists and other opponents of Nazism had begun. In many streets Jews, old and young, men and women, herded by Storm Troopers with drawn truncheons, and surrounded by jeering crowds, were forced onto their hands and knees to scrub the Schuschnigg signs off walls and pavements. At SA barracks other Jews, including doctors and professors, were forced to clean out the latrines, in one case using for this the sacred prayer bands, the Tefellin, from a nearby synagogue.

Earlier that afternoon I had nearly been myself on the receiving end of attention from the local Nazis. The *Daily Express* office in Vienna was in a flat, which also served as the correspondent's home, in a small square, the Modenaplatz. I was standing by the window of the flat with Roland Bochow, a Reichs German from Berlin who had become the assistant correspondent of the *Express* in Vienna, when I saw a khaki-clad squad straggling across the grass of the square. At the front was a tall, gangling Storm Trooper in a brand new khaki uniform. Behind him came a dozen or so other Storm Troopers in a variety of garbs. Some had khaki shirts and black trousers; others khaki shirts and *Lederhosen*; others the white shirt, black trousers and swastika armband which was the most easily adopted version of a Nazi uniform. Their leader was trying to get them into some form of marching formation, but they looked a sorry lot. I taunted Bochow with the bearing of his new allies. 'You'll never get Austrian Nazis even to march in step,' I said – and then I paused, for I realised the squad were crossing the road towards the entrance to our block of flats.

A few minutes later we could hear the clang of heavy boots on the stairs, and the doorbell rang. Bochow said quickly, 'I will see to this.' I could hear voices raised when he opened the door, then argument, and suddenly Bochow's voice, in sharp Prussian tones, ordering them away. He came back into the room, aggressive, but also a little shaken. 'These Austrian fools,' he said. 'That bloody janitor who looks after this building has been up to tricks. He had denounced you as an enemy of Nazis and a friend of Jews, and persuaded the local SA to come round and teach you a lesson. They were going to wreck the flat and beat you up. I gave them a piece of my mind, I can tell you. And as for that bloody janitor, I will see he is out of his job before the week is over.' From the window, we watched the squad file dispiritedly away. They halted in the middle of the square, and gathered round, arguing. One man clearly wanted to return, and kept trying to get the others to follow him. But in the end they dispersed.

*

My journey back to Paris provided a strange postscript to this first Nazi conquest. On the train, on a hard wooden seat in an open plan third class carriage, was a girl in her late teens, manifestly British, with a swathe of blonde hair across her forehead, a delicate complexion, and cheeks which seemed to have still the fullness of adolescence. On her dress was pinned a swastika badge. I recognised her as Unity Mitford, friend and ardent admirer of Hitler, one of whose sisters had married Sir Oswald Mosley and another Esmond Romilly. She answered my questions angrily and disdainfully.

'I was heartbroken when I did not see Hitler when he arrived at his birthplace at Linz,' she said. 'Another English friend, who was with him there, said it was the most wonderful experience of his life. But I saw his entry into Vienna, and perhaps after all that was best. Afterwards I saw him for a few minutes in his hotel. He was tired, but seemed very moved by it all. I think it was wonderful.'

The other friend who had been with Hitler in Linz was G. Ward Price of the *Daily Mail*, the most prominent apologist in the British press for Hitler and Mussolini. At Linz he had stood on the balcony alongside Hitler, watching the Reichswehr march in, and had broadcast in English over the German radio, in their live transmission of the scene, his delight at it all.

With Austria in his grasp, Hitler was in a position to move against Czechoslovakia. When, therefore, in July 1938 Arthur Christiansen sent me to cover the Runciman mission I knew I would be reporting not only news but history.

CHAPTER THREE

A Republic at Bay

On his second day in Prague, 4 August, exactly twenty-four years since Great Britain had entered World War I, Lord Runciman put on a top hat and a morning coat, and went off in a heat wave, with temperatures of over 82° in the shade, to pay a series of formal calls on the leaders of the Czechoslovakian Government. As his car drove across the red sandstone Karlsbridge, with two police motor-cycle outriders in front, and mounted up through the winding, tree-shaded streets of old Prague, the scene was full of reminders of what was at stake for this young new republic.

The Hradschin Castle, with its sheer brownstone walls, and the high, pointed spires of St Vitus's Cathedral, which stood in its inner courtyard, had for three hundred years been the bastion from which the Germanic Habsburgs had ruled the Czechs. Along the road which wound downhill past the castle had come in 1620 the battle-stained but victorious Habsburg knights and their peasant levies who had overthrown the Czech nobles in the battle of the White Mountain, a pine-fringed tableland on the outskirts of modern Prague. It was a battle which brought to an end the ancient kingdom of Bohemia, which had been established a thousand years earlier by the Slavonic Czech tribes who had migrated here on their wild, shaggy ponies from the steppes of Central Asia. The good king Wenceslas of the carol had been amongst its early rulers, and his name was celebrated in the wide main boulevard of modern Prague. But Bohemian independence, like that of neighbouring Moravia, had been crushed at the White Mountain, and from 1620 until the First World War the Czechs were to remain under the Habsburg heel – or, as it appeared to the ordinary Czech, under the heel of the Habsburg German policeman, the German tax inspector, the German aristocrats whom the Habsburgs brought in, or promoted, to rule the Slav peasantry and the Slav workers. German was the official language, German the main tongue in the schools.

Then came World War I, and the winning of Czech and Slovak independence. One key element in the way independence was

36

gained could be seen by Lord Runciman in the uniforms of the sentries who presented arms as his car swept into the courtyard of the Prime Minister's residence. For they wore, not the somewhat greenish khaki of the modern Czechoslovak army, but the World War I uniforms of the French, Italian and Czarist Russian armies, Czechoslovak prisoners and deserters in that war had been grouped into foreign legions to fight against their former rulers. Pale blue of the French *poilu*, with a floppy, dark blue beret; grey green of Italy, with felt hat upturned at one side; khaki, and flat-topped forage cap of Imperial Russia; each of these uniforms appeared in the three companies of the Legionary unit which provided the castle guard.

These wartime legions provided a strong reinforcement to the claims made by Professor Thomas Masaryk at the Versailles Peace Conference for the setting up of an independent republic for the Czechs, and the Slovaks, and the Ruthenians who lived on the borders of the Ukraine. The Allied leaders agreed, and since the natural western frontier of such a state was formed by the great curve of the Sudeten Mountains, three and a half million Germans of Sudetenland were incorporated into it. It seemed logical enough at the time. The Sudeten Germans had never been part of Germany, but had always, as nation states emerged in Europe, been ruled from Vienna. Only now, with Hitler demanding to rule not only the Reich of the German Kaisers, but a new, greater Reich into which all of German race, whatever their present nationality, should be incorporated, had the presence of this non-Slav minority within the confines of the young new republic become an issue to trouble the Chancelleries of Europe.

Thomas Masaryk had been President of the Czechoslovak Republic from its inception until his death in December 1937 – his funeral in Prague had been one of the last stories I covered before moving to Paris. He had been succeeded by his close friend and collaborator, Edouard Benes, a quiet, scholarly man whose lack of ostentation, and stubbornness, and reasoned approach were characteristic of the Czech people. His prestige was great, and the Czechs gave him their absolute trust. Benes had been in his youth a good footballer, a fact I was careful to record for the *Daily Express* readers, in my efforts to arouse their interest in this distant land. He waited now to receive Lord Runciman in the high-ceilinged room, with its tall windows overlooking the long curve of the Moldau River, in which he was to endure not only one but two betrayals of his country – for he was again President when in 1949 the communists took over.

The Prime Minister, Dr Hodza, was a Slovak, the son of a wealthy peasant. Stocky, well dressed, precise, with pince-nez and a stubborn chin, he looked like a successful bank manager. Hodza had in pre-war days been a representative of the Slovak minority within the Hungarian Parliament, and had not that instinctive antagonism towards the formerly dominant Germans which welled up in the minds of most of the older generation of Czechs. He was in favour of compromise towards the Sudetens – if compromise rather than capitulation could be achieved.

The Foreign Minister, Dr Kamil Krofta, a white-haired, low-voiced man of sixty-five, was very much Benes's man. He had resigned his professorship of history at Prague University to join the government on Masryk's death. He worked in the Czernin Palace, formerly the home of the Czernin family, one of whose members, Count Czernin, had been Austrian Foreign Minister in World War I, and had signed the Treaty of Brest Litovsk with the Bolsheviks. Part of the building was now a barracks, and as Runciman's car approached it was halted by a column of troops swinging past, without rifles, roaring a Czech peasant song. Krofta was a kindly, genial, unostentatious man who could be seen in the mornings taking his dog for a walk in the park at the back of the Czernin Palace, prepared to wait his turn at the corner stall to buy a bag of fresh apricots or strawberries from the peasant woman who ran it.

Back in the Alcron Hotel that evening Lord Runciman met leaders of the Sudeten Germans. Henlein was not among them. Hitler had instructed him to play it tough with Runciman, so he was to insist – and prevail in his insistence – that Runciman must come to him in Sudetenland, not he to Runciman in what he saw as alien Prague. His lieutenants were men cast very much in the Nazi mould. For a brief period their names and their faces were to be in newspapers all over the world, until they slipped back into comparative obscurity once they had played the parts Hitler had allotted them. There was Ernst Kundt, the ex-front-line soldier, son of a washerwoman, whose pennies had gone to educate him before the war. Wearing a simple, ready-made suit and an old overcoat, his face was deeply lined, and he wore a dark Hitler moustache. His expression was cheerful, despite its aggressiveness. He was to win the confidence of the Runciman mission. 'Kundt is an honest man,' one of them said to me. When fighting had been started in the

Sudetenland, he alone of the Sudeten leaders did not flee from Prague. He was more of a sincere man with a grievance than a blind, fanatical supporter of Hitler.

Another distinct Nazi type was Sebekowesky, a smooth, astute young lawyer, a relatively new recruit to the Party, but rising rapidly in it, sincere no doubt in his beliefs, but also in the belief that this was the way to advancement. Their propaganda chief was Oscar Ulrich, bald-headed, with a gold tooth and pale horn-rimmed spectacles which gave him a bland, semi-oriental expression. He had been at one time a chinaware salesman in Britain.

The toughest of them all, Karl Hermann Franck, Henlein's deputy (and perhaps the real Nazi driving force behind Henlein's more genial facade) was also absent this first evening, though he was to join in the formal talks with Runciman. Tall, gaunt, stern faced, he had the air of the fanatic. He too was an ex-soldier, who had fought in the Austro-Hungarian army in the Great War. A misfit after the war, he had set up a small printing firm in Karlsbad, which just managed to keep itself from bankruptcy when Henlein set up his Sudeten German Party in 1933. Franck became one of his first supporters. From his printing works he did the Party's early printing. As the Party expanded, and the sales of its pamphlets, its books and its posters greatly increased, Franck began to flourish, and now drove about in a big black Mercedes Benz.

These Nazis were not, however, the only leaders of the Sudeten Germans. The Social Democrat Party still existed in the Sudetenland. Its leader was a young, slightly built, friendly lawyer, Wenzl Jaksch. I took to him immediately when we talked after his first meeting with Runciman. His thin, humorous face lit up with a smile as he explained that the meeting had not gone very well. 'Lord Runciman emphasised that we Social Democrats were only a small party compared to Henlein's. I agreed. I told him our problem is that we are a party of peace and freedom, ideals which are not very popular these days, so we don't compete very well with parties which don't believe in such things.'

Jaksch had an easy, laughing courage, moving freely about Prague despite frequent threats from the Henleinists. He managed to escape from Czechoslovakia in 1939, survived the war, and returned to become a post-war leader of the revived Social Democrats, only to lose his life in a car crash outside Bonn in 1948.

When this first hot, steamy week which the mission had spent in Prague came to an end, Lord Runciman, true to the habits of his caste, departed to the country for the weekend, having accepted an invitation to the stately home of one of the country's aristocrats. The trouble was that the only aristocrats in Czechoslovakia were those left over from the days of the Habsburgs, most of whom were of German race, so it was to the castle of the Germanic Count Kinsky near Brunn that this impartial British arbitrator set off for the first break in his duties.

*

Runciman's weekend off meant time off for the press as well. I was able to start learning something about the people of this land whose fate was to bring us to the brink of war, and who were now living through the last eight weeks they were to know as a truly free people, before being trapped in a bondage which, in its differing forms, has lasted until this day. In those weeks which I shared with them I found Prague an easy city to come to love: modern, garish Prague as well as the old and handsome Bohemian city.

Impressions crowded in on my mind – crowds packing the wide pavements of the Wenchelas Square on a Sunday, strolling slowly up and down in their Sunday best; material well being, with shop after shop packed with cheap silk stockings, cheap dresses and suits, cheap shoes – cheap and good; delicatessen shops by the score, where a midnight snack might consist of half a roast duck, a plate of Russian salad, and half a dozen cucumbers; constant noise from trams, and constant grime from the smuts of soft coal which fell everywhere, from factory chimneys and household chimneys alike; taxis driving at breakneck speed; Slovak peasant women in brilliant costume selling piles of embroidery from stalls outside the international hotels; the gigantic sixteen-inch shell, and a host of smaller shells, with beside each the armour plating, suitably pierced, which it could penetrate, displayed in a shop window in a side street as if it were like any other merchandise, products of the great Skoda works so soon to fall into Hitler's hands; the rows of sexy French magazines, the elegant forerunners of *Playboy*, which appeared on every street bookstall, even in the hotel lifts, but which no one ever seemed to buy; the night club which claimed to be 'the only baroque night club in Europe', with ornate gilt balconies, and a pianist who looked like Aldous Huxley, and a troupe of dancers from Riga – itself another city tasting its last months of freedom.

When the crisis unfolded in September this club was to become an unofficial foreign press centre, for it served excellent food into the small hours. Many a late story datelined Prague was to be telephoned from its telephone booth, whilst in the background the dance floor was packed with people slapping their thighs and twirling their fingers in 'The Lambeth Walk', the dance the tune for which was to provide the background music for Britain as it stared war in the face that September. With its defiant if bogus Cockney tones, it was not a bad anthem for the times, and the Czechs took to it avidly, proclaiming that they too were determined to be

> 'taking it free and easy
> doing as you damn well pleasy'.

I explored the narrow, cobbled streets of old Prague, where gateways gave you sudden glimpses of old, stone-banked gardens, and willow trees with the Moldau swift and brown beyond. Almost every house had its sign – here three violins, there a stork, or a pelican, or a lamb – painted above its doorway. From the old Karl Bridge I watched bathers in canoes shooting the rapids formed by the weir across the river. Old men fished from the base of the powder magazine tower where students had held back the Germans in the Thirty Years War, and where Elizabeth of Bohemia, daughter of James I of England, had sheltered with her husband from the attacks of the ruler of the Palatine. I went up the river on a slow paddle boat, to spend weekends in a cottage in pinewoods, where we bought milk from a great stone monastery whose farm was run by brown-robed monks. In the local inn we ate huge, butter-drenched meals, in which *Schweinscarre mit Kraut und Knödel* seemed to have the stature of a national dish. In the fields the peasants gathered in the rye harvest, the famous golden rye of Bohemia.

Of course it was not all milk and honey in this young republic. There were the unemployed – 100,000 of them – a big total for a small country; wages were low, if social benefits were high; there were ugly neon lights, and stark modern buildings, in a particularly hideous grey concrete, amid the old castellated towers. But there was a sense of vigour, and an absence of marked distinctions between wealth and poverty which reminded me of Australia and New Zealand.

As if aware that the days of freedom were numbered, people poured out to enjoy the sunshine of that fine August. Along the Moldau the brown bodies of the bathers seemed almost to hide the green of the fields. At Barandov, in the lovely cliffside restaurant, couples danced in the warm moonlight. In the nearby concrete and glass modern villa of a film producer, writers and directors and actors and actresses from the film studios which had made *Extase* and *Matricula* sipped Melnik wine, and worried about the future. On the villa's flat sunbathing roof an anti-aircraft gun had been placed during the 21 May crisis. 'The officer in charge was a Sudeten German,' our host told me.

A wine hall on the river's edge was packed and in full song. Troops in coarse khaki, men in shiny, tight-fitting suits, fair-haired, sunburnt women in bright cotton dresses sat at the long tables roaring out the words of a Slovak peasant song, laughing, drinking the light golden beer of Pilsen, or the sharp red wine of southern Slovakia. The woman accordionist who led the orchestra changed suddenly to another tune, less rollicking, more military. The crowd half sang, half hummed the refrain. It was clear that the words were not yet familiar to them. But when the chorus came, they were all in, with a crash of voices:

> Come on Adolf, we're ready.
> Come on Adolf, come ahead.

This audience was clearly not afraid of the German divisions manoeuvring along their frontiers. They sang with a lusty self-confidence and ease of mind which had nothing artificial or strained about it. The song, written after the 21 May crisis, matched their feelings. There was no sign that they were singing to reassure themselves, to screw up their determination. They were expressing their feelings that, whatever might come, they were ready for it. It reminded me of the happy-go-lucky, slightly jeering but in no way false confidence of the Madrilenos in the face of Franco's bombs.

Many times in the next few weeks I was to feel a similarity between besieged Madrid and threatened Prague. In both cities the dominant feeling was of people who have made up their minds to risk death rather than to yield, who have come to – and passed – a decisive point from which there was no going back. Their minds were easy, for their decision was made. Come what may, we will fight, said the common people of Prague in their every action in those days of early August 1938 – and given the lead they would have kept their word. A middle-aged man who sat by me in the train one day, when I was on my way to a riverside beach for a swim, had served in the United States Marines during the war. 'It may be our

lot to go down to servitude again,' he said. 'But if we do, it won't
be without a fight.'

This deep-seated confidence was not based on any misreading of
the facts so far as they, the mass of people, knew them. Had not 21
May shown that if you stood up to Hitler, he backed down? Had
not Britain and France stood by them on that day? Had not France
repeatedly said she would honour her treaty obligations? And were
there not always in the background the khaki-clad millions of the
Russian armies, that Red Star in the East to which these fellow Slavs
now looked eagerly? Again and again this defiance was expressed to
me. There was the Czech mill owner from Sudetenland who said,
'We will all go, every old man, every boy, even the women if
necessary, if he attacks us.' In the village inn, near the monastery
where we got our milk a burly soldier on leave went further: 'We
should start the fighting ourselves, and have done with it. I got two
wounds in the last war, and I'll go again willingly'. The peasants at
the other tables nodded their approval.

'And to think that your Government is planning to sell these
people down the river,' said Maurice Hindus, as he lay in the sun
at Barandov and read *The Times*. Hindus, whose books had brought
us in New Zealand our first detailed, if slanted information about
the Soviet Five Year Plans, proved to be a dark-haired, craggy-
faced man in his forties. In his talk, if not yet in his writing, he was
already showing signs of disillusion with Stalin, whose personality
and policies he had in the past effusively praised. Though I agreed with
his evaluation of British policy, his words and his tone irritated me, for
he was only one of many American journalists who were very ready to
urge Britain and France to stand and fight, but were apt to shrug
their shoulders if we suggested that America might join in, and do
the same.

CHAPTER FOUR

A Brush with the Gestapo

As Lord Runciman settled down to the task of hearing formal evidence, working in the panelled, fussily furnished sitting room of his suite in the Alcron Hotel, Dr Goebbels gave him a striking reminder of Nazi propaganda skill. He built up the death of a Sudeten German in an inn brawl into a case of political martyrdom, and ensured that the dead man was given a hero's funeral. It was no doubt an easy enough task for Goebbels, for he had long since transformed the murdered pimp, Horst Wessel, into a German hero, and had made the Horst Wessel song into Germany's second National Anthem.

On the night of Sunday, 7 August, Wenzel Beyerl, a 28-year-old woodcutter was stabbed to death at Gasterwald, a lonely Sudetenland forest village. Beyerl was a Henlein supporter, and he had quarrelled, during a session of heavy drinking, with a fellow villager, another Sudeten, Robert Hoiden, who was a Social Democrat who had lived for many years in Austria. The facts were not in dispute. I checked most of them literally on the spot, where the sticky stain of Beyerl's blood still showed by the roadside. He had been followed from the inn by Hoiden, who had stabbed him five times in the back. Hoiden worked in a glass factory whose tall white chimney showed up incongruously amid the dark, bleak, deserted pinewoods – a factory whose workers formed a Socialist enclave in this Henleinist territory.

The German radio jumped on the story right away. 'More Czech brutality' it thundered. The broadcasters had one difficulty to overcome. They did not want to admit that Sudeten German had been fighting Sudeten German, that the support of the people of the Sudetenland for Henlein was not rock solid. They overcame that by arguing that since Hoiden had at one time lived in Austria, he was a dirty red from red Vienna, and therefore an honorary Czech.

Beyerl's funeral was turned by the Henleinists into a major propaganda demonstration. The body, in its white peasant coffin, was laid on a platform covered with red Henleinist flags and guarded by four men in the grey shirt uniform of Henlein's Storm

Troopers, the FS, or Volunteer Defence Service. Three Henleinist deputies, members of the Prague Parliament, strode militarily to and fro in grey uniforms which were exact copies of the black German SS uniform. Local Sudeten Nazis, in white shirts, black ties, and black trousers held up sometimes by Sam Browne belts, sometimes by brilliant coloured braces from their Sunday suits, lined the rough forest road. In sharp contrast was the dark green greatcoat of the local gendarmerie commander, a short sword in a scabbard at his waist. Further back, their green uniforms brilliant against the dark hills, stood a squad of gendarmes, bayonets fixed on the loaded black Mausers, gleaming spiked helmets on their heads.

Onto this scene strode the tall, gaunt figure of Hermann Franck, Henlein's deputy. He saluted the bier perfunctorily, conferred with a plain clothes police offcer and with the gendarmerie commander. The funeral cortège formed up, a choir sang the Henleinist song '*Wir Bleiben Deutsch* – We remain forever German'.

Suddenly from a wooden peasant house on the other side of the road came one of the most terrible cries I have ever heard. Beyerl's mother emerged, a bent figure in black, with a black handkerchief over her head, and a candle clutched in her hand. Rocking herself slowly to and fro she cried, 'My son, my son, my Wenzel.'

Slowly they brought her down to the bier. Beside her walked the dead boy's stepfather, a heavily moustached peasant uncomfortable in his rough best suit. Franck and the other Sudeten Nazi leaders shook the mother's hand, said some words to her. The village priest, a young man, nervous and seemingly uncertain of himself, began to intone the burial service, and the mother began again this terrible, heart-wrenching wail.

The ranks of the storm troopers stirred. You could sense the feeling running through them. 'These swinish Czechs. What brutality to bring this sorrow on this poor peasant woman.' Hatred glowed in their eyes as they stared towards the Czech gendarmes, who stared equally contemptuously back. The hatred which Goebbels sought to foster was growing with every moment.

The priest finished, the funeral procession formed up, and with drums rolling portentously in the forest, moved off towards the graveyard. There Franck delivered an oration in Henlein's name. He emphasised the Party view that the murderer was a deserter from the German people. 'In our eyes he was no German. He was a traitor.' He paused, and once again the mother's terrible cry, almost animal rather than human in its suffering, tore the silence. Below the churchyard were the rolling pine hills of the Bohemian forest, a dark brooding world as sombre and as full of foreboding as any forest in the tales of the Brothers Grimm. From country like this, further to the south, had sprung Hitler's forebears, the Schickelgrubers. Today, under the grey clouds through which the sun struggled, menace overhung it.

Down in the village the gendarmes, their faces still marked with scorn rather than fear, strode through the funeral crowd towards their headquarters in the village school, which was packed to the windows with their reinforcements. At the start of the ceremony I had thought their bearing was scornful to the point of provocation. I was less sure after I talked to the stepfather. He told me that Beyerl's mother, a Catholic, had wanted a simple Catholic funeral, but that all the comfort she might have gained from the quiet rites of her faith had been lost amid this panoply of scarlet banners, and grey uniforms and rolling drums. The Czech gendarmes certainly had no doubts. They saw this as a sordid local quarrel inflated by the Nazis into an incident to go all over the world as a breeder of further hatred. They knew their foe. And as they strode down the village streets the crowds drew back as if a leper were passing.

My reporting of the funeral at Gasterwald got me into trouble with the Henleinists. The next time I called at their offices in Prague their chief publicity officer, Herr Ulrich, had a cutting from the *Daily Express* in front of him, with passages in my story underlined in red ink. My reference to the funeral as a propaganda occasion had aroused deep resentment, he said. When I argued that this was a fair interpretation, he fixed me with a hard stare. 'You must realise, Herr Cox, that feelings amongst our rank and file are running high, particularly amongst our members here in Prague. If you continue to write in this vein you may find that some of the more rash of them take matters into their own hands. And that would be a pity.' The gold tooth in the front of his mouth glinted in a half-smile. It was, I suspected, a hollow threat, and indeed may have been partly animated by his personal annoyance at an earlier story of mine. I had described him not only as having been at one time a chinaware salesman in Britain, but as one who specialised in a particular line – chamberpots. I decided however that it would be sensible for me to move from my present hotel, the Esplanade, which had no security precautions, into the Alcron where police were always on duty.

I had also to bear in mind that an incident during my days as correspondent in Vienna, in which I had stumbled upon some of the Gestapo's secrets, could have got me, if not onto a Gestapo black list, at least onto a dark grey one. It arose from a story which involved Roland Bochow, the refugee from the Nazis who had been appointed by my predecessor as an assistant correspondent in the Vienna office. A burly man in his forties, he had been born in India, of German parents who had been interned and – he claimed – badly treated during the First World War. Bochow spoke almost perfect English, which he had learned when working as a planter in Malaya. He had been forced back to Germany by the slump, and had found new employment as an official on the personal staff of von Papen, the East Prussian landowner who had been one of Hilter's main Nationalist rivals for the Chancellorship. When Hitler became Chancellor in 1933, he had, in order to reassure the aged President Hindenberg, had to appoint von Papen as his Vice-Chancellor. When Hindenberg died in August 1934, and Hitler merged the offices of President and Chancellor to become the absolute ruler of Germany, he shunted von Papen aside to the post of German Ambassador in Austria.

In Berlin during the pre-Hitler period Bochow had become an important contact for Sefton Delmer, the star *Daily Express* correspondent. That link had saved Bochow's life during the turbulent days of late June 1934, when Hitler had moved against the commander of his storm troops, Ernst Roehm.

On the morning of 30 June 1934, the day on which Roehm was arrested and shot, Bochow had been at work in von Papen's offices in Berlin. He was well aware that matters were moving towards a showdown not only between Hitler and Roehm, but between Hitler and von Papen, who, even though Vice Chancellor in Hitler's Cabinet, had criticised the Nazis openly in a speech a fortnight earlier, at Marburg University. A corridor, which also served as a reception and waiting room, separated Bochow's office from that of his immediate superior on von Papen's staff, a young Junker called von Bose. Suddenly Bochow heard voices raised, and then two shots, from von Bose's office, which had its own separate entrance from another corridor. Bochow had only seconds within which to act. He hit upon a brilliant scheme. He took his hat off the hatstand in the corner of his office, walked out into the waiting room and took a seat, with his hat on his knees, on one of its chairs, as if he had come in for an appointment.

'My main worry was the commissionaire behind the reception desk,' Bochow told me. 'I had given him a rocket that morning about not keeping the place tidy. He could easily have given me away.

'The next moment the door of von Bose's office opened, and an SS officer appeared. He was stowing his revolver, which was still smoking, into its holster. Behind him I could see two other SS men rolling up von Bose's body in a carpet. The officer glared at me and asked who I was, and what I was doing there. I gave a false name, and said I had had an appointment with von Bose. I even managed a joke. I said, 'But I seem to have chosen the wrong day on which to come.' The commissionaire, thank God, said nothing.

'The SS officer told me to get out. I walked down the three flights of stairs, wondering if I would get to the door before the commissionaire changed his mind, and told the truth. I could see the sunlit street in front of me, and was just moving through the main doorway, when suddenly two SS men, who had, unseen by me, been stationed one on each side of the doorway, crossed their rifles in front of me and shouted, '*Halt.*' I barked back at them in my most Prussian, commanding tones, 'I am from the Gestapo.' They hesitated, and then raised their rifles and said, 'Very good.'

'I took the underground to my home in the suburbs, reckoning it would get me there faster than the SS could move by road. At home I gathered my wife and my two boys, in order to drive them to the Swiss frontier. As I was backing the car out of the garage, I heard a shout from a policeman further down the street. I died half a dozen deaths in my seat as he hurried towards us. I assumed word had come for my arrest. But he had merely noticed that, in reversing, I had damaged a small tree which had recently been planted near the street verge. For what seemed an age he noted down my name and address, and told me I would be charged with damaging public property.

'I got my family to the border near Berne, where they were able to cross safely into Switzerland. I did not dare accompany them, because it was almost certain that by then instructions to arrest me would have been sent to all frontier posts. I left the car in the German frontier town, in the hope that the SS would assume I had crossed the frontier, and took a train back to Berlin. There I used the last of my money to pay the premium due on my life insurance, in the hope they would pay up if I was killed. Then I phoned Delmer, and borrowed some money from him. With that I took a

Foreign Correspondents en route to the Anschluss, March 1938, in a photograph which shows the creases of the years. The author is at the far right: H.R. Knickerbocker in centre, in spectacles: Walter Kerr seated far left.

The Czechoslovakian army on manoeuvres.

In Vienna after the Anschluss, Hitler proclaiming the incorporation of Austria into the German Reich.

train to a place on the Czechoslovakian border which I knew from former holidays, where the frontier line ran through thick forests. I was able to slip across it, and make my way to Prague, then on to Vienna.'

On Delmer's recommendation Bochow had been taken on as assistant in the *Express* office in Vienna. He had found himself a flat next door, where he lived with his wife Hansi and his two sons, aged six and nine. He found himself just round the corner from his old boss, von Papen, whom Hitler had rusticated to the post of German Ambassador to Austria. Bochow re-established his links with von Papen, but discreetly, as both men assumed they would be under the surveillance of Gestapo agents operating in Vienna. Bochow was in close touch with another member of von Papen's entourage, the Baron von Keppler, who had been on the SS's death list in 1934, but had got away to Switzerland, and now held a post in the Vienna Embassy under his old chief. A third trusted figure in this group was Keppler's secretary, a small dark-haired girl in her twenties, whose Christian name was Rosa, and who had a flat opposite us in the Modena Platz.

I never really liked or trusted Bochow – nor, I suspect, did he me. But we worked together easily and well, for we shared a common fascination with the shifts and manoeuvrings of power, and a common relish in finding out about them. Bochow had some excellent sources – I assume through von Papen – and he took considerable risks in passing on information, much of which I am sure had been imparted to him on a confidential basis by the man whose trusted servant he had been.

It was this fascination with getting to the bottom of a story which landed Bochow – and myself – in trouble with the Gestapo. It arose over the most famous British traitor of the thirties. In November 1937 Lieutenant Norman Baillie Stewart of the Cameron Highlanders was released from Maidstone prison after serving a five-year sentence for handing over to the Germans secret information about British tanks and British tank tactics. Celebrated as 'The Officer in the Tower', because the first news of his arrest had come when he was imprisoned in the Tower of London awaiting trial, Baillie Stewart had after his release suddenly disappeared from England. It was believed that he might have headed for Vienna.

The Viennese police followed a practice very helpful to journalists. All hoteliers and boarding house keepers had to report to the police the names and home addresses of anyone who checked in with them. If you wanted to track down a visitor, you had only to fill in a card at police headquarters giving the name and most recent address of the person you were seeking, and twenty-four hours later, if they were in Vienna, your card came back with the record of the place at which they had registered. Bochow filled in a card for Baillie Stewart. In the space marked 'Last Known Address' he put 'The Tower of London'. The system functioned admirably, and informed us that a Herr Baillie Stewart was registered at the Pension Minerva. I hurried round to the Minerva, which proved to be on the third floor of a large, gloomy nineteenth-century apartment block just off the Karntnerstrasse, in the heart of the city. When there was no answer to my ring on the door bell, I pushed open the heavy oak door and found myself in a well-lit, spacious lobby with, in one corner, a modern telephone switchboard, much larger than would usually be installed in such a place.

A young dark-haired efficient looking woman was dealing with a caller on it, and looked up with annoyed surprise when she found me standing by her. As soon as she saw me she swept with a single gesture the three or four telephone leads from their connections on the board. To my inquiry for Herr Baillie Stewart she retorted angrily that no one of that name was staying at the pension. The police record must be a mistake, she argued. As I turned to go, the door opened, and a tall, fair young man with a hurt and yet stubborn expression came in, accompanied by a good-looking woman in her late twenties, with shoulder-length blonde hair, and wearing a smartly cut raincoat. Since girls even more than money had been the chief bait employed by the German secret service to entice Baillie Stewart, this seemed all in character. I addressed the man in English as Baillie Stewart. He looked surprised, but nodded acknowledgement, and was about to answer my query about how long he planned to stay in Vienna when his blonde companion brusquely intervened. She drew him swiftly into the hall, and then turned on me and said in excellent English, with only faint traces of a foreign accent. 'That is not Mr Baillie Stewart. You are mistaken. I must insist you leave this place immediately.'

None of my protests that the man had acknowledged that he was Baillie Stewart, and that I was a British correspondent, proved effective. So I made my way back to the Modenaplatz, and talked the problem over with Bochow.

We had at least half a story, and an exclusive one at that, in the fact that Baillie Stewart was in Vienna, and we downed a few whiskies to celebrate the fact. These may have been the reason for the rash step which Bochow next took. He suggested that he rang the Pension Minerva, using not the office telephone, which might well be bugged, but the telephone which had long been installed in the hall of my flat, and which was listed under the name of the man from whom we leased the place. This was an old-fashioned apparatus, which had, in addition to the usual handpiece, a small round spare receiver on a cord, which could enable a second person to hear the conversation.

I listened through this whilst Bochow rang the Pension Minerva. A clipped, north German woman's voice replied, admitting that Herr Baillie Stewart had stayed at the pension, but had now left. Bochow, adopting his most abrupt, arrogant Prussian tones, demanded to know where he had gone. The woman refused to say more. Bochow, his voice increasingly imperious, insisted that he must know Herr Baillie Stewart's new address. His manner rather than his words proved effective.

'Who is speaking?' the woman demanded.

'Herr Baumgarten,' responded Bochow, 'and I want an immediate answer.'

There was a moment's silence, then a respectful reply. 'Just a moment, Herr Baumgarten.' A minute or so later, she was on the line again. 'Herr Baillie Stewart has left for Budapest. He can be found at the usual address there,' she replied, and hung up.

Bochow put the telephone back on the hook, and turned to me, his huge frame sweating with strain. 'I have done something very foolish, very foolish,' he said. 'You must promise to me that you will never tell anyone the name I used then. It was stupid of me to use it. It is a name which is a password in the German Secret Service, a password I learnt when I dealt with the service on behalf of von Papen in Berlin. You must forget it, and forget this incident. Otherwise I could be in severe trouble.'

This conversation made clear to me that the Pension Minerva with its large switchboard and its female minders was a safe house for the German Secret Service. To cover Bochow's tracks I confined my report to the facts that Baillie Stewart had been in Vienna, and had gone on to Hungary, where he went to ground skilfully, evading us all.

I thought no more of the matter until a week later, when I was engaged in one of the more pleasant aspects of a foreign correspondent's duties, that of reading the local morning papers in bed before breakfast. The bedside telephone rang, and a man, in sharp, clipped Prussian tones asked to speak to Herr Bochow. When I said he was not there, my caller demanded his home number. I explained that we never gave the home numbers of our staff. In icy tones the caller continued:

'I suggest you contact Herr Bochow and tell him to telephone me immediately at the Hotel Imperial.'

'Who is speaking?' I enquired.

'Herr Baumgarten,' came the reply.

I rang Bochow. Within minutes he had arrived from his home next door. He was grey and shaking. Early though it was, I poured him out a large whisky. 'This man has been sent from Berlin,' he told me. 'He demands that I see him at the Imperial Hotel at ten this morning. I am in real danger. This is the German Secret Service in action.'

We arranged that I would station myself in a café across the Ringstrasse from the Imperial. If Bochow had not emerged by eleven o'clock, I was to ring von Keppler of the German Embassy. Since calls to the Embassy would certainly be monitored, Keppler would be waiting at his home.

About ten minutes to eleven Bochow emerged from the Imperial accompanied by a burly man with a square, close-cropped skull – almost the cartoonist's prototype of a German. I could see from the relief on Bochow's face, as they crossed the road that all was, for the moment at least, going well. The newcomer introduced himself, not without relishing the irony, as Herr Baumgarten. In good if stiff English he came quickly to the point. Any reference by me either to the telephone call, or to this morning's events would bring me trouble. 'You could find Vienna a very unpleasant place if you do not agree,' he said. 'Unpleasant not only for you but for your wife and child. We may not be the government here – yet. But we have means of getting our own way in matters like this.'

His message delivered, Herr Baumgarten relaxed. He insisted that Bochow and I dine with him that night. It proved to be a long night, in which we all drank a lot, and in which Herr Baumgarten boasted that he had been in England recently on a special mission. It was to try to buy up the British news magazine *Cavalcade* (one of the British imitations of *Time* magazine, all of which were doomed to failure) with a view to making it a journal advocating the restoration of the Duke of Windsor as King. It was nearly three in the morning when Bochow and I finally steered our visitor back to the Imperial, and made our way through the cold autumn streets to the Modenaplatz. Of his interview that morning, Bochow would say only one thing. 'They have given me a further chance – but they've warned me it is my last.'

I took it upon myself to decide to keep my mouth shut, and my typewriter silent, about the events of that day. I did not believe the *Daily Express* would have appreciated my making a martyr of myself – as Christiansen confirmed emphatically when I later in London told him the whole story. Even less would they have appreciated it if I had got Bochow into a concentration camp for what had, after all, been a zealous piece of news gathering.

Bochow did not suffer in the long term for this indiscretion. Immediately after the Anschluss he was summoned to the headquarters the Gestapo had set up in Vienna, and there told he was in the clear. I do not know what actions he had engaged in to win this rehabilitation, but certainly he was the only one of von Papen's close associates in Vienna not to be either executed or sent to a concentration camp. But I had now, in this new land under threat by the Nazis, to work on the assumption that I had been noted down as certainly no friend of the Reich.

CHAPTER FIVE

A Castle – and Princesses

If the Henleinists in Prague were not forthcoming with information for the foreign press, nor were the members of the Runciman Mission. Both the Foreign Office officials on his staff were certainly no adherents to the idea of open diplomacy. The senior of them, Runciman's chief policy adviser Frank Ashton-Gwatkin, could not hide his dislike of the press. He increasingly infuriated the American correspondents by the tight-lipped disdain with which he would refuse to amplify the daily communiqués, which merely listed Lord Runciman's engagements. The other official, Frank Stopford, though excellent company, witty, full of anecdotes about strange happenings in diplomatic missions in which he had served, was an expert at escaping behind an enigmatic smile when pressed for information. 'After all, war or peace may depend upon what we are doing now. One false word, one mistaken remark by us could bring the whole delicate structure of mediation crashing down,' was the refrain. Nor was the third member of the group, the Conservative MP Mr Geoffrey Peto, any more help, though I discovered I had a personal link with him. He was the present owner of Sandford Park, the Oxfordshire manor house which my forebears had sold after my grandfather had emigrated to New Zealand. He was, alas, to emerge as an ardent appeaser.

This secrecy brought a furious row with the press when, on 18 August, Lord Runciman met Henlein for the first time. The day before it had become clear that Hitler had decided to step up the pressure. Henlein's Party had turned down the Czech offer of partial home rule, not just for the Sudetenland, but for all five provinces of Czechoslovakia – North and South Bohemia, Moravia, Slovakia and Ruthenia. This meant that the Germans would have had no one province which they could have dominated, for the boundaries of each of the two Bohemias, in which most of the Germans lived, though following natural geographical and economic lines, had been drawn so that almost as many Czechs lived in them as Germans.

Herr Kundt rejected these proposals as 'a mere phantom of home rule', and concluded on a menacing note – 'The patience of our people, which has seen no sign of good will on your part, is less than our patience.' As he and his men walked down the stone stairs of the Kolowrat Palace, after delivering their message, and came out in to the evening sunshine, news of their decision was brought to Lord Runciman in the Hotel Alcron. He decided he must tackle Henlein himself about this attitude even if that meant a move of appeasement. When Henlein would not come to Prague (pleading his safety could not be guaranteed, which was nonsense, for the last thing the Czechs wanted was to provoke Hitler) he offered to go to Henlein. A meeting was arranged for the next day at Schloss Rothenhaus, the castle of Prince Max Egon von Hohenlohe, at Langenburg in the Sudeten mountains fifteen miles from the German border.

The Schloss was a great square country house set among beech and pine woods. The problem which Runciman faced – and which the Czech Government and the world faced – was writ large in the scene that morning, as Lord Runciman's car made its way westwards across the plains, past fields where Czech peasants were gathering in the harvest, to where, like a wall on the horizon, stood the mountains of Sudetenland. Sheer and definite on the skyline, the hills looked that day just as Bismarck had described them, as 'a fortress built by God in the heart of Europe'.

Just before midday Lord Runciman and Lady Runciman in one car, and Ashton-Gwatkin and Geoffrey Peto in another, turned off the main road into the castle drive. Gamekeepers of Prince Hohenlohe's staff, Henleinist badges in their coats, gave the Nazi salute as the cars passed. Ten minutes later two open cars, travelling at high speed, turned in through the same gates. The gamekeepers' salutes were even more emphatic. In the front car were Henlein and Karl Hermann Franck. Franck was in the grey uniform he had worn at the funeral a week earlier. Henlein, bespectacled, suntanned, wore a brown sports jacket and neatly creased grey flannel trousers, like an English bank clerk on holiday. The cars moved on through a gateway into an inner courtyard. The British, American, French and Czech corespondents who had raced after Runciman in a cavalcade of dusty cars, were left outside this gateway, by the side of the castle drive, to await events.

After lunch, just before the talks began, we could see Prince Max and his wife and their guests sitting in the sun on the castle terrace, sipping their coffee. Before them was the rolling parkland of the

castle grounds, like that of a great British country house. Children
played with a brown retriever, laughing and tumbling on the lawn.
The gamekeepers, reinforced by grey-uniformed Sudeten storm
troopers, kept guard discreetly, hidden by shrubs and trees. Voices
and laughter rang out in the stillness. Here was the Cliveden touch,
the art of country house diplomacy, being applied with skill in
Central Europe. Everything in this environment combined to
convey an impression of peaceful, genial folk, with a real
appreciation of life, people whose surroundings seemed to guarantee
peace and reasonableness. The contrast with the hot offices of
politicians in noisy Prague was sharp. And behind these tall
windows, with their view over the green and gold summer
landscape, Konrad Henlein, Hitler's Sudeten lieutenant, was
quietly demanding that the Czechs should hand over to his control
these frontier mountains, which were the one safeguard which the
Czechoslovak democracy had against German dictatorship, and
which were the only truly defensible frontier between Berlin and the
Black Sea.

The talks lasted five hours. All that time we waited in our cars in
the drive, though we could see clearly the correspondents of Sudeten
Nazi papers and photographers in their grey Party uniforms in the
castle courtyard, coming and going freely from the house. At six
o'clock Lord and Lady Runciman drove off to Prague. A few
minutes later Henlein left, sitting alone in the back seat of a car
which swept past us at high speed. Then Mr Ashton-Gwatkin came
out to read a press communique. It told us nothing more than that
the meeting had taken place, and that Konrad Henlein had put his
views to Lord Runciman. When Walter Kerr, in the name of the
highly influential *New York Herald Tribune*, asked Ashton-Gwatkin
how he expected us to write our despatches without any
information, the British official answered short-temperedly, 'You
can use your imaginations.' When we protested that Sudeten
journalists and photographs had been admitted to the castle
courtyard, whilst we had been kept outside, Ashton-Gwatkin
snapped back, 'You ought to consider yourself lucky to be allowed
within the grounds at all.'

All of this led me to an error in my story. Amongst the people we
had seen from time to time in the castle courtyard was a dark-haired
woman in an elegant summer dress. No one had identified her, but
when we got back to Prague one of the evening papers was carrying
a photograph of Princess Stephanie Hohenlohe, a cousin of the owner

of Schloss Rothenhaus. Princess Stephanie was an ardent Nazi, a Viennese with wide contacts with England, who had launched a number of Nazis on London society. The woman in the photograph looked very like the woman in the courtyard. Perhaps because I was infuriated by Ashton-Gwatkin's attitude, I allowed myself to jump to the conclusion that this ardent pro-Nazi, also of the Hohenlohe clan, had been at the castle during these talks. It was the kind of gossipy angle which the *Express* loved, and they made the most of it. The next day the denials came in thick and fast, from Princess Stephanie herself, from Prince Max, from Runciman. But the story had attained a momentum of its own. It was picked up by *Time* magazine, and spread round the world.

It was the type of slip which could have cost me dear. But in the event it proved a protection rather than a danger. For the Princess Stephanie was, it seems, friendly with Lord Rothermere, and for some complicated reason which I never bothered to fathom, Beaverbrook was at that moment by no means averse to seeing Rothermere embarrassed.

This was as well, for the tone of my stories, reflecting as they did my belief that the British might be about to sell out the Czechs, was not finding favour. Christiansen raised this with me in a letter of 17 August:

I think your despatches are very good indeed, as you know. But I get an undercurrent of depression from them which shows to me a foreboding of trouble that you have.

Maybe you are right. But I tell you this: in the five years I have been Editor of the *Daily Express* there have been many, many nights on which the news seems enough to turn a man's hair white. We have gone on during those times, vigorously and cheerfully, saying 'Everything is going to be all right' and so far we have been right!

The trouble is you sometimes get your nose too near the grindstone; things look a bit too gritty.

I don't write this to you in order to ask you to alter the tone of your despatches, but to suggest to you that you should stand back and survey the possibilities and probabilities as though you were living in Wigan and not in Prague.

Kindest regards.

I took it at the time as a sign that Christiansen was out of touch with what was happening in Europe, that it showed how limited, even if keen, was his perception of events outside the British Isles.

But this may have been a misjudgement. I think it more likely that complaints were coming through from Beaverbrook, and this was a kindly move by Christiansen to warn me – and also to deflect that criticism. For he could always say, 'I have sent Cox a strong letter telling him to get back on course.' Whatever the reason behind the letter, I certainly made no attempt to change the tone of my reports, because I believed the facts would soon justify them.

CHAPTER SIX

Foreign Correspondents

The meeting at Schloss Rothenhaus marked the end of the first stage of Lord Runciman's work, that of establishing the facts. There was no doubt that Henlein would accept nothing less than the demands he had made at Karlsbad in April for the creation of what would be virtually a Sudeten German state within the Czechoslovakian Republic. Runciman now moved to his second task – mediation. Since there was no chance that Henlein, with Hitler at his back, would move an inch, mediation could only mean one thing – cajoling or forcing the Czechs to yield.

This Lord Runciman and Mr Ashton-Gwatkin set about doing, spurred on from London by a realisation that the Germans were gathering their armies on the Czech borders, and that the Nuremberg Rally, due to begin on 6 September, gave Hitler an ideal chance to inflame German opinion, and prepare it for war. The story of the four weeks in Prague which followed the Henlein-Runciman meeting of 18 August was therefore one of relentless pressure on the Czechs, with Runciman adopting indeed not so much the role of mediator as of arbitrator, ultimately ruling that Henlein was entitled to have what he demanded. The Czechs were caught between the twin pressures inherent in the nature of the Runciman mission. If they resisted what he thought reasonable, they risked not only losing the support of the British Government, but of providing an excuse for the French not to honour their treaty with Czechoslovakia. If they gave way to Runciman's proposals, which increasingly took the form of Henlein's proposals, they risked breaking up their own country and opening its borders to Hitler. Sadly and bitterly they chose the second course: sadly and bitterly their Foreign Office spokesman made plain to us, each evening, what further retreats had been agreed to: sadly and bitterly each evening I reported these to London.

With each day, too, the Sudeten Nazi attitude became more arrogant. To deal with Henlein Mr Ashton-Gwatkin had to embark on a second journey to Sudetenland, this time to Marienbad.

Henlein exploited the propaganda value of the visit to the full. Before he met the British official, he held a meeting of his senior leaders in the Hotel Weimar in Marienberg. No ordinary room would do for the occasion. He insisted that the room which Edward VII had occupied during his pre-war visits to the spa be opened up. It had remained closed ever since 1914. Now the dust covers were removed, the daguerreotype of the Emperor Francis Joseph came down from the wall. When the meeting was over, Henlein came out on the balcony to receive, Hitler fashion, the cheers of the crowd. The hotel proprietor had the scene photographed, ready for use in his publicity once the territory had passed to Germany.

Meanwhile at Nuremberg prominent Britons were gathering as Hitler's guests at the annual Party Rally. The guest list showed the kind of attention Hitlerism commanded in Britain at the time. Lady Stamp, wife of the chairman of the Great Western Railway, sat next to Rudolf Hess at a tea party for VIPs. Her husband was there, and Lord Clive, Lord and Lady Brocket, Lord and Lady Hollenden (he had been High Sheriff of London), and Lord McGowan, the chairman of ICI. Another guest at Nuremberg, the MP Sir Arnold Wilson, had long advocated appeasement of Hitler. He had asked me to lunch at the Athenaeum in 1934 after my articles on the Nazi Youth Labour Camp had appeared, to chide me for criticising the Nazis. His pro-Nazism rested on a desire to avoid another war like the one in which he had served in 1914–18. When war did come, he took the honourable course, and though well into his forties enlisted in the RAF, and died as the air gunner in a bomber shot down over Germany.

As the crisis deepened, the journalistic stars of the day came to join us in Prague. Tom Driberg, then writing the William Hickey Diary column on the *Daily Express*, drove out by car from London. Under his hand, the Hickey column was far from being the collection of society gossip and scandal into which it later degenerated. It was for the most part an account of events witnessed or experienced by Driberg, combining meticulous observation with shrewd reflection, presented in clear, scholarly, at times pedantically exact prose.

Driberg was thirty-three years old. Tall, poised, wary, apart, with a remarkably large head, smooth dark hair and wide set, dark eyes, he had a curiously sleek look, as if covered by a fine silken veil. Within Fleet Street he was widely known to be both a homosexual – a fact he admitted much later, in his autobiography – and a

Communist, a fact which he readily acknowledged when, later that year, Beaverbrook carried out a survey of the political views of the staffs of his newspapers. What was not known was that he was also a member of MI5.

Driberg had his own chauffeured car. His driver, a stocky, bullet-headed ex-sailor dressed in a well-cut black suit, soon emerged as having another role than that of just a chauffeur. Obsequious to Driberg in public, in private he was curt and almost arrogant. In England they shared a house together, and, in one late-night drinking session in our hotel, confided to me their great wish was to adopt a child. They were angry that the law would not allow an all-male ménage to do that, and became even more angry when I made plain that I thought the law was right.

For me the most interesting new arrival was Vincent Sheean. His book *In Search of History*,[1] recounting and analysing his journalistic experiences in the twenties and early thirties, reflected exactly my own fascination with news as instant history, and had reinforced my determination to get into international journalism. Known as Jimmy to his friends, Sheean was a tall man with greying hair, a wide, sensitive mouth and an amused, if sardonic, dignity. There was poetry as well as perception in his writing. It is illustrated in the closing sentences of his account of the defeat by the Spaniards of the Moroccan rebel leader, Abd-el-Krim:

> And the bones of my friend Mohammed ben Madj, after so many summer's suns, must long ago have added their pinch of dust to the dust that whirls and sifts across the Moroccan plain. The traveller in such regions, riding through it, does well to wrap his turban around his face to keep it out of eyes and throat; it will sting none the less for being the dust of an honest man.

Sheean, who was in Prague with his wife, Diana, a daughter of the actor Sir Johnston Forbes Robertson, was writing for an American news features agency, which syndicated his articles to papers throughout the States. Hemingway's reporting from Spain was for the same agency. It provided a valuable function, for writers were freed from the need to meet daily deadlines, and could report and interpret events in depth. Virginia Cowles, who had recently come to London from America, was to adopt the same technique for the *Sunday Times*, with marked success.

1 Published by Hamish Hamilton, 1935.

Two of my former colleagues in Vienna, G. E. R. Gedye of the *Daily Telegraph*, and Douglas Reed, formerly of *The Times* and now of the *News Chronicle*, had moved to Prague. Both had served in World War I, Eric Gedye in the infantry, Douglas Reed in the Royal Flying Corps. Both felt deeply that all that had been won in that war at such great cost was being thrown away by Chamberlain's misreading of the nature of Hitler and of Nazism. They were very different in character. Gedye was eager, extrovert, cheerful: Reed was reserved, living a secretive life with his Hungarian mistress. Each of them was to write books which had deep influence on public opinion – as could happen with books in those days when they could be quickly produced, close on the heels of events, and when the television picture had not crowded aside the written word. Douglas Reed had had to resign from *The Times* in order to bring out *Insanity Fair*, an account of the rise of Hitlerism up to, and including, the Anschluss. His policy towards Hitler was the direct opposite to that of the editor of *The Times*, Geoffrey Dawson, the high priest of appeasement. Gedye's book, *Fallen Bastions*, was to appear after the fall of Czechoslovakia. Though the *Daily Telegraph* had been wary of Hitler, and had acquiesced in, rather than advocated Munich, the contents of *Fallen Bastions* were too strong meat even for that paper. Gedye had to go off and work for the *New York Times*.

This list of correspondents had a major gap in it, though it was one few noticed at the time. In this crisis which was to bring Britain to the brink of war, no reporter or commentator for BBC radio was stationed in Czechoslovakia, or visited the country. This was so, even though Edward R. Murrow had demonstrated, during the Anschluss, the power of radio to provide its own vivid and instant, on-the-spot coverage of a big event. CBS was to repeat this process during August and September 1938, with over one hundred special broadcasts from Prague, Berlin, Nuremberg, London, Paris and other centres. Their main rival, NBC, also moved into direct news coverage, and enlisted my friend and colleague, Walter Kerr of the *New York Herald Tribune*, to do news talks for them from Prague. I went with him to the Czech broadcasting headquarters in Prague when he did the first of these, the first time I had been in a broadcasting studio.

Of the pressmen who crowded to Prague, the most influential was almost certainly Claud Cockburn whose cyclostyled weekly news sheet *The Week* was then at the peak of its influence, eagerly scanned by foreign diplomats, and eagerly drawn upon by every foreign correspondent in London. His description of the pro-appeasement group centring upon Lady Astor, Lord Lothian and Geoffrey Dawson of *The Times* as 'the Cliveden Set' – Cliveden being the Astor country house near Maidenhead – was not only a brilliant propaganda coup but a statement very close to the truth.

I had come to know Cockburn well during the siege of Madrid in 1936. Tall, bald, pale, with large, alert, sardonic eyes behind horn-rimmed spectacles, with jowls which managed always to look darkened by five o'clock shadow, and with an almost mockingly upper-class voice, Cockburn's utterly confident, intellectual assurance would have been intolerable had it not been offset by his sense of humour. Even the gravest events had for him their comic side, and you were not likely to be long in his company without finding yourself caught up in a burst of laughter. This was a quality which made Claud Cockburn not only good company but which, skilfully interwoven with his doctrinaire Marxism, was to make him the most formidable propagandist of the Left in Britain in the thirties. A mocking adjective, a witty anecdote, a deft quip would ensure that key passages in *The Week* would be repeated in clubs and pubs and over dining-tables because they were funny, as well as shrewdly politically angled. Cockburn's humour was all the more politically effective because, though hard-hitting, it was seldom rancorous, owing more to the philosophy of 'what fools these mortals be' than to the usual scaffold-side jesting of left-wing extremism. But he kept such light touches for *The Week*. His reports under the name Frank Pitcairn in the *Daily Worker* were cast in the sternness of Party orthodoxy.

Claud Cockburn viewed not only the Spanish Civil War, but all events in this turbulent decade from the Marxist standpoint that truth was not an absolute, but was what helps advance the class struggle. If this involved distorting or even faking events, he did so with gusto. In his autobiography (*I Claud*, Penguin Books, 1967, p. 192) he describes with hilarity how he invented an anti-Franco revolt in Tetuan in order to affect a French Government decision on arms for Spain. In that same year he equally readily propagated false reports that the Trotskyist POUM in Barcelona had plotted a rising against the Republic, so justifying the imprisonment and execution of many members of the POUM by the Communist-dominated Spanish Republican police.

Cockburn later sought to justify his view that all journalism is in part propaganda in a passage in his autobiography which has been taken as Holy Writ by later generations of self-termed 'committed journalists', who have numbered in their ranks many television reporters and producers ready to use the privileged position accorded them to mingle opinion with information.

> To hear people talking about facts [Cockburn wrote] you would think they lay about like pieces of gold ore in the Yukon days waiting to be picked up – arduously, it is true, but still definitely and visibly – by strenuous prospectors whose subsequent problem was only to get them to market.
>
> Such a view is evidently and dangerously naive. There are no such facts. Or, if they are, they are meaningless and entirely ineffective; they might, in fact, just as well not be lying about at all until the prospector – the journalist – puts them into relation with other facts; presents them, in other words. Then they become as much as part of a pattern created by him as if he were writing a novel.[1]

But there are such facts, and common sense tells us we face them every day of our lives, when we learn on the news that snow has fallen across the country; that Club A has beaten Club B in a cup tie; that mortgage rates have gone up or down. These are plain unvarnished facts that do not depend upon the manner of their presentation by any journalist. All that matters is that they be stated accurately. If anyone doubts the validity of hard facts, he need only to serve on a battlefield. An enemy tank suddenly discovered on the far side of a hill is certainly not 'meaningless and entirely ineffective' to the troops on the spot, something which would have validity only if it were dressed up in some form as a 'tank of the reactionary imperialist forces' or of 'the terrorist insurgent forces'. It is simply a tank which might kill you, a fact if ever there was one.

Claud Cockburn remained a dedicated Communist until the 1950s. He swallowed the change in the Party line in September 1939, even though that meant putting his cause above his country, and he never openly disavowed his faith. Cockburn's various works of autobiography make plain that his experience of reporting the Wall Street crash of 1929, which he covered for the London *Times*, had convinced him that Marx was right, and that capitalism was doomed to crash and make way for communism. Given that, it made sense to align oneself with the future. That Cockburn proceeded to do with unhesitating vigour, and with scorn for lesser beings who failed to see the light. There was also in Cockburn a

1   *I Claud*, Penguin Books, 1967, p. 147.

great deal of the autocrat, drawn to a system which he found not only intellectually satisfying, but which favoured elites, and particularly intellectual élites, amongst whom he instinctively numbered himself.

CHAPTER SEVEN

'The Truth Will Prevail'

On Monday, 5 September, the Prague Government finally gave
way to Runciman's pressure, and agreed to a plan which gave
Henlein the home rule he had demanded. Their reward was to find
in the London *Times* two days later an editorial advocating, not
home rule for the Sudetens, but outright cession of Sudetenland to
the Germans. 'It might be worthwhile', the key passage read,
'for the Czechoslovak Government to consider whether they
should exclude altogether the project, which has found favour
in some quarters, of making Czechoslovakia a more homogeneous
state, by the secession of that fringe of alien populations who
are contiguous to the nation with which they are united by
race.'

The English papers got to Prague in mid-afternoon, and the few
copies of *The Times* were snatched from the hotel news stands by
waiting foreign correspondents. Set in the neat clear typeface of
Times New Roman the words in the leader column looked
innocuous, like a sentence in an academic dissertation. But in
Central Europe they seemed to be in lettering two inches high, a
proclamation of the death sentence on a nation. Seven words made
this impact – 'which has found favour in some quarters'. These
were taken as an indication that *The Times* was relaying the British
Government's view. It mattered little that the next day the Foreign
Office denied that this editorial reflected British Government policy.
The opinion was by then widespread that if *The Times* took this view,
then dismemberment of Czechoslovakia was the aim, if not of the
British Government, of powerful forces which sooner or later would
sway the British Government, of people like the Astors and Lord
Lothian and Dawson of *The Times*. I had met Lothian at Oxford,
when he was head of the Rhodes Trust. He had scorned my
intention to go into journalism. 'Real power rests with
Government,' he said. 'We decide what to do, and then send for the
newspapers and tell them to sell it to the public.' His mind, once
made up, would take a lot of shifting. Claud Cockburn may have
over-stressed the role of Cliveden, the Thames-side country house

of the Astors, as the meeting place of the appeasers, but he had certainly not misjudged their intentions.

Cockburn's *The Week* for 8 September gives an interesting indication of his methods. Not content merely with underlining the significance of the *Times* editorial, he asserted that the leading article had been referred before publication to the German Embassy, in London, and had been approved by them. No evidence for this has ever emerged. This report was almost certainly a fabrication, a textbook example of Cockburn's view that truth is not an absolute, but is what helps your side in the class struggle.

Events now gathered pace. On 12 September Hitler was thundering from the tribune at Nuremberg his demands for the Czechs to hand over Sudetenland by 1 October, addressing himself to Benes and the Czech Government for the first time in this dispute. Until then he had spoken only through Henlein. Within minutes of the end of his speech, the Henleinists were out on the streets of towns and villages in the Sudetenland, chanting, '*Ein Volk, ein Reich, ein Führer*' and attacking the police with stones, glasses and chairs.

By the weekend, rioting in many Sudeten towns and villages developed into open revolt with shots fired at the police, Czech and Jewish shops looted, customs houses and police stations attacked. More than a score of Czech gendarmes were killed, many more wounded. In one battle, at Heberskirk, on the morning of 14 September, fourteen gendarmes and twenty-eight Sudetens were killed. The gendarmerie were seriously handicapped by orders from the Ministry of the Interior in Prague to 'do nothing to aggravate the situation', a policy urged on the Ministry by the British and French ministers in the capital. Yet when martial law was proclaimed in the Sudetenland on Tuesday, 13 September, the fighting quickly died away. The Henleinist squads took off their swastika armbands, restored their guns to their hiding-places, and withdrew from the streets. Henlein himself, and Prince Max Hohenlohe, Lord Runciman's host at Rothenhaus, decamped across the frontier in Germany, with Henlein proclaiming in a farewell message the new slogan: 'We want to go home to the Reich'.

The rioting put paid to the Runciman Mission, which may have been one of its aims. Runciman and Ashton-Gwatkin had been standing by for talks with Henlein on Monday, 12 September, when the Sudeten leader telephoned to cancel these, claiming that in Eger there had been 'a terrible massacre, with hundreds dead, mostly

children'. This was a lie. Yet four days later Runciman and his
mission left for London, claiming that the Sudeten problem could
not be solved within Czechoslovakia. He was to recommend to
Chamberlain that all frontier districts where the Sudeten population
was in an important majority should be ceded to Germany – so
providing the British Prime Minister with a justification to
dismember Czechoslovakia. Chamberlain did not delay. On
Thursday, 15 September, he flew to Berchtesgaden for the first of
his fatal talks with Hitler.

During the weekend that followed, the last weekend of normal life
which the twenty-year-old Republic was to know, the people of
Czechoslovakia waited in a mood of stunned stoicism to learn their
fate. Sunday was a day of brilliant sunshine; the pavements in the
Wenchelas Square were thronged with the traditional Sunday
promenade. An outburst of cheering came from a group in front of
one of the show cases in which newspapers were displayed for
passers-by to read. A new turn in the crisis? No, just a win for
Prague in a key football match. In the courtyard of the Hradcany
Castle a great pile of sand had been placed, to be used against
incendiary bombs. Children played on it in the sunshine, laughing
as they shaped it into sand castles.

The next day Czechoslovakia learnt the contents of Chamberlain's betrayal. In mid afternoon the British Minister, Mr Basil
Newton, and the French Minister, M Delacroix, drove to the
Hradcany Castle. History allowed itself a grimace of irony, for the
Legionary guards who presented arms as the French Minister's car
passed were that day wearing the uniforms of the French Army in
which their forebears had served. I hope M Delacroix averted his
gaze, for the message he and his colleagues bore was a demand for
the dismemberment of the Czechoslovakian Republic. France and
Britain called upon Prague to hand over to the German Reich all
areas of their country in which more than fifty per cent of the
inhabitants were of German stock.

Though the portents for such a move had been clear ever since
Chamberlain stepped into his plane at Heston, the news
nevertheless came as a profound shock to the Czechs. They had
never believed that the French, who were bound to them by a formal
alliance, would desert them, even if Britain did. I was in Wenchelas
Square when the first newspaper-seller came running through the
crowds, shouting news of the plan. People seized the papers, and
stood reading them on the pavement, turning to the first passer-by

to comment. Small crowds gathered, arguing and gesticulating. One was at the foot of the statue to King Wenchelas, at the place where, thirty years later, the Czech student, Jan Pallach, was to burn himself to death as protest against yet another betrayal, this time by the Soviet Union. By now the British morning papers had arrived. The *Daily Express* carried across its front page the words 'The *Daily Express* declares that Great Britain will not be involved in a European war this year or next year either' – that ill-fated slogan which was to haunt Beaverbrook to the end of his days.

The first reactions of the people of Prague were disbelief, followed by anger, and then defiance. That too was the response of the Government, which next day gave a firm though courteously phrased 'No' to the proposals. At the same time they gave the army and police orders to deal firmly with a new development – organised incursions across the border into Sudetenland by bands of Sudeten guerrillas, equipped with German arms and supported by German Nazi units. Customs houses were attacked and burnt, Czech police and officials killed or kidnapped. It was the start of a carefully orchestrated cross-border insurrection, designed to give the outside world the impression that Czechoslovakia was breaking up from within.

Late that Tuesday night, after I had sent off my story to London, I walked to the Charles Bridge. In the Government buildings on the hillside above lights still glowed. In the chilly late summer night air, they seemed a symbol of a country determined to fight rather than yield. I woke the next morning to find that these were illusions. At two o'clock on the morning of that day, Wednesday, 21 September, the British and French ministers were back at the Hradcany, having demanded an interview with President Benes. An exhausted President dragged himself from his bed, and dressed to receive them. They presented an ultimatum. Neither France nor Britain would stand by Czechoslovakia should her refusal to cede the Sudetenland to Germany lead to war. Mr Chamberlain was off to Godesberg that day·for his second meeting with Hitler, and he wanted an immediate answer.

The weary Czech Cabinet were called to the Hradcany. They argued and debated throughout the Wednesday morning and afternoon. Finally at five in the evening they capitulated.

By that time the wide thoroughfare of the Wenchelas Square was a great mass of waiting people. Loudspeakers had been placed on lamp-posts along its length, and over these, at six o'clock, came the news that the Government had yielded to this fearsome pressure. The crowd began to surge towards the Charles Bridge, and across it towards the Hradcany. It was growing dark now, and the castle rose dark against the sky, with only an occasional light showing. A black-out had been ordered on all Government buildings, in case Goering's air force struck without warning.

At the head of the crowd half a dozen people carried the Czech tricolor, the same red, white and blue of the French who had failed them. Singing the National Anthem, chanting, 'We will not give in: We will keep our frontiers', the huge procession surged on.

There was little fanaticism, only a mixed air of confusion and determination. Here was a man carrying a briefcase, on his way home from work. There a group of students. Behind them factory workers in black leather jackets, their hands still black from the work bench. Women led children by the hand. Well-dressed people came out of cafés to join the march. They all pressed on up the hill, under the blue-shaded street lights – another air-raid precaution.

At the foot of the narrow street winding towards the castle the way was blocked by fifty mounted police, and a double line of foot police. The crowd made one attempt to break through, and two policemen were pulled from their horses. But violence was not their aim. Instead they stood in the darkness, singing and chanting their slogans until after a couple of hours they began to drift away.

Above them, from the flagpole on the Hradcany, the President's flag still flew, with on it the words 'The truth will prevail'. They were proud words, which my grandfather had taken as the text of his inaugural lecture when he became one of the founder professors of New Zealand's first University in 1871. They are no doubt true – but even then they seemed sadly incomplete. Today any Czech must ask himself how long will it be before the truth does prevail in his country. He could indeed be forgiven if the ultimate blasphemy occurred in his mind, if he asked himself whether the truth might perhaps prove to be that of the torturer O'Brien in Orwell's *1984* , rather than of the hero-victim, Winston Smith?

The next day there was an even larger mass demonstration, as hundreds of thousands of people massed in the Wenchelas Square, and before the Parliament buildings, and moved slowly up and down, waving the Czech flag. Many were workers, their lunch boxes in their hands, carrying banners saying, 'We made the arms: let us use them.' They had marched in columns from the outer suburbs and even from surrounding villages. When at ten o'clock the loudspeakers announced that the Hodza Government had resigned, and that a Government of National Defence had been formed with at its head General Jan Syrovy, the cheering shook the windows of the Ambassador Hotel from which we were watching. Syrovy, with a patch hiding an old wound in his right eye, had been the legendary commander of the Czech Legion in Russia, the force which had battled against the Germans and then had fought its way to freedom, across Siberia, against the Bolsheviks.

The next day reports came through from Godesberg that Hitler had stiffened his terms still further, to a point at which even Chamberlain found them unacceptable – at least to a point at which Chamberlain feared he might not be able to get the British people to swallow them. The British Prime Minister returned sadly to London, and the British and the French advised the Czechoslovak Government that they could 'no longer take the responsibility of advising Czechoslovakia not to mobilise'. At twenty minutes past ten that evening a general mobilisation was proclaimed throughout the Republic.

It gave me – for what that was worth in such times – a scoop. At five minutes past ten that evening I had just finished dictating my copy to London when the Czech journalist who worked as assistant in the *Daily Express* office in Prague signalled to me to stay on the line. He was, like almost all fit Czechs of his age, an army reservist. A friend in the War Ministry had telephoned him to say that a general mobilisation was to be announced in a few minutes' time. His friend was warning him, not as a journalist, but to enable him to get home and say goodbye to his wife before rushing to his depot. I dictated then and there a further story to London, giving news of the mobilisation. I had just finished when all telephones were cut off, in readiness for war. No other newspaper correspondent got the story through to London that night.

The proclamation of the mobilisation was broadcast in Czech, then in Slovak, then in German, then in Hungarian, in Ruthenian, and finally in Polish – the many languages of the Republic. It precipitated an extraordinary spectacle. Men rushed wildly through the blacked-out streets to get to their homes for their equipment. Waiters in restaurants took off their aprons, late-night shop-keepers closed their premises, cars in the streets were halted by the police and asked to take men to their assembly points. Soon the streets were full of men, each with his small suitcase, hurrying towards barracks or the railway stations. One man walked with at his side his ten-year-old son proudly carrying his suitcase. With little traffic in the streets, the dominant sound was of hurrying feet, insistent in the darkness. At every street corner, in hotel lobbies, on station platforms, men and women were taking their swift farewells. Guards appeared in front of every public building, and in the Alcron Hotel the management produced a gas mask for each guest.

It was a night when a nation faced a supreme test, and found itself unafraid, when it thought it had a chance to fight for its freedom. Three years later, when I found myself with a Free Czech battalion on the outskirts of Tobruk, I met two men who had been mobilised that night. Their faces lit up when they recalled it. 'We only wanted to fight,' they said. 'Why couldn't you have let us do so?'

CHAPTER EIGHT

Betrayal

We now had to make our own plans to deal with war, if it came. The experts predicted that Prague would be bombed flat within days of the outbreak of hostilities, so Kerr, Sheean and I set about finding a base outside the city from which we could work, should the need arise. We found such a place in house No 94 in the village of Seberov, just beyond the city outskirts – a neat brick peasant house overlooking a village pond, crowded with ducks and geese. The woman of the house showed us a painting of the pond with two photographs of young boys set in it, like a Surrealist picture, and told us that these were her sons, both of whom had been drowned in the pond three years ago, when ice had suddenly cracked under them. She was now pregnant again.

On the ridge outside Prague, on the way back, we paused to look down on the city with its grey roofs packed around the high walls of the Hradschin Castle, where the President's flag was a dot of red and white against a very blue sky. Sheean said, 'That's just how it will look to the bombers when they come.'

We never went to live at Seberov. We went there only once again, on the night of 26 September, when Hitler was due to speak at the Sportspalast in Berlin. If he was going to attack Czechoslovakia, this seemed the moment for him to do so. We listened to the speech in the kitchen of No 94, where they had their wireless set. Through the static we strained to follow the speech, waiting for a declaration that at that moment bombers were on their way to Prague. The pregnant woman sat with her hands folded round the child inside her, and with the picture of her drowned sons behind her, and when Hitler raved against Benes she said, 'He sounds just like our dog does when he's angry.' Her husband told us later that he was very worried about her, as she had had two miscarriages already, and the baby was lying the wrong way, and might kill her. He was very quiet and gentle with her, and she was rather cross with him, as pregnant women can be. It was on to such individual burdens, borne that night in millions of homes across Europe, that Hitler was now preparing to add, sooner or later, the terrible further burden of war.

But no declaration of war came that night, and we were able to drive back through the darkness to Prague, knowing that Hitler had confined himself to one final threat. 'Either Benes will accept this offer by October 1st, and give the Sudeten Germans their freedom at last, or we will come and fetch that freedom.'

This ultimatum left four days, time enough, as it proved, for the final betrayal at Munich to be arranged and executed. We used this time to further our plans to cover a war, buying winter clothing and some reserves of food, and arranging for special supplies of petrol. My main concern was that if war came, I would find myself cut off in Eastern Europe, separated from France, where my wife and son would be in the heart of one of the main targets for bombing raids, the city of Paris. We lived in a flat at St Cloud, on the southern outskirts of the city. It was just upstream from the great riverside Renault car factory at Billancourt, a military target if ever there was one. What is more, Cecily was pregnant – our second son was to be born in March 1939. We had agreed that if the French mobilised, and war seemed likely, she should take Peter, now a year old, into Central France. But that posed the nightmare burden of arranging evacuation by train in a foreign land. Our own private lives were clearly no more prepared for war than were the arrangements of the French and British Governments, now hastily organising the digging of air-raid trenches and the filling of sandbags.

Within twenty-four hours of Hitler's Sportspalast speech came, however, the first sign that Britain and France would after all cave in. That evening Chamberlain made the broadcast in which he mourned the fact that Britain was preparing to go to war because of 'a quarrel in a faraway country between people of whom we know nothing'. The Czechs heard this with concern, and anger. So too did the British correspondents in Prague, though with wry smiles as well. For we thought we had done quite a bit since early August, and even before, to try to inform and alert the British public about this land and this crisis.

Then came the news that Chamberlain and Daladier were flying to Munich, and finally, late on Thursday, 29 September, the dreadful and dreaded news that the great powers had dismembered the Czechoslovakian Republic. Not only were the Sudeten areas ceded to Germany, but other territories were handed over to Poland and Hungary. All of this was to be done in such haste that hundreds of thousands of anti-Nazi Germans and Jews would now fall into Hitler's hands, and face either the concentration camp or death. Henlein, on the German radio the day after Munich, said of his Sudeten opponents, 'We shall imprison them until they turn black.' This was the same Konrad Henlein whom Ashton-Gwatkin had described as 'an honest man whom one can trust to keep his word'.

Leon Blum was to record that he heard of the Munich settlement with mixed feelings of relief and shame. My own reaction was the same. I was relieved that my wife and son were free from the threat of the bomber, and that I would not find myself – for the time being at least – caught up in war. But here in Prague, where the price for this relief would have to be paid, the sense of shame soon became uppermost, as did the realisation that we had bought a reprieve at a terrible cost.

This was borne in on me sharply on the afternoon of 30 September, when the new Prime Minister, General Jan Syrovy, set out over the air the full grim tale of what had been inflicted on his country at Munich the day before. I listened to the broadcast in the sitting room in which Runciman had worked in the Alcron Hotel. It had a big wireless set, specially installed for the mission. Milos Schafranek, of the Czech Foreign Office, and his wife and two other Czechs were there, and Jimmy Sheean and his wife, and my *Daily Express* colleague Bill Morrell. We tuned in and got the steady tick-tock, tick-tock, which was the station identification signal of Prague, a sound we had often heard from the loudspeakers in the streets. It sounded now like a life ticking itself away, a grandfather clock in the room of a dying man. Then Syrovy came on, his thick voice making one think of his thick figure, and his black eye patch. I could not understand his words, so I watched Schafranek's face, as it grew greyer and thinner.

Half way through, Morrell came in with the English papers which the afternoon plane had brought in, and opened out the *Express*. It had one huge word as its headline, in type two inches high – 'Peace'. Above it was repeated the declaration that 'Britain will not be involved in a European war this year or next year either'. Schafranek picked up the paper, and a look of horror and disgust and then of scorn came over his face, and he put it down as if it were something physically rotten. All the time Syrovy's voice went on, telling the people to trust him and keep calm and hold together in this hour of need. I felt shame flood through me, and anger that we had betrayed not only these people but ourselves. I vowed then and there, in that fusty Central European hotel room, that when war came I would fight in it, and not merely write about it, that I would make such personal recompense as I could for that evil done in all our names on that September day in Munich.

Meanwhile, the news had to be covered. Hitler was due to cross the frontier in three days' time, to make good his boast to bring the Sudetenland within the Reich by 1 October. I set out for Eger, crossed into Germany, and drove on to Beyreuth, where the Wagner Festival, beloved of Hitler had just ended.

The next day we added our car to the line of press vehicles following towards Karlsbad the cavalcade of nine six-wheeled black Mercedes Benz cars, in one of which rode the Führer, in a brown raincoat and flat-topped forage cap. A young German press officer, in an elegantly cut Storm Trooper uniform, incensed that we had no formal credentials, tried to get us turned back, but the long column of cars was under way, and to extricate us from it proved impossible. He was even more annoyed when I pointed out that one banner greeting Hitler contained a grammatical error.

In every Sudeten village the swastika flags were out and the people lined the roads, arms outstretched. Outside Karlsbad a German armoured brigade was drawn up by the roadside, tanks and field guns, anti-tank guns and light anti-aircraft guns set side by side on the grass verge, their crews stiffly to attention at their sides. Many of the guns had flowers in their muzzles. At one point a column of motor cycle troops was drawn up. Each machine had one soldier riding the cycle, a rifle slung across his back, another seated in a side-car, armed either with a rifle or a light machine gun. I had not then the military training to assess this weaponry. But when later I became an infantry intelligence officer, I knew that I had seen that morning at least two of the main types of German tanks, the silhouettes of which I learnt to look for as they came over the desert horizon towards us outside Tobruk in the autumn battles of 1941. I remembered those motor-cycle troops, too, for the first German prisoner I had to interrogate in Greece had been the side-car passenger in just such a combination, which had run into a New Zealand ambush north of Thermopylae. His uniform was soaked with the blood of his comrade, who had been shot riding the motor cycle.

All that was in the unseen if readily imaginable future that October morning as we followed Hitler into Karlsbad. From the balcony of the municipal theatre he made a short, fierce speech. We were within feet of him as he spoke. At Eger the day before he had proclaimed to the Sudetenlanders, 'We were ready to draw the sword for you.' Now his voice took on a steely vehemence as he declared, 'That I should one day stand here before you I never for a moment doubted.' The words were banal enough, but his tone had a sudden, manic intensity which would have been frightening in an ordinary individual. In a speech by the head of a great state, by a dictator who, by lifting a finger, could let loose the fire power of those troops we had seen ranged by the roadside, they had the force of an electric shock, silencing the crowd for several seconds before the Storm Troopers set under way a new frenzied outbreak of 'Sieg Heil, Sieg Heil', No one, hearing that speech, could doubt that this man would ultimately bring war to Europe, that he wanted not just territorial gain, but territorial conquest.

In the villages between Karlsbad and the purely Czech areas the Czech gendarmes and officials were moving out, and Henleinist Storm Troopers were everywhere hanging out swastika flags, and in one place were hustling a group of grey-faced, terrified civilians away up a side street. Some shops were already daubed with '*Jude*'. On the edge of one village two grey-haired men in green-faced hunting jackets and *Lederhosen*, with the gnarled faces of peasants, ran to embrace one another. '*Endlich Heim ins Reich*' – 'Back home in the Reich at last' – one said. Did, I wonder, the Sudeten peasantry really talk in such sentimental, propagandist tones, or were they just echoing what Henlein and the German radio had dinned into their ears?

The road took us through wooded hills where lay the pill-boxes and underground fortifications which the Czechs now had to abandon. Across one field a line of khaki-clad Czech infantry, carrying light machine guns and boxes of ammunition as well as their rifles, were moving towards a lorry waiting to evacuate them. At the rear was a young officer, map case under one arm, field telephone under another. Tears coursed down his sunburnt cheeks.

Back in Prague the hotel lounges were now thronged with new faces, those of taut, grey-visaged men and women, political refugees or Jews who had fled from Sudetenland, and sought now to flee from Prague. Amongst them was Gregor Strasser, one-time Nazi and former confidant of Hitler, against whom he had turned ten years before. Though he was probably the refugee from Nazism whom Hitler would most have liked to have seen dead, Strasser was undismayed by this huge defeat the forces against Hitler had suffered.

A hardened soldier from World War I, his mind was on where the next stand could be made. Rumania? Turkey? He canvassed both with vigour. I learnt an important truth from Strasser that day, that the best antidote to defeat is to prepare for your next battle. It was something which I was to find, when I became caught up in soldiering myself, that came instinctively to all good commanders, whether they had charge of a platoon or an army.

One refugee had sold us occasional news stories in Vienna. Though Czech by race, he had an Austrian passport, and had fled to Prague when the Anschluss came. He felt the Gestapo closing on him, and when not only the British and Americans but even the Jugoslavs refused him a visa, he literally foamed at the mouth with fear – the only time I have seen such a phenomenon – as he walked agitatedly up and down the *Daily Express* office in Prague. He was a meagre figure, almost certainly a spy for several countries, but he was a human being. So I raided the *Express* cash reserves, and gave him fifty pounds – a big sum in those days – and told him to try to buy a visa on the black market. He got one to Jugoslavia only to be gathered in by the Gestapo there in 1941.

The time had come for me to leave Prague. I drove south with Jimmy and Diana Sheean. Along the road towards the Reich frontier in what had been Austria, we passed the Czech army in retreat. There were lines of field guns drawn up by the roadside, cavalry in village squares, lorry upon lorry filled with dejected men. At Bratislava the Czechs allowed us through their frontier barrier, but the German police officer on the other side would not let us pass. The frontier was closed until German troops had moved up into a newly ceded strip of land. 'I am sorry,' he said, when he saw my British passport, 'because you are on our side now.'

We turned towards the Hungarian frontier, which also ran up to the outskirts of Bratislava. It was dark now, and on the frontier road was a line of troops trudging dispiritedly through the darkness, leading horse-drawn carts piled high with equipment. A brilliant rim of flame broke from the windows and doorway of a concrete pillbox, whose wooden fittings had been set on fire.

I asked the troops if the Hungarian frontier was still open. 'They are all open. There aren't any frontiers any more anywhere around here,' their corporal replied bitterly. 'Everyone just takes what he wants now.'

The Czech customs station was deserted, its flagstaff broken, its doors open. The red and white frontier barrier was down, locked into place. We drove around it, across an open, bumpy field, towards the Hungarian post. They let us through without argument, and we were soon on the main highway towards the Hungarian border and Vienna. It was a long drive, and Sheean kept himself going with draughts of neat whisky from a bottle he kept on the floor by the gear handle.

It was well after midnight when we reached Vienna. I spent that night in a gilded bed in a gilded bedroom in the Sacher Hotel. The next morning I took the Paris train from the Westbahnhof, the station at which I had arrived so hopefully as a student five years before, on my first visit to Austria.

In Paris I found that Cecily had just returned from Limoges. When events reached their crisis on the weekend between the Godesberg and Munich meetings, she had put into operation our plan for her to move away from our dangerously placed flat at St Cloud. Though by now three months pregnant, she had struggled aboard a hideously overcrowded train with our one-year-old son Peter, and had made her way to Limoges. Our Bretonne maid Yvonne had returned to her home near Lorient, and our Danish nurse Else followed Cecily to Limoges. In a letter to her parents Else recorded those days:

Limoges was an awful town, rather big and dirty. The hotel was untidy, everything was untidy and dirty. The only attractive thing in that town is *la patisserie*. I never tasted such wonderful *patisserie* as in Limoges.

You ought to have seen us the evening we came back from Limoges. Mrs Cox went out to buy some food while I put Peter to bed. When Mrs Cox came back with the parcels we moved two arm chairs into the kitchen and then we started to cook and fry and we ate and drank half the night. We were awfully hungry.

We went back to Paris on Monday. Yvonne arrived on Tuesday. Mr Cox arrived today, dead tired and terribly disappointed. He is only 28 years old but looked more like 40. And when we heard how the circumstances are in Prague today, and how the Germans rule, you can't but think that in spite of it all it might have been better to fight the Nazi regime now. Experts say a new crisis could take place in springtime and the war will break out within two years.

CHAPTER NINE

The Great Munich Lie

I returned to a France and an England where public life was dominated by the Great Munich Lie, by the assertion that the Munich settlement had brought, in Chamberlain's words, 'Peace for our time', and had marked the end of Hitler's aggression in Europe. Only events could prove whether this was false or true. If you argued that it was an illusion, that Munich had bought merely a respite, at huge cost, and that war would assuredly come, you were deemed to want war to come. Moreover, as the evidence began to mount, week by week, that Hitler was as belligerent as ever, the appeasers became all the more vehement in their defence of Munich, until at times their intolerance of criticism had itself undertones of totalitarianism.

This came across strongly when the Commons debated the aftermath of Munich early in November. I was in London on leave, and Guy Eden, the *Daily Express* Lobby Correspondent, got me a seat in the lower Strangers Gallery at the House of Commons. This small gallery (now a broadcasting booth) was on the floor of the Chamber, which made one seem part of the proceedings, rather than just an onlooker.

Clement Attlee from the Labour front bench attacked the Munich agreement as a great defeat for Britain and for the cause of law and order. Chamberlain was quickly on his feet, his voice cold with venom. 'If the Right Honourable gentleman really believes that,' the Prime Minister said, 'then I am sorry he should say so publicly. It is not one of the characteristics of totalitarian states, at any rate, that they are accustomed to foul their own nests.'

To attack a fellow Parliamentarian for openly criticising the Government's policy was an odd attitude for the Prime Minister of a Parliamentary democracy to adopt. To cite the totalitarian states in support of that attitude was not only odd but sinister, when it was clear that the way in which Hitler ensured that no criticism should 'foul' Germany's nest was to use the truncheon and the concentration camp.

(*Right*) Princess Mara
Scherbatoff, in the Paris office
of the *Daily Express*.

(*Below*) View from 32 Rue de
Cavaire, St Cloud.

Chamberlain and Hitler at Munich.

Chamberlain at Heston airport on his return to England from Munich.

The absolute certainty of the appeasers that they were right, their bland refusal to contemplate that there had been any alternative but to surrender Czechoslovakia, was chilling to encounter. I came up against it in the heartland of appeasement, in the editorial offices of *The Times*. Ferdinand Kuhn, the chief correspondent of the *New York Times* in London, had been one of my earliest friends in Fleet Street. He had an office in the *Times* building in Printing House Square. He was so struck by my account of the injustices done to the Czechs, even down to the arbitrary course of the new frontier line, that he took me to see Robin Barrington-Ward, then assistant editor of *The Times* (he became editor in 1941). But Barrington-Ward had no doubts at all about what Chamberlain had done, or what *The Times* had advocated. I appreciated the forces which had led him to this view. He had served for more than three years in the trenches in the last war, winning a DSO and a Military Cross and three mentions in dispatches. He was determined to prevent another generation from going through such wasteful horrors.

That evening Barrington-Ward rejected everything Kuhn and I had to say with such cold certainty that Kuhn was provoked into saying to him, very quietly, 'Should you not bear in mind from your own history books the words Fairfax used to Oliver Cromwell, "I beseech ye, by the bowels of Christ, consider ye may be mistaken" ' – words which were later to be flung at Chamberlain in the House of Commons by Amery.

Since the *Daily Express* was in the front rank of those preaching that Munich meant peace, I felt deeply that I should resign. One major fact dissuaded me. Cecily was having a difficult pregnancy, afflicted by a skin rash which the doctor (but only after the baby was born) discovered was due to a food allergy. It irritated her by day, and tormented her with sleeplessness by night. To have called upon her, with another child just over a year old, to uproot herself from Paris, and set about rebuilding a new home in Britain, when we had no savings, and there was no certainty I would get another job, would not only have been unfair, but unreasonably dangerous. Sinclair Lewis, in his novel *It can't happen here*, written to warn of the dangers of creeping Fascism in America and Britain, makes one of his characters exclaim, 'What crimes are committed in the name of a man's wife and children.' But it is also a crime to endanger the health, perhaps even the lives, of your wife and children.

There was, too, another argument. Despite its editorial policy, despite Beaverbrook's memorandum to Christiansen, the *Express* had printed my stories from Prague unchanged and intact except when cut for reasons of space. The paper had done this, although on at least one occasion it had carried leaders virtually contradicting the deductions I was drawing. If I resigned, I gave up this chance to depict to millions of people events as I saw them, and would perhaps make way for someone who would present them from an appeaser's angle. I decided upon a compromise. I would stay with the *Express* until after the baby was born, and then make a move.

I took out some of my frustration by using part of my leave to canvass for Lindsay of Balliol in the Oxford by-election where he was standing as an anti-appeasement candidate in a contest with Quintin Hogg. One fellow canvasser was an old friend from my undergraduate days, a young history don at Merton called Bill Williams. So strongly did he oppose Munich that he had joined the Territorials. When war came he was called up into the King's Dragoon Guards, and in due course was posted to the Middle East. In March 1941, as an officer with an armoured car unit in Cyrenaica, he was in command of the armoured car which first sighted the vanguard of Rommel's forces advancing from Tripoli. After fighting in the open desert, and in besieged Tobruk, Bill Williams was posted to GHQ in Cairo as an officer in Intelligence. There he caught the attention in 1942 of the newly appointed General Montgomery, who promoted him to be Chief Intelligence Officer of the Eighth Army, setting him on the road which was to bring him, at the war's end, to the rank of Brigadier Williams, DSO.

Another man with whom I tramped the leaf-strewn streets of Oxford that autumn was my fellow New Zealander John Mulgan, who was working with the Oxford University Press after taking a first in English. For him too a hard war lay ahead. He joined the Territorials, and as an officer in the Royal West Kent Regiment was to fight at Alamein, and then to serve behind the enemy lines with the Greek Resistance for nearly two years, only to die suddenly in Cairo just before the war ended.

The areas in which we canvassed were solidly pro-Chamberlain. We received many rebuffs, and insults, some of which we brought upon ourselves, for we interpreted the role of canvasser as being not merely to ask people how they were going to vote but of urging them to vote our way. I felt a hatred for the beefy, sleek, loud-voiced Conservative officials, many from their Party HQ in London, who gathered in the bars of the big hotels at the end of the day's campaigning. They embodied for me the selfish shortsightedness of the abandonment of Czechoslovakia. I felt the same for Quintin Hogg, even though I knew him only as a distant, boyish figure on Union Jack draped platforms. Hogg was to prove himself a brave soldier. The next time I encountered him was when we were in the same ward in an army hospital in Jerusalem, where he was recovering from a wound in the knee, received when he manned a Bren gun in the open desert against low-flying Messerschmitt fighters. And he was to prove himself after the war an equally doughty fighter for human freedom. But in October 1938 he was caught up in the wrong cause.

CHAPTER TEN

Beaverbrook

In mid-October Lord Beaverbrook paid his first visit to Paris since the Munich crisis. One of the hazards of the job of *Daily Express* correspondent in Paris was that the city lay on the route between Beaverbrook's London home, Stornaway House, and his Riviera villa at Cap d'Ail. The rich travelled by train in those days, and Beaverbrook and a small entourage of two or three would travel by the Golden Arrow to Paris, and stay a night or two at the Ritz before continuing by the Blue Train to the Cote d'Azur. Whilst he was in the city, the Paris correspondent had to be ready to be summoned at short notice to Beaverbrook's suite in the Ritz, to answer questions about developments in France or give his views on whatever subject was uppermost in his lordship's mind at that moment. I learnt quickly to brief myself fully on the state of the rolling stock on French railways. One of Beaverbrook's hobby horses was to get wooden-walled passenger carriages, of which there were still many on British railways, replaced by metal-walled ones, which would be less dangerous in accidents. The French were in the process of making that change, and it was well to have the latest statistics at one's fingertips.

Soon after I had been transferred to Paris I was warned of an even more alarming prospect. Beaverbrook was considering acquiring an apartment in Paris, as a more permanent base there. When he heard that Cecily and I had found a superbly placed flat in a new block at St Cloud he insisted on inspecting the block. The visit was not without its problems. Beaverbrook was delighted with the view from 32 Rue du Calvaire and by the fine series of rooms on the front, and then demanded to see the smaller rooms at the back. Cecily took him to look at them. In one room our nine-month-old son was asleep in his cot. He was a fine, strong baby, and he looked his best, his fair hair outlined against a blue blanket. Beaverbrook swung round to Cecily and asked:

'Is that your child?'

'Yes,' she answered, with rightful pride.

84

'If it was mine I would take him out and drown him,' came his retort.

Cecily was equal to the occasion. 'Lord Beaverbrook,' she replied quietly, 'you must have been very unlucky with your children.'

I was not surprised, but I was relieved to learn a day or two later that his lordship had decided against buying himself a Paris flat.

Lord Beaverbrook did not seem perturbed by Cecily's riposte and as the weeks went by Christiansen passed on to me occasional words of praise from him for my work. I was however taken completely by surprise when, late in June 1938, Christiansen telephoned me to say that Beaverbrook wanted me to be appointed as one of his leader writers. It was a job which I was immediately sure I did not want. I recoiled from it partly because I was increasingly concerned about the pro-appeasement stance which the paper was beginning to adopt, but partly also because I did not want to work in a post where my own judgement would be swamped by that of the proprietor. Yet that was something which was inescapably part of the role of leader writing for a Beaverbrook paper. I wanted to exercise my own judgement, as I could to a considerable degree in evaluating and covering daily news. I did not want to put my pen – or, more exactly – my typewriter, at the service of someone else's ideas. This was not the outcome of intellectual vanity or pride (though no doubt that came into it) but from a sense that if I once became Beaverbrook's man, in the sense which was implicit in being his leader writer, I might never become fully my own man again. I was later to observe that those who, by joining the Communist Party, agreed to abdicate their own judgement in favour of the Party line, seemed to be intellectually scarred for life, even if their Party membership had been relatively brief. The same could be true, I feared, if I toed the Beaverbrook Party line. It was not only that I realised that in journalism one's own power of judgement was an essential and invaluable asset, but I knew that unless I developed it as far as I could at this stage of my life, it might be dangerously blunted and damaged.

The pro-appeasement policy which also worried me had been detectable in an article in the *Evening Standard* as early as April 12 1938, a month after the Anschluss, an article which played down the dangers of Hitlerism. It was under the title of 'No War in Europe'. The astute Sir Bruce Lockhart, then on Beaverbrook's staff, noted in his diary that evening that though the article was signed by Frank Owen, it was 'obviously written by Lord Beaverbrook'.

On 23 May, after the weekend of alarms along the Czech frontier,

Beaverbrook's policy became more explicit. On the front page of the *Daily Express*, over Lord Beaverbrook's signature, appeared this message:

> Britain will not be involved in war. There will be no major war in Europe this year or next year.
> The Germans will not seize Czechoslovakia.
> So go about your business with confidence in the future, and fear not.
> Provide us with aeroplanes, anti-aircraft guns, and ammunition.
> Develop our own Imperial resources, and give our races prosperity and happiness at home.

This was the first use of the 'There Will Be No War' slogan which was to become the hallmark of Beaverbrook's policy between then and the outbreak of war in September 1939. It was an exceedingly dangerous slogan, because it was a half truth, and a half truth can very often be more deadly than a lie. Fully spelt out, it should have read, 'There will be no war this year, or next year either, *if we let Hitler have his way,* or, alternatively *because Mr Chamberlain intends to let Hitler have his way.*' For there was no question of Hitler giving up his expansionist aims. Even a cursory study of his writings and his speeches ruled out that possibility. Yet the price tag of appeasing Hitler was carefully omitted from the *Daily Express*'s 'No War' slogan, so lulling the British public into a false sense of security at the very moment when they needed to be alerted to the dangers ahead. At the same time it encouraged the Nazis in their expansionist policy – for they quickly supplied in their own minds the missing second half of the sentence.

The slogan was, in fact, a skilful, though disguised advocacy of a policy of appeasing Hitler. Though the word appeasement had not yet passed into common currency, this message of 23 May 1938 aligned Beaverbrook as one of the first and one of the most formidable of the advocates of appeasement. Beaverbrook and his apologists have since defended his attitude by pointing to the fact that an integral part of his policy was British rearmament – or, as his lordship insisted that his leader writers phrased it, a policy of 'filling the gaps in our defences'. This was good so far as it went, but such rearmament could, if we abandoned our alliances in Europe, at most help us to survive a war when it came. If, however, we stood firm over Czechoslovakia, we had a chance – the last chance – of preventing that war by halting Hitler in his tracks, a process which could have led to his overthrow by the more cautious elements in the German High Command. And even from the point of view of rearmament, it made sense not to abandon an ally as well armed as Czechoslovakia. The armament of her thirty to forty divisions which, as the outcome of Munich, was in a matter of months to make its way into German hands, was equivalent to the output of British arms factories during the first two years of the war. Sir John Colville, who as Churchill's Private Secretary at 10 Downing Street, came to know Beaverbrook well, categorised Beaverbrook at this time as 'an arch-appeaser of the dictators'.[1]

I had not thought all these issues through at the time when the invitation to become one of Beaverbrook's leader writers came, but they were clear enough in my mind for me to be sure that I wanted no part in advocating this aspect of his policies. I had, too, another strong objection to moving into an editorial writer's sanctum: I had not become a journalist in order to tell other people what they should do. I was an historian at heart, not a preacher or advocate. I wanted to tell other people what was happening in the world around them, tell them as frankly and as clearly as I could, and leave them to make up their own minds about things. I believed that if people could learn the truth, they would act sensibly upon it.

I decided to base my case against becoming a leader writer on the second of these grounds. That left me some chance of remaining an *Express* reporter – a job in which I had been given a high degree of freedom. So I told Christiansen that I could not take the job. 'You realise it's the Old Man's wish; if you won't do it, you will have to tell him yourself,' was Christiansen's reply. 'He will be in Paris tomorrow.'

In his suite at the Ritz, with its pink silk-lined walls and gilt Louis XV furnishings, Beaverbrook was seated in a high-backed chair. On the table before him stood the dictaphone he frequently used, a machine on which messages, spoken into a small, trumpet-like mouthpiece, were recorded on a drum, like those of the earliest gramophones.

The wide mouth, which in a grin seemed to extend from ear to ear, the large head on the neat body, the wide-set, keen eyes which studied me had already been the subject of innumerable photographs, drawings and caricatures. In particular I was familiar with David Low's portrayal of him as a grinning, mischievous imp. I had, in my encounters with him, so far had no experience of

1 *The Fringes of Power*, Sir John Colville, Hodder & Stoughton, 1985, p. 733.

this lighter side of his character. That he was to display only later, particularly during the war, when we met on a different basis. Perhaps I took life too seriously in the thirties – at any rate with my elders – for me to stimulate his mischievous wit. It was the tough magnate, not the Puckish jester, whom I faced that afternoon.

Yet he welcomed me warmly, indeed affectionately, and came immediately to the point. 'Christiansen tells me he's going to make you a leader writer,' he began – which was hardly the version of the proposal which Chris had given me.

'Yes,' I replied. 'And I've explained to him that I don't want to be a leader writer. I want to remain a reporter.'

He pretended to be surprised at my decision, though he clearly knew of it in advance from Christiansen. I explained I had come a long way from New Zealand to see and learn about Europe, and that I wanted to stay in the field, where the news took place, rather than retreat to an office to write about it. He deployed the contrary case – that leader writing was the way to power, power over people's minds, power and advancement within a newspaper. He argued the case always in my own interest, not at all from that of the paper, and argued it patiently, without anger or tension. I made my own case with, I hope, as much calm. Then he shook his head. 'Well, if your mind is made up . . .' and he picked up the speaker of the dictaphone.

'Memo for Mr Christiansen. Kaarx' – my name was drawled out in his Canadian accent into what seemed like polysyllables – 'Kaarx doesn't want to be a leader writer. Better let him ride.'

I returned home shaken, but confident that I had done the right thing. 'There's no doubt about these big men,' I told Cecily that evening. 'They respect you if you stand up to them.'

I would have been much less confident had I known the full terms of the memorandum which reached Arthur Christiansen the next day. I learnt of it only in April 1940, when I told Arthur Christiansen that I was not prepared to go to Norway as the *Daily Express* war correspondent, as I intended to join the army. We were drinking in a pub off Fleet Street, and he grew indignant. 'After I saved you from getting the sack in 1938, you owe it to me not to walk out on me now, when I and the paper need you,' he said.

How could he have saved me from getting the sack? I had heard Beaverbrook himself dictate a memorandum telling Christiansen to let me ride. Christiansen's answer was to take me through the black-out across Fleet Street to his office, where he dug out the file. The memorandum was there, neatly typed. It was a fuller message than the one dictated in my presence. It read:

> Cox does not want to be a leader writer. Better let him ride.
> Sack him within a month.

I had survived on the paper, Chris explained, only because he had won for me a short-term reprieve, on the grounds that I was needed to cover the Runciman Mission story. My work in Prague had then, he said, been good enough for him to avoid implementing Beaverbrook's command.

The leader-writer post which I had turned down went to Michael Foot, whose journalistic efforts until then had been confined to left-wing journals like the *New Statesman*. A young, dark-haired, bespectacled figure, he was with Beaverbrook in the familiar suite at the Ritz when I was summoned there in that post-Munich autumn. I had had contact with Foot on only one previous occasion, at the War Memorial in Oxford on Remembrance Day 1932. The Oxford University Labour Club had organised a line of demonstrators to hold up anti-war banners when the official wreath-laying ceremony took place at the Memorial. I was in my first term at Oxford, and the dangers of another war of which I had become aware in the Soviet Union and Germany during the summer were fresh in my mind, so I decided to join the demonstration. Michael Foot was one of those organisers marshalling us into line amidst the jeers of passing motorists. For in those days Remembrance Parades were held always on November 11th, which that year was a weekday.

I do not know if this incident remained in Michael Foot's mind, but he gave no sign of remembering it when we met in this more exotic setting. Beaverbrook addressed Foot in warm, friendly terms, as if to indicate to me what a good job I had passed up. But I noted too that he also took care to dictate to Foot in my presence a couple of paragraphs for a future editorial, as if also to remind me – and Foot – who was the boss. Foot's main work for Beaverbrook was to be with the *Evening Standard* which, when war came closer, Beaverbrook allowed to take a non-appeasement stance.

Looking back over the years, I am not surprised that Beaverbrook should have wanted me to be fired from his employ once I had refused the leader-writing offer. For he was offering me not only advancement, but his friendship, admission to that entourage of

intimates who formed his personal court. What Beaverbrook wanted
from his lieutenants was not only that they should do his work, but
that also they should become virtually his sons. He gained this from
many of them, from Peter Howard and Frank Owen, and particularly from Michael Foot, who indeed came to love him like a
son. That was a role I could never have played.

It is commonly believed that the influence of Beaverbrook on his
close entourage was malign, that Sir Stafford Cripps was right when
he accused Beaverbrook of having 'an intentionally demoralising
effect on his young men'.[1] Yet those who did join Beaverbrook's
court have not shown many signs of regarding themselves as having
been corrupted by 'Robin Badfellow' – as Muggeridge termed
Beaverbrook when he worked for him on the *Evening Standard*. Frank
Owen, it is true, had he not been drawn into Beaverbrook's web,
might have moved over from the Liberals to Labour, and have taken
his place alongside Gaitskell and Evan Durbin, Douglas Jay and
Hector McNeil as a minister in the post-war Labour Government,
instead of ending his days as a hard-drinking literary pensioner of
Beaverbrook, hammering out a life of Lloyd George which won few
plaudits. But Owen was not the first or the last Fleet Street figure
to regard alcohol and journalism as natural partners, and he did
after all in his lifetime edit with distinction two Fleet Street
newspapers. Michael Foot executed the leader-writing job with
loyalty and avidity, and yet emerged five years later with his socialist
principles apparently unscathed – certainly in good enough shape
for him ultimately to lead the Labour Party.

Peter Howard, who accepted and shared Beaverbrook's views
more completely and more enthusiastically than any other of his
acolytes, did break with him decisively, and went on to become
ultimately the leader of Moral Rearmament. Others who served
Beaverbrook for long periods got as much as they gave. Sefton
Delmer remained faithful to the man who had brought
him into journalism until he was ultimately cold-shouldered
from the Beaverbrook court by a monarch who sought new
courtiers. Arthur Christiansen might well have found himself
hemmed in as a highly gifted chief sub-editor had Beaverbrook not
recognised and supported his talent. In return for the right to edit
the *Daily Express*, Chris endured with equanimity many strains and

1 Quoted by Cecil King in *With Malice Toward None*, a diary entry for 9 September 1942.

even cruelties across the years. 'I never went on holiday without Beaverbrook ringing me just before I left, and planting some anxiety calculated to destroy my peace of mind whilst I was away,' Christiansen told me once. Beaverbrook's final words to Christiansen, after at last firing him from the *Express* Newspapers in 1953, were a classic of mischievous cruelty. He accompanied Christiansen to the lift in his apartment block, and as the lift began to descend said to him, 'Going down, Mr Christiansen, going down.'

It is true, as the diaries of Sir Bruce Lockhart reveal, that Beaverbrook could, apparently deliberately, humiliate those who worked for him by demanding their attendance at short notice and at all hours, and add the further indignity of dictating leaders or passages for the gossip columns to them whilst stalking about his room naked after a shower. But such callous indifference to the time or the habits of subordinates is a common characteristic of many men of power. Churchill had no hesitation in keeping the Chiefs of Staff up to the small hours of the morning, despite the enormous other pressures on them, often simply to have an audience for his reminiscences. Lloyd George heaped many petty indignities on his staff, not only in the discharge of his official duties, but in covering up the arrangements for the amours which gained him the nickname of 'The Goat'.

Beaverbrook was no more demanding than were these men of their close associates. The criticism of his actions may therefore have derived more from the nature of the ends to which he directed the talents of those who served him, ends which were not so much evil as mischievous. It is not surprising that those of Beaverbrook's contemporaries who were on the receiving end of this mischief should have seen as wicked the use of able young men for this purpose.

CHAPTER ELEVEN

France After Munich

In France *le mensonge de Munich* was sustained with fervour by the Foreign Minister, M Georges Bonnet, and by the large section of the press which, for one reason or another, wrote what the Government wanted. The general public were more cynical. 'See you again next time' was a common farewell spoken to one another by the reservists who had been called up to man the Maginot Line, as they were demobilised in early October. But relief that war had not come was widespread.

It endured even when, barely six weeks after Munich, an event in the heart of Paris set in train actions which were to reveal the true nature of the Nazi regime in which both the British and French Governments were reposing their trust. On 7 November 1938 I reported: 'At 9.30 this morning Henschel Feibel Grunszpan, a 17-year-old Polish Jew, shot dead Herr von Rath, a 32-year-old Third Secretary, in the German Embassy here.'

Two days later came the Nazis' reply to Grunszpan's deed, the pogrom of *Kristallnacht*, the night of broken glass. Jewish shops, Jewish homes, synagogues were smashed, burned and looted throughout the Reich. Thirty-five Jews were killed, 101 synagogues destroyed by fire, another 76 so badly damaged they had to be demolished, 7,500 shops wrecked.

Faithfully, the bulk of the French press played this down, as M Bonnet was in the midst of negotiations with von Ribbentrop for a Franco-German declaration that neither side would in future resort to war against the other. The French Foreign Minister wanted a piece of paper to match that which Mr Chamberlain had so proudly flourished on his return from Munich, as proof that he had secured 'peace for our time'. Von Ribbentrop was prepared to come to Paris and sign such a declaration provided the French gave him a reception 'at least equal to that shown when the King and Queen of England came to Paris' (German Foreign Ministry Archives). The French matched this in at least one respect, by receiving him at one of the special inner railway stations not open to the public.

In Ribbentrop's case, this was to be the Gare des Invalides, in due
course to become familiar to millions of visitors to France as the
post-war Paris air terminal. It had for the French the great
advantage that, unlike the Bois de Boulogne station where the
British King and Queen had been received only four and a half
months before (though that now seemed in another age), it would
not involve a drive of any length through streets where the German
Foreign Minister might meet either hostile or at best indifferent
crowds.

So on a morning of brilliant late autumn sunshine we of the
foreign press found ourselves once more standing alongside a red-
carpeted platform, where M Bonnet, smiling with real warmth,
hurried forward to greet the former Pomméry champagne salesman,
now returning triumphantly to Paris in the role of Foreign Minister
of Hitler's increasingly powerful Reich. Von Ribbentrop allowed
himself some cordiality. He saw the fine weather as a good omen for
the talks. 'I saw France last night under the beauty of a magnificent
moon,' he added. The Garde Republicane presented arms with
their carbines, and in an oddly tense silence a group of Germans
resident in Paris shot out their arms in the Nazi salute from where
they stood under two swastika flags – the only ones apparent in
Paris that day. Mobile guards and gendarmes lined the short route
from the station through which the long black car carrying von
Ribbentrop made its way across the Place de la Concorde. No
crowds turned to wave. The few onlookers were silent, a silence
accentuated by the halting of the traffic to allow the car and its
motor- cycle outriders to pass. Its destination was the Hôtel Crillon,
that hotel which had been the headquarters of Lloyd George and the
British delegation at the Versailles Conference less than twenty
years ago.

The Franco-German declaration, signed that night in the famous
Clock Room of the Quai d'Orsay, may have removed France's
anxieties about any future German demands on Alsace and
Lorraine, but it did nothing to diminish French anxieties about a
new problem which had suddenly surfaced. Just a week earlier
Mussolini had suddenly made clear that he was going to take a leaf
out of his Axis partner's book, and set in train his own revanchist
demands. On 30 November the black-shirted Fascist deputies in the
Chamber of Deputies in Rome had, in the presence of the French
Ambassador, suddenly risen to their feet and chanted, 'Tunisia,
Corsica, Nice' – all territories under French sovereignty or

French control to which Italy was now laying public claim.

So, in early December, I found myself on the way to Tunisia, to report once again on a dictator's claim on a neighbour's territory. Tunisia, though still nominally ruled by its Bey, was a French protectorate. It had almost as many Italian settlers as it had French – indeed, Mussolini claimed the Italians were in the majority – but there was little chance that it would form another Sudetenland. Its military importance to France was too great. A French staff officer explained this to me on the shore of the Gulf of Tunis, just above the white-walled, minareted village of Sidi Bou Said, and close to the ruins of Carthage. Offshore the dark shapes of two French submarines showed up as dark dots against the brilliant blue sea that stretched away towards Cape Bon.

'Twenty minutes' flying time from here is the Italian island of Pantelleria, which Mussolini had turned into a major military base,' said the officer. 'Another half hour's time by fast bomber lies Sicily. We are almost an extension of Europe here. If the Italians controlled Tunisia they would cut the Mediterranean in two.'

Five hundred miles to the south-east another officer drove with me to the frontier of the Italian colony of Libya. At the desert border post a sunburnt Italian Carabinieri officer and the two Libyan cavalrymen on duty gave us the Fascist salute, and chatted in a friendly way. On the Italian side the tarmac road doubled in width, forming the wide military Via Balbia which stretched from this border to the frontier of Egypt at Sollum. Along it an Italian invasion force could have moved rapidly from Tripoli towards Tunisia. But it would have made little progress inside the French-held territory. Forty miles from the border just south of the Mareth Oasis, the French had built a desert Maginot Line. Along one side of a rocky desert gully (the word 'wadi' had not yet passed into everyday English) the camouflaged cupolas of gun positions could be glimpsed, almost indistinguishable in the sandy ground. Barbed wire entanglements, five rows deep, and a triple line of upright steel rails formed a barrier to troops and tanks. The line ran in a forty-five-mile curve from the Mediterranean shore to the Matamata mountains, steep and grey against the hazy desert sky. It was a formidable line, and I reported confidently that it formed an impassable barrier against an army approaching from Libya. It was an accurate enough prediction, for when an army did advance against it four and a half years later, the Mareth Line held firm, in the battle in which Montgomery launched his desert Eighth Army against Rommel's Afrika Korps, who made at Mareth their first major stand after Alamein. But the rest of my prediction proved less sound. I wrote that the Mareth Line was protected to the west by the Matamata Mountains, 'roadless, waterless and impassable'. This was true, but what I did not foresee was that, with modern motor transport, these mountains could be outflanked by a wide sweep through the desert further west, a move which was to be carried out by General Freyberg and the 2nd New Zealand Division in 1943, forcing Rommel to withdraw from the Mareth fortifications.

For my work, those ten days in Tunis marked an important development. The *Daily Express* gave me space on the leader page to sum up and evaluate what I had seen and learnt in that time, not just to report but to delineate the underlying contours of events which I had reported from day to day. It was a satisfying form of journalism, which I was to develop further during the coming months. Of all my work as a writing journalist, it is by these leader page articles I would most want to be judged.

We were working – though we had no inkling of it at the time – in the final stages of the era of the descriptive writer in daily journalism. Within the next decade radio would oust the newspaper as the main means of conveying a picture of events – and radio would in its turn swiftly be thrust aside by the even more powerful reporting instrument of the television camera. We were amongst the last practitioners of the art of depicting in words, for the immediate information of the public, the events of the day. Once broadcasting, and in particular television, became dominant in this field, the role of the writing journalist was increasingly to be confined to interpreting, analysing and evaluating, rather than to depicting and describing. 'I am a camera with its shutter open,' Christopher Isherwood had written in the opening passage of *Goodbye to Berlin*, and in the field of daily news our eyes and our ears were the camera lenses of the time. We had the responsibility and the pleasure of practising the craft of instant history.

It was a fascinating and fulfilling, if harassing, task. There was the search for the event; the noting, amidst the tumult and confusion, of its salient features and of significant and vivid detail, the quickly scribbled interviews with participants; then, as often as not, the long drive back to base, slumped in the back of a bumping car, formulating the story in your mind, seeking similes and metaphors, groping for an effective opening sentence and a strong conclusion; the hasty typing on a rickety table or washstand; the race to the telegraph office or the anxious wait for the telephone call to London. It was an odd way in which to practise an art – for certainly the skill of capturing the essence of a fast-moving event, and transforming it into words which would convey the truth of it to millions of readers the next day was an art form. Descriptive written journalism went out, however, in a blaze of glory. These, its dying years, produced some of its best practitioners – Douglas Reed and de Caux of the London *Times*, George Steer of the *Daily Telegraph*, Alan Moorehead and Alan Wood of the *Daily Express*, William Forrest of the *News Chronicle*; and, in its last post-war phase, Patrick O'Donovan and Hugh Massingham of the *Observer*. It was a good company in which to serve.

This report from Tunis nearly got me into serious trouble with the Italian authorities. When I reached Rome on my way back to Paris I was greeted by Frank Gervasi, of the International News Service. 'I would get on to the train for Paris right away,' he counselled. 'The Propaganda Ministry are after your blood. They say you have insulted Fascist youth.' The trouble stemmed, I discovered, from a mishearing by the *Daily Express* telephonist who had taken down my article from Tunis over a bad, crackling telephone line. In describing how highly organised, on Fascist lines, was the Italian colony in Tunis, I had said, 'This minute, as I write, thirty little Sons of the Wolf Fascist organisation are drilling in the school courtyard next door with little wooden rifles.' It had appeared in the paper as 'dirty little Sons of the Wolf'. I took Gervasi's advice and I was thankful when early the next morning I found myself safely on the French side of the border.

*

The winter of 1938–39 in Paris remains in my mind as a sour and dark period, a time of snow-bordered pavements, of low, ochreous skies, with overlying all a sense that what lay ahead was war, or, worse still, betrayal without a fight. Cecily was tormented and increasingly exhausted by the skin affliction brought on by her allergy. The *Express* news desk, with the international scene for the moment relatively calm, stepped up its demands on the Paris office for yet more stories of crime and scandal. When on New Year's Day 1939 it called for coverage of a cockfighting tourney in Calais, due to be attended by members of the British aristocracy, it seemed to me that news values had reached rock bottom. With war looming,

Lord Beaverbrook and Arthur Christiansen.

Hitler entering the Sudetenland, October 1938.

German troops crossing the Charles Bridge in Prague, March 1939.

the paper was prepared to devote space to this degrading and brutal occasion. Fortunately I was saved by a change of plan. A reporter and photographer were sent from London. When the story, full of vivid detail, appeared in the paper it bore the name of a relatively new recruit to the staff, George Millar. His disdain for the story, as he has since made clear, was no less than mine, but he had tackled the task with a more cheerful acceptance of the foibles of human nature than I could summon up that winter.

Early in the New Year it was clear that the Spanish Republic was nearing its end. On 26 January 1939, Barcelona fell, leaving only the beleaguered central zone around Madrid and Valencia in Republican hands. The progress of the war had been a constant background to the other stories on which I had been engaged during the previous two years, something never far from my thoughts. Day by day, once I had dealt with the news items of immediate concern to my duties, I had turned to the reports from Spain, to follow the ebb and flow of battle around Madrid and along the Ebro, in the Basque country and in the Asturias, reading these with mixed feelings of guilt that I was not still in the midst of the battle, and envy for those who had followed the long struggle at first hand.

In Paris the Spanish Civil War was close at hand. Through the French capital moved a steady stream of correspondents and propagandists, politicians and spies, on their way to and from Madrid and Barcelona. I spent many hours with new arrivals from Madrid and Barcelona on the terrace of the Café Flore or the Deux Magots, the two cafés on the Boulevard St Germain which were replacing the Dome and the Coupole in Montparnasse as the Paris meeting place for expatriates. From these travellers, more than from the newspaper reports, I gathered the sense not only of war weariness but of disillusion within the Republic. The discipline of the Communist Party, which had been so important in the defence of Madrid, had become a two-edged weapon, cutting against liberty within Republican Spain as well as against Franco's forces. Through their control of the police, and of the dreaded SIM – Servicio de Investigacion Militar – the Communists were able in 1937 to crush the Trotskyist POUM. George Orwell, who had served in the POUM militia, was lucky to escape with his life. The Spanish Communists also enabled the OGPU to extend to Spain the Stalinist purges then at their height in Russia. Kleber, the Red Army officer who commanded the first International Brigades, was one such victim. He was at first demoted to a lesser command in Spain, and then recalled to Russia, where he disappeared without trace. General Berzin, the senior Soviet officer in Spain, was also executed.

I was reluctant to accept the ever-increasing volume of evidence that things were going sour in Republican Spain, and clung hard to my belief not only that the Republic would win through, but that the bright new world which seemed to have dawned for the ordinary people of Spain in the summer sunshine of 1936, and had still been a glowing prospect that autumn in Madrid, might yet come about. My closest Spanish contact in Paris, a former press attaché at the Republican Embassy there called Massip, who had been ousted from that post for being too liberal, constantly warned me that these were vain hopes. A slim, dark-haired Catalan, he felt that whichever side won in Spain, individual liberty would now be the loser. 'There are two enemies of man,' he would declare. 'Nature and the State. Both have to be tamed if man is to be free.'

By the end of January 1939 such discussions had been overtaken by events. With the fall of Barcelona some 400,000 refugees fled along the mountain roads and tracks into France, in a long terrible cavalcade of suffering, a nightmarish foretaste of what was soon to be witnessed on roads all over Europe. Alan Moorehead, who had become my assistant in the Paris office, went to the frontier, and his descriptions of this disaster, and of the brutally harsh treatment meted out to the refugees in France, demonstrated fully for the first time the capacity for vivid reporting which was in World War II to win him enduring fame. The story proved, too, to be a milestone in British broadcasting. The BBC sent Richard Dimbleby to the Franco-Spanish frontier near Port Bou. From there he broadcast an eye-witness account of the mass Republican evacuation, the first such account carried by the BBC from their own reporter of these events of the turbulent thirties.

On 27 February 1939, France recognised Franco's regime as the legal Government of Spain, though another month was to elapse before the Republican forces in Madrid, Valencia and Alicante were finally overthrown. In Paris the Spanish Embassy passed formally out of Republican hands at five that evening. All diplomatic staff had long since left the building in the Avenue Georges Cinq. Shortly before five o'clock struck on the clock of the nearby American church, a grey-haired porter emerged from the Embassy with a few belongings wrapped in a newspaper under his arm. He closed the gates, and walked slowly away towards the Champs Elysées, quickly swallowed up in the throngs of smartly dressed men and women hurrying along the pavements. A few minutes later a long black car drew up, and a burly man in a black coat and homburg hat, accompanied by two excited young women in furs, unlocked the Embassy door and took possession in the name of Franco. It was the end of an era, not just for Republican Spain, but also for the hope which had flared brilliantly if briefly for many of us.

During the post-Munich months I forged a friendship with Madame Genevieve Tabouis, then at the peak of her influence as a columnist. She was the wife of a former diplomat, and her column in the radical daily paper *L'Oeuvre* was regarded as a major source of inside information, quoted constantly by the news agencies, and relayed throughout the world.

Madame Tabouis was a small, neat, vibrant, handsome woman in her mid-forties with grey, carefully coiffured hair. She was passionately opposed to the Munich settlement, and to the policies of Georges Bonnet and liked to bring together people who shared her views at the apartment she and her husband occupied just off the Boulevard Haussman. It had been once a highly fashionable area, but most of the *haute monde* had now deserted it for the new apartment blocks and mansions between the Arc de Triomphe and the Bois. I found myself a fairly frequent guest at these lunches, many of which were attended by army officers like General Juin who were deeply worried by the shifting balance of military power in Germany's favour. Tabouis and I fell into the habit of exchanging information regularly. Frequently, often early in the morning, my telephone would ring at St Cloud and the now familiar voice would pour out a torrent of news and rumours and interpretation. I had learned to cross-check carefully anything she told me, but Tabouis not only put me onto a number of usable stories, but also kept me abreast of the way French informed opinion was moving. I came to have a very real affection for her, particularly because of her fierce patriotism and her determination to see France stand up for itself. We were never on Christian name terms – indeed in those days surnames could often reflect as close a link as do the instantly used Christian names of today – but we worked easily together, sharing not only news, but laughter at the sardonic turns of events in those bitter days.

Paris had become a gathering place for exiles from Nazi Germany. Amongst them was a girl in her early twenties called Charlotte Reimer, whom I had last seen on that day in 1934 on which the Storm Troopers had given me a taste of their methods when I failed to salute the swastika. She had a German father and an English mother, and I had been given a letter of introduction to her from friends in London. Her parents had left Germany when Hitler came to power, but she had stayed because Karl, the young German to whom she was engaged, and who had been prominent in the Communist Youth Movement, was imprisoned by the Nazis.

Charlotte proved to be a small, dark-haired, vital figure, speaking perfect English. She surprised me by asking if I would take her to lunch the next day in a restaurant on the top floor of a leading department store, in the heart of Berlin's West End. It was a fashionable and costly place, the Fortnum and Mason's of Berlin, and my funds did not run to such luxuries.

'I will pay,' she explained. 'If we get there early, and get a table by the window, it is possible to see into a corner of the courtyard of the Moabit prison. The prisoners are allowed into the yard for exercise between midday and one o'clock. If I can see that Karl is amongst them, then I know he is still there, and has not been taken off to Dachau or some other concentration camp. The police have beaten him terribly, but so long as they hold him, he has a chance. Once he is handed over to the Nazis, they will destroy him.'

We were in good time, and secured a window table, from which it was possible to see, some blocks away, a small patch of courtyard surrounded by high grey walls, and to detect tiny figures moving across it. Charlotte sat, outwardly appearing nonchalant and talkative so as not to arouse the suspicions of the waiters or the people at other tables. Only one hand, clenched around her napkin until her fingers seemed almost bloodless, revealed the strain she was under. Around us women in the flowing gowns of the time, furs draped across the backs of their chairs, lacquered hair showing under expensive hats, laughed and talked to their escorts – many of whom were in well-cut Storm Trooper uniforms. As cover for her scrutiny of the prison yard, Charlotte pretended to be pointing out the sights of Berlin, spread out in the sunshine below us. We were half way through ordering our meal when I noticed her grip on the napkin suddenly relax. Her eyes softened with relief, and once the waiter had gone she nodded, and began to ask eagerly for news of London. Only when later we got to the relative privacy of the street outside did she say that she had seen Karl walking with two other prisoners, and with an apparently undamaged stride.

I saw her again that evening, and marvelled at her courage – for she was a German citizen, and constantly in danger of arrest – at staying on in Berlin when she might have fled to safety. When I left her at the doorway of the ponderous, old-fashioned apartment building in which she had a room, and watched her start briskly up the stairway, she looked vulnerable and very much alone. Her spirit of defiance may well have had something to do with the fact that when, a few minutes later, I encountered the marching Storm Troopers in the dark Berlin Street, I deliberately refrained from saluting their swastika flag.

Now Charlotte appeared in Paris, together with Karl, whom I had glimpsed that day from the roof-top restaurant, as he trudged round the exercise yard of the Moabit Prison. He had been released after serving a five-year sentence, and he and Charlotte had managed to escape from Germany, and were now married, and in exile in Paris. But they were in trouble, and sought my help. The Stalinist purges had spread to the emigré world in France, and Karl and Charlotte, who had also become a Communist, were under suspicion from their Party colleagues, accused of having played in with the Gestapo to ensure their escape from the Reich. An emigré Communist tribunal was investigating them. It could help, they argued, to prove their case if I could certify to it that I had seen Karl in Moabit Prison on that particular day.

So on a bright summer afternoon in July 1939 I had found myself in an office in an old building just off the Boulevard St Germain, facing four men and a woman who sat behind a big oak desk piled high with papers. The air was thick with tobacco smoke, and through the tall windows came the familiar sounds of Paris, the blare of taxi horns, and the whistles of traffic policemen. Karl and Charlotte sat, anxious and intent, on two hard chairs at the side of the room, as I gave my account of that day four years earlier. I was cross-questioned for about half an hour. My evidence could not have been of much help to them, for they were both expelled from the Communist Party, and their photographs printed in the emigré press as people to be shunned. This may have been fortunate for them, for they set about emigrating to North America, where Karl built up a new existence as a clothing manufacturer, his political days very much over. He was more fortunate than the members of the tribunal which had condemned him. They were handed over to the Nazis when France fell, and died in concentration camps.

One mysterious Left Bank figure of this period was a German of

Czech origin, born in Brunn, who went by the name of Andre
Simone but whose real name was Otto Katz. Simone-Katz was a
small pale man in his early forties, who appeared self-effacing, but
was in fact skilfully self-assertive. One of his cheeks bore the scar of
a street fight with the Nazis in pre-1933 days, a characteristic which
led Edgar Mowrer of the *Chicago Daily News* to describe him as 'the
Jew with a duelling scar'. After the rise of Hitler, Katz had escaped
to Paris, where he led the Comintern propaganda on behalf of
Republican Spain, exaggerating or fabricating pro-Republican
news items for the left-wing French press.

My links with Simone (as I knew him), were not concerned with
Spain, for which I had no news responsibility, but with French
politics. On these he not only had good sources, but an avid interest
in discovering what was happening, which made him a useful
contact. In the twelve months leading up to the outbreak of war he
not only put me on to a number of good stories, particularly
concerning the flow of Nazi money into the French press, but had
a hard shrewd mind against which to test the multitude of rumours
and reports which swirled around Paris, where politics, society and
journalism intermingled on several levels.

Simone preferred for us to meet on the Right Bank, well away
from the Latin Quarter and Montparnasse cafés frequented by his
fellow Communists. He favoured in particular the downstairs room
of a large garish café on the Boulevard des Capucines, close to the
Place de l'Opéra. It had red leather and velvet banquettes, black-
topped tables, and bright strip lighting, and was frequented by
vividly dressed and vividly made up prostitutes who plied their trade
both in the café and on the pavements above. Into this gaudy setting
would suddenly appear the incongruous figure of Simone in a pale
khaki raincoat, with a bundle of newspapers under his arm. 'You
can buy nice girls here,' he said to me the first time we used this
rendezvous, in tones someone might have used in recommending
the cakes on offer in a *patisserie*.

Our discussions soon fell into a set pattern. It was the period when
the Stalinist trials were at their peak, and almost every day the
papers would carry reports from Moscow of one more unbelievable
accusation, one more unbelievable confession. I would challenge
Simone on the latest of these. He would be ready with his riposte,
often thrusting into my hand some lengthy cyclostyled statement
from Moscow, badly translated into English, of a so-called
confession. I still have the 800-page hardback copy of the official

court proceedings *In the Case of the anti-Soviet Bloc of rightists and Trotskyites* which he gave me. Each of us having in this way established our fundamental difference of political approach, we would settle down to our scrutiny of the French political scene, about which Simone could often be sardonically witty, for mixed with his dogmatism was a sense of humour. Then, as suddenly as he had arrived, he would gather up his papers, mutter about an urgent further meeting he had to attend, and disappear up the stairs. I used to wonder if these swift entrances and exits were a skill imparted by the Comintern to their key operatives.

One story which Simone and I, by pooling our information, successfully cracked concerned the manoeuvre of Daladier and Bonnet to do a secret deal with Italy, in which they would make some concessions about Djibouti, Tunis and the Suez Canal, whilst at the same time outwardly taking a determined stand against the Italian claims. Early in February 1939 Bonnet sent Paul Baudouin, president of the French-controlled Bank of Indo-China, to the Italian Foreign Minister in Rome, Count Ciano, to offer a deal. The Italians loyally informed their Axis partner. This alarmed the Nazi Government, who had no wish to see France solve her problems with Italy, and so be left free to face up to Germany. Ribbentrop therefore leaked details of the secret talks to pro-Nazi forces in Paris. I picked up a hint of these: so too did Simone. I consulted Tabouis, and within twenty-four hours both she and I were able to break the story. Daladier and Bonnet denied it furiously, but the talks were ultimately called off.

My problem, once I established the story, was to get the *Daily Express* to use it. Their sub-editors, ever sensitive to what would interest people in drab back streets in the Midlands, had little taste for stories about complex diplomatic manoeuvrings about remote places with unpronounceable names. I had to sell the story not only to our readers, but to the hard-headed sub-editors who guarded their portals. To do this, I exploited the fact that the three principal French figures involved all had surnames beginning with the letter B – Bonnet, Baudouin, and a third emissary, de Brinon. So I built up the story as 'The Mystery of the Three Messieurs B'. It proved a selling line, and Arthur Christiansen's 'suburban housewife in Walsall', at whom we were told to aim, was for several weeks kept well abreast of these developments. Remote though the places involved may have seemed in 1939, within the next few years men from Walsall and a multitude of similar towns in Britain were to move through Djbouti to free Abyssinia, and to fight fierce battles in Tunisia.

CHAPTER TWELVE

The Munich Lie Exposed

On 15 March 1939 the Great Munich Lie was at last exposed. At six o'clock that morning German troops crossed the frontiers of the rump state of Czechoslovakia and moved to occupy Prague, just three hours after the aged President Hacha had, in Berlin, signed away control of his country to the Germans. By mid-afternoon the *Paris Soir*'s front page was covered with photographs of the stunned crowds, tears coursing down their faces, watching German tanks and lorried infantry move down the Wenchelas Platz where, only six months before, I had seen the people of Prague demonstrate in their thousands their desire to defend their land. I could readily envisage the other scenes the cameras did not catch, as the squads of Gestapo and of the SS hustled people from their homes into the backs of vans, on their way to the concentration camp and the blood-stained interrogation cellar. I hoped that Jaksch, and Schafranik and Ripka and the host of others whose sole crime was to love their country, had been able to escape. But at least in Britain and France the air was now clearer, and the lie had been given to the belief that Hitler had been sated at Munich, and that if we were polite to him peace was assured.

Yet I was not surprised when, that afternoon in the Commons, Chamberlain showed no sign of giving up his illusions about Hitler. Far from condemning this new move, the British Prime Minister did not speak of Czechoslovakia as having been invaded. Instead it had 'become disintegrated'. Sir John Simon explained that the guarantees which at Munich we had given to protect the frontiers of reshaped Czechoslovakia could not be applied, as that Czechoslovakia had ceased to exist. Chamberlain stressed that he had no wish to associate himself with any of the charges of breach of faith on Hitler's part which were being 'bandied about'.

This speech was prominently displayed in the Swiss newspapers which I bought the next morning on the platform in Zurich, on my way by train to Bucharest. Rumania, with its rich oil reserves, and its own homegrown Fascist movement, the Iron Guards, seemed set to be the Nazis' next target. I broke my journey in Budapest. Our correspondent there, an old friend from my Vienna days, had been mobilised. But his young, dark-haired wife was in their flat overlooking the Danube, and it was there, on their short wave radio, that I heard the BBC report of Neville Chamberlain's speech at Birmingham on the evening of 17 March. It contained an astonishing change of tone. Now he spoke of Czechoslovakia having been invaded, of its independence having been lost, of Hitler having 'taken the law into his own hands'. Chamberlain promised to consult with France and with the countries of the Commonwealth, who, like Britain, were not 'disinterested in South-East Europe'. Were we at last preparing to stand and resist? Was indeed this speech intended to deter a further move in the Balkans, with Rumania as its target?

Bucharest in the early spring of 1939 was an imitation Paris, part flashy, part musty in a way which seemed characteristic of those Balkan countries which had for centuries been under the Turks. Along the wide tree-lined Chaussée, a would-be Champs Elysées with its own Triumphal Arch (which, on close examination, proved to be made of concrete), stucco-fronted mansions stood like stage sets in Hollywood. The side roads were muddy and unpaved, ending abruptly in open country, and over it all was the immense, arching sky of the Danube delta. Droskies, wooden arches curving above their shafts, and pulled by magnificent, long-maned horses, rattled through the streets alongside modern cars and lorries. On the crowded Calle Victorei you gathered at eleven in the morning to take a glass of champagne and eat caviare, served by the scoopful. In the early warm evening air you dined in a garden restaurant where officers in sky-blue uniforms, direct from the pages of a Ruritanian romance, bent to kiss the hands of vivid-lipped women who strove to emulate the chic of Paris, but somehow never seemed to achieve more than a rather strident version of it. Even the bronze of their gleaming hair, which those knowledgeable in such matters assured me was its true colour, looked as if it was the product of a dye. Yet though so much of this culture was ersatz, the place had an abounding vitality, a sense of being the capital of a land of rich natural resources – which it was – which overcame its falsities.

The British Government had by now become convinced (on the basis of what has since been shown to be inaccurate information) that Hitler was indeed about to seize Rumania, and King Carol was pressurised into mobilising a substantial part of his armed forces. The order calling up reservists was published on the evening on which I was travelling by train towards Arad, on the Rumanian–Hungarian frontier. I awoke to find that at every station at which we halted the platforms were crowded with peasants reporting for duty; tall, moustachioed men in rough sheepskin jackets and high black woollen caps, their legs bound with straps of bast, and often with bast shoes on their feet. Their womenfolk, young and old, in bright green and red dresses, with white kerchiefs on their heads, talked and wept and gesticulated. As the train drew out they gave way to a shrill, undulating wail which struck straight at the emotions, the anguish of simple people caught up in events which they feared – and rightly feared – would prove both painful and long.

As station after station yielded up its reservists, the carriages of the train became jammed with men and bundles. They spread into the *wagon-lit* carriage, filling the corridor and ultimately crowding into the first class compartment into which my sleeping berth had been transformed. The *wagon-lit* attendant protested at the door that they should not disturb 'the gentleman'. One big peasant answered swiftly in Rumanian. I asked the attendant what he had said. 'He says that this is war – and in war there are no longer gentlemen, only men.'

Throughout the Balkans that March, the last time I was to visit them until, two years later, I found myself as a soldier in Greece, there was a sense of dislocation, of stones loosening which would soon precipitate a landslide. In the black earth of the Danubian plain, in disputed territory long claimed from Rumania by Hungary, troops in the yellowish khaki of the Rumanian army dug trenches and trained their machine guns on either side of the road leading to Budapest. They had to keep an eye to their backs all the time, for this was a Hungarian-speaking area, reft from Hungary at the end of the Great War, eager to be united to Hungary. Their spokesman was the Roman Catholic Bishop of Arad, who was extremely cordial to me, not only because he wanted to plead the case of the Hungarian minority but because he was an avid reader of the *Sunday Express*, an *outré* activity for a cleric in those days. His dark brown eyes glowed with excitement when I assured him that I had indeed seen Lord Castlerosse, the gossip columnist of the *Sunday Express*, in the flesh – a fitting phrase for this Irish peer, who must have weighed close on eighteen stone.

In Zagreb, Matchek, the Croatian leader, spoke warily of the need for self-rule for the Croats within Jugoslavia. Zagreb was a quiet city, Austrian in appearance (Croatia had been part of Austro-Hungary until 1918), with yellow stucco buildings and tree-lined streets where the sound of horses' hooves outdid that of the occasional car or lorry. Brown-eyed, wide-browed girls walked past, as proud as the girls who had walked last summer through the streets of Prague. The young men at the corner laughed, trying to catch their glances. Around the reception desk in my hotel crowded a group of Jewish refugees, just in from Prague, their luggage piled high behind them. One middle-aged woman put on the desk a brand new British passport and said in German, 'I go on to London tomorrow.'

In Vienna camouflaged Reichswehr lorries moved through the streets, and steel-cowled Reichswehr troops marched along the Ringstrasse with set faces. At Leonding, the boyhood home of Adolf Hitler, near Linz, a banner, stained by recent snow, swung above the muddy road. It proclaimed, 'A New Thousand Year Era Begins. Heil Hitler.' Beyond Munich red lights glowed in the darkness, warning aircraft to keep away from Dachau concentration camp.

CHAPTER THIRTEEN

Troubled Spring

The spring months which followed, though overhung by the threat of war, were at least free of the cant and falsehoods of the post-Munich period. Beaverbrook allowed the *Daily Express*, after at first opposing the guarantee to Poland, gradually to shift its position to one of standing firm against further German aggression. 'We have forty-nine million foreign secretaries in Britain these days,' it declared in a leader, 'and they all seem to want to make a stand.' So the paper went along with them, at least as far as ceasing to pretend that Hitler did not pose a threat. I could work for it now in a much easier frame of mind, no longer feeling that I was caught up in a conspiracy – however frank I might try to make my own reporting – to lull the public into an attitude of false security.

Our personal lives were brighter too. On March 8 our second child was born in the American Hospital at Neuilly. It was a boy, and we gave him the name of Patrick. It was the name of Cecily's younger brother, and this was our bid to offset the fact that two days after the baby's birth Lieutenant Patrick Turner of the Royal Marines had died at sea, having jumped overboard from HMS *Ramillies* off Malta in an effort to save one of his men, who had fallen from the deck in a rough sea.

With the baby's birth Cecily's allergy had disappeared, and she was soon fit enough to live a full life again. Late in April we took a holiday at the village of Sils Maria in the Engadine in Switzerland, the last we were to have for many years. We climbed to the edge of the snowline. Where the white crust crumbled and melted, white crocuses sprang up amidst the flattened grass. There was still snow enough on the tops to provide a passage for the coffee smugglers, dark figures on skis making their way across from Italy, watched through binoculars by the Swiss frontier guards. The warmer weather brought landslides to the steep mountainsides, setting cascades of rocks tumbling and bounding down the bare screes, to splash like shell bursts into the blue waters of the lake. In a wooden chalet by its waters Nietzsche had written *So Spake Zarathustra*. Here he penned his picture of the man of the future, 'anti-Christ and anti-nihilist, conqueror of both God and Unbeing', a vision which had helped to inspire Adolf Hitler towards deeds the full horror of which we had in that spring of 1939 not yet envisaged.

Yet even in this remote valley in this most neutral of countries there were reminders of the threat of war. The Swiss had called up their reservists for army manoeuvres, and grey-uniformed troops, skis on shoulders, trudged through the village street at dawn. On the road which wound down from Maloja to Lake Como gun barrels showed in the slits of fortresses cut into the living rock. Across the Italian frontier Como lay benign and lovely, a stretch of pale blue silk in the spring sunshine. We drank apéritifs at a lakeside café just a kilometre or so from the spot where, six years later almost to the day, Mussolini and his mistress Clara Petacci were to be seized by the partisans, and taken off to be killed and hung by their heels from the awning of a filling station near Milan.

In May I took a late ski-ing holiday at Lac de Tignes, in the Haute Savoie. In those days you had to climb by foot for half an hour from the now-drowned valley floor to reach the plateau, ringed with mountain peaks, where one lone chalet stood, and where today a whole town has been erected. There were no ski lifts, and we climbed with skins tied under our skis to the tops of the runs, coming down in twenty minutes across a stretch which had taken three hours to ascend. Except for one other visitor, a Swiss, the hotel was occupied by a film unit making a feature film. A score or more of the world's foremost skiers were taking part in it, and at the end of the day's filming they would swoop down the slope carrying huge loads and cameras and other gear on their backs. It was late enough in the season, too, for avalanches to be a constant feature, roaring and thundering every half hour or so from the high peaks, during the heat of the day. I went back to Paris fitter than I had been for years.

That spring and summer gave us a last rich taste of a Paris which was never to be the same again. The rate of exchange made the pound worth a lot in francs. With the generous living allowances the *Daily Express* paid to its men abroad we could live well. Many mornings I rode in the Bois de Boulogne, cantering along the sandy rides which wound for miles amidst the oaks and beeches of that huge park. There were pleasant tennis courts at St Cloud, and good swimming at the Porte Molitor and even in a huge wooden swimmimg pool moored in the Seine close to the Quai d'Orsay, in river water as yet remarkably unpolluted by passing barge traffic. In the evening the highly efficient services of the French post office enabled me to dine out, and yet stay on the job. The telephone exchange would divert any calls coming in to your number to any other number you designated. Several of our neighbourhood restaurants became in this way out-stations of the *Daily Express* office. Two were our particular favourites – Pierre in the Place Gaillon, and the Roy Gourmet in the Place des Victoires. At their doorways trays of oysters and sea urchins and lobsters were ranged in straw baskets. Inside were coarse white tablecloths, and constantly bustling, ever friendly waitresses, and family parties with napkins tucked under their chins, discussing eagerly what they should eat, what they were eating, and – over the cognac *pour la dégustation* – what they had eaten. Wild strawberries sprinkled with white wine were a speciality of the Pierre, and *canard aux olives* and *ris de veau au Marsala* those of the Roy Gourmet.

On a Saturday evening we could go up market and up town, to Fouquet's which offered a *table d'hôte* dinner and a half bottle of wine per person for the then modest equivalent of ten shillings sterling, or Pruniers for *quenelles de brochet* of exquisite texture and taste. We used the great restaurants, like Maxims and the Tour d'Argent and Le Grand Vefour only sparingly, if we had guests to entertain who needed to be impressed. And Le Pré Catalan in the heart of the Bois on a warm summer evening was subtle luxury at its peak.

After dinner at Fouquet's we could cross the Avenue Georges Cinq to listen to the pianist at the Boeuf sur le Toit, the pleasantest bar in this part of Paris. Though the Boeuf had a reputation as a meeting place for homosexuals, they formed – at least to the outward eye – only a small part of the clientele, and in the custom of the day did not flaunt their tastes. Throughout the period from Munich to the outbreak of war one tune was to be heard in every Paris bar and nightclub, the slow, poignant lilt of 'J'Attendrai', fitting exactly the mood of fatalism, melancholy and yet hope of the time. Noël Coward's words 'Ah, the potency of cheap music' were never more true than in the thirties. Perhaps because hit tunes were fewer, and held their place longer, perhaps because the tunes were in themselves more memorable, a handful of songs formed a constant background music to the march of events. Prague had gone valiantly forward in the summer and early autumn of 1938 to the tune which was sweeping London – and indeed New York – 'Doin' the Lambeth Walk'. *The Times* had even noted, in a fourth

leader that if war were to come, 'Doin' the Lambeth Walk' might
prove to be the equivalent of 1914's 'Tipperary'. So 'J'Attendrai',
the tune to which the reservists had gone off in September 1938 to
man the Maginot Line, was to remain the theme song of France in
the last months of peace in 1939. It was indeed to be the most
evocative tune of its period until Eric Maschwitz's 'A Nightingale
Sang in Berkeley Square' was to catch exactly the mood of nostalgia
and daring of the summer of 1940, when it became the favourite
record played on their gramophones by young fighter pilots as they
awaited the order to scramble during the Blitz.

Alternatively, on those summer nights of 1939, we could drive
across to the Rue St Anne, near the Opera, to hear Suzy Solidor
sing in the *boîte* which bore her name. The walls of its one long,
narrow room were hung with modern paintings, some seascapes
from her native Brittany, others portraits of the *chanteuse* herself by
leading artists of the day – Domergue and van Dongen, Yves
Brayer and Jean Dunard, even a drawing of her by Jean Cocteau.
Suzy Solidor herself, tall, with a strong, curved Viking nose, wide-
set eyes and ash-blonde hair in a page boy bob – *à la Jeanne d'Arc*
as the French said – sang or recited in a warm, strong, mezzo-
contralto voice which seemed to belong more to the outdoors than
to this crowded Parisian room. Her voice was part of the ambiguity
which surrounded Suzy Solidor, an ambiguity which was perhaps
the secret of her attraction. It was partly sexual, but partly also that
of the contrast between the wind-swept Atlantic coasts of her youth
and this elegant and indeed decadent Paris. The *chanteuse*'s long
gleaming Schiaparelli and Chanel evening dresses, often a metallic
gold or silver or jet, were the highest of *haute couture*. Yet the bare
shoulders which they fashionably displayed were the rounded,
strong, sunburned shoulders of a swimmer, and her gaze, above the
crimson curve of her sharply outlined lips was as much that of the
mariner as of the *grande elegante*. And which she changed abruptly
from the haunting rhythms of her famous 'Les Filles de Saint Malo'
to Cole Porter's 'Night and Day', the contrast, and the ambiguity
was a mixture which intoxicated Paris, and it became the fashionable thing for society hostesses to bring their dinner guests on to
Suzy Solidor's to round off the evening.

One of the few people impervious to her personality was Lord
Beaverbrook. At his request, I took him there on one evening. The
visit was not a success. Beaverbrook did not have enough French to
follow her songs, and though Suzy Solidor made a point of coming

to our table (I had ensured that she had been advised in advance of his visit), and spoke to Beaverbrook in fluent English, each was too strong a personality for there to be any rapport. It was on this occasion that I first realised that what Beaverbrook demanded – at any rate in his leisure hours – was not so much friends, as a court.

There were also, in that Paris of 1939, excellent places for that most English of occasions, afternoon tea. Rumplemeyer's and La Marquise de Seville offered millefeuilles and éclairs and surprisingly good Indian and china tea, as well as a range of the tisanes loved by the French matrons who, dressed as if for Gold Cup day at Ascot, chattered eagerly at the tiny tables. Almost equally in vogue with Parisian society was the tearoom run by W. H. Smith's above their English bookshop in the Rue de Rivoli, which served good strong Indian tea, and crumpets and buttered anchovy toast.

More spectacular, and very much of its period, was the scene in the late afternoon in the huge gilded foyers of the two main tourist hotels off the Champs Elysées, the Georges Cinq and the Prince de Galles. Between five and seven o'clock, particularly on a Saturday, they saw an extraordinary parade of the rich and the would-be rich, where the *grandes* – and not so *grandes* – *cocottes*, silver fox furs draped over the arms of their gilt chairs, mingled – without any apparent embarrassment to either side – with Parisian matrons and rich Americans. It was Veblen's theory of conspicuous consumption displayed in its most vivid form – and, it seems, for the last time in Western Europe. For when the rich emerged again after the war, they took care to keep the display of their wealth within their own increasingly guarded compounds.

The theatres too were crowded that summer. Cocteau's *Parents Terribles*, in the Theatre Marigny near the Rond Point, drew crowds whose elegance made the scenes in the foyer during the entr'acte as dazzling as anything on the stage, with the latest work of the great couturiers – Schiaparelli, Chanel, Worth, Paquin – being worn with a casual pride. A similar parade, where the faces rather than the clothes caught the eye, took place between acts at the Comedie Française, where Voltaire in marble sardonically watched from his armchair the crowd pacing the long broad hallway. In this throng one evening was a woman whose somewhat coarsened features exuded an extraordinary vitality and confidence, a quality emphasised by her hat. In the fashion of the time it was in gleaming black straw, fitting with a narrow brim, like the hat of a village curé, but decorated with a shaft of fur rather like a monkey's tail. She stalked around, talking animatedly, contemptuously indifferent to the fact that the appendage to her hat was apt to thrust itself into the faces of others strolling in the foyer. Pierre Lazareff, who was with us that evening, identified her. *'C'est la Comtesse Hélène de Portes, la maîtresse de Paul Reynaud.'*

Yet these pleasant times were overshadowed by the constant realisation that war could be on us before the year was out, a threat which loomed like a distant thunderstorm on a sunny day. It both sharpened and soured our enjoyment. We lived that summer in a way in which, I was later to experience, men and women live together during periods of leave from the battlefront, with gladness and sorrow intertwined. It was a sensation at its sharpest at the beginning and the end of the day. I woke to the superb vista of the Bois beyond our windows, with one sturdy son running across the sunlit room towards us, and another cheerful in his cot, only to feel the sudden pang of their vulnerability. At night when we came home the Bois would be black, with the Eiffel Tower outlined against a sky glowing with the city lights. The broad line of the Seine below us, gleaming in the moonlight, was not only beautiful but, one realised, a source of danger, a clear guide to enemy bombers, so easy to envisage sweeping in from the east, leading them to the new bridge under construction just upstream, and to the roofs of the huge riverside Renault factory, busy now on night shift building tanks and trucks for France's rearmament programme.

The *Daily Express* office in Paris was housed in two large rooms in the modern seven-storied building of the leading French popular paper of the day, the *Paris Soir*, in the Rue du Louvre. It was set in a mixed quartier of tall, grey-stuccoed, wooden-shuttered building where finance, newspapers, small workshops and good restaurants jostled one another. The Paris Bourse, a grey, columned building, like a discoloured Greek temple, was close by, and during dealing hours the clamour of its dealers, many of them bargaining on the wide steps of the building, brought echoes of penned animals in distant stockyards. The Bank of France, the National Library, and the colonnades and garden of the Palais Royale were at our back. So too were several of the most celebrated Maisons Closes of Paris, one, the House of Nations, offering its delights in bedrooms each decorated in the style of a different country.

Paris Soir was an evening paper, owned by a millionaire textile magnate turned newspaper proprietor, M Jean Prouvost, and edited by Pierre Lazareff, a small, eager Jew, with thick, pebble-lensed spectacles, whose family stemmed from Poland. Lazareff was a genius in news presentation – quite the equal, in French terms, of Arthur Christiansen. He used his front page largely as a billboard for the contents of the inside pages, with huge headlines dramatising the main story, and a lavish use of pictures. His wife, small, dark, and good-looking, was an equally successful editress in her own right and under her own name of Hélène Gordon. She had built up the women's weekly *Marie Claire* into part of the fabric of French life. Under them the *Paris Soir* building, jutting like the rounded prow of an ocean liner on to the small Place d'Aboukir, pulsated with life, as motor cyclists dashed up with the latest copy or cans of film, as elegantly dressed reporters, overcoats slung like cloaks over their shoulders, moved gravely towards the lift. I relished the vitality of it all, enjoyed being greeted as *'cher collègue'* by Pierre Lazareff as, in his high-pitched, confident voice, he would call me into his office ostensibly to tell me some item of political gossip, but really to share with me his pleasure in the pattern of a page or the use of a photograph.

A central figure of the *Daily Express* Paris office was the secretary, a White Russian, Princess Mara Scherbatoff. Tall, dark, calm, with a rounded, Slavonic face, she glided rather than walked, moving with an erect, easy dignity no doubt acquired by generations of her forebears on the parquet floors of lofty palace rooms in St Petersburg and Moscow. She moves *comme la Reine Elizabeth*, the commissionaire in the hallway of the Paris Soir building would comment admiringly, going on to explain that the queen he had in mind was not the recently crowned Queen of England but the new great liner portrayed in newsreels of the time making its way serenely across the seas.

Mara Scherbatoff was the oldest of four equally beautiful sisters, one of whom was the head mannequin at Balenciaga. They lived with their old Swiss governess in a flat in Passy. Scherb, as she was called by everyone, had no shorthand, and her typing was slow, but she spoke English, French and Russian perfectly, and provided an admirably steady, as well as a glamorous centre to the swirl of a newspaper office.

My work was made the pleasanter in the summer of 1939 by the arrival in the Paris office of a new assistant who delighted in handling the sex and scandal stories so beloved by the London news desk. He was a sturdy, middle-aged, whimsical Scot called Donald Augustin Robertson – though no one ever called him anything but

Robbie – whom the paper had hurriedly posted abroad until a row he had had with the Metropolitan Police had died down. Sent to cover a story of a gang battle in London's East End, Robbie had seized a moment when the desk in the Poplar police station had been left unmanned. Posing as a detective, he summoned a suspect from the waiting room into a nearby interview room, grilled him and got the full story, and then departed before the station sergeant knew what had happened. His resultant story had produced demands for Robbie to be charged with impersonating a police officer. Christiansen suddenly remembered Robbie had learnt French during World War I, and attached him to the Paris office. He transformed my life. Not only did he take over all the so-called human interest stories, but he did them with marvellous gusto and humour.

Robbie had one of those varied backgrounds which characterised Fleet Street men in the days before journalists were mass produced from universities and schools of journalism. He had at one time been a violinist on the music halls. He played well, but it was his gimmick rather than his music which could bring down the house. Before each performance he would carefully pace out the distance between where he would stand to play, and the edge of the orchestra pit. As he reached the crescendo of his main piece, he would seem to be so wrapped up in the music, so carried away by his feelings and his concentration, that his gaze would turn upwards. At the same time he would begin to move forward, step by step, closer and closer to the edge of the stage, until with the next step it would seem certain that, with eyes averted, he must plunge on to the heads of the orchestra. The audience would watch, riveted, until with one foot outstretched, apparently about to step into space, he would bring the piece to a triumphant end. Relief from the tension – as well as appreciation for his playing – would ensure a tumult of applause, a fact which would delight as well as puzzle the music-hall managers.

Robbie's arrival enabled me to undertake some investigative journalism into the flow into France of Nazi money to be used for anti-Semitic and anti-British propaganda. The name of Bonnet, the Foreign Minister, kept cropping up in rumours about the distribution of these funds. My inquiries led me to some strange sights – to a flat in the fashionable Paris suburb of Passy where even the wallpaper had been stripped from the walls, leaving only the stained and scratched plaster, in a police search for evidence: to a frightened woman in Angers, south-west of Paris, who was so relieved to discover that I was not yet another detective coming to grill her that she poured out her story to me; the trail led from her to a blonde German au pair girl who left abruptly for Holland just an hour before I reached the home where she had been employed. I discovered that there had indeed been a Bonnet engaged in handling money from Germany. It was not, however, the Foreign Minister, but a newphew of his, who held a minor post in Pari-Mutuel, the French totalisator system.

The clues ultimately led back to Otto Abetz, the Nazis' chief agent and unofficial ambassador in Paris. Though he was a close friend of both Georges and Madame Bonnet, the evidence against him was strong enough for the French Sûreté to expel him from the country. I traced the blonde au pair to the Hague, and was about to go off to interview her there when J. B. Wilson, the *Daily Express* news editor, intervened. He had studied a photograph of the girl, with long hair falling over a sunburned shoulder, taken on the beach in Holland. 'Cox is not at all her type,' he opined. 'A dark sardonic type is likely to be much more her line. Send Montagu Lacey.' And so Lacey, from the London staff, departed for Holland, and proved Wilson's judgement correct by producing a lengthy interview – and photographs which delighted Christiansen.

This story gained me considerable publicity in Paris. The French papers, inhibited as they were from investigating too closely the affairs of their own ministers, avidly reprinted my findings. This was particularly the case with the left centre *L'Ordre*, for which Tabouis now wrote, and which was edited by a massive veteran of Verdun, Emil Buré. '*Cox, de la grande quotidienne anglaise, le Daily Express*' became a much-quoted source in his pages.

In July I visited Verdun, the World War I battlefield which to the French meant all that the Somme and Passchendaele meant for Britain – and indeed more, for it had been fought on French soil, and had its fortresses fallen in 1917 the way to Paris would have been open. The ruined Fort Douaumont was still surrounded by rusty barbed wire entanglements, overgrown trenches and mine craters. Behind it a huge ossuary presented a dignified, cathedral-like front but through the basement windows at the back could be seen the bones and skulls of tens of thousands of unidentified bodies. Beside it was the Trench of Bayonets, where the tops of twenty-four rifles, with long thin bayonets attached, showed in a ragged line above the earth which filled the trench. Beneath, it was claimed, the holders of the rifles stood, buried, engulfed by the earth thrown up by a land mine which had exploded as they prepared to go over the top in a charge.

Even the hideous concrete walls which had been built around the trench, making it look like a municipal water works, and the broken strings of rosaries, scraps of ugly purple wreaths, and stray bits of wood and paper which littered the trench surface could not destroy its poignancy. Even more moving were the mile upon mile of cratered ground which covered these rolling hills, pockmarked by countless shell holes. The green leaves on new, stunted bushes could not hide these craters, filled with stagnant water or churned gravel or rank grass. It made me think of telescopic photographs of the moon's surface. This was the outcome of a war fought only twenty years earlier – and a presage of what a new war could mean for us, the generation who would be called on to fight it.

On that sunny afternoon, with the larks singing high above these ravaged hills, it was almost more than the mind could take in that such events could ever be deliberately set in train again. Yet even here the signs were clear. Beyond Douaumont a new barrier cut through the old, rusty barbed wire. The road, a notice said, was closed to all but military traffic. Lorries carrying material for new fortifications ground their way along the dusty track.

CHAPTER FOURTEEN

'There Will Be No War'

Towards the end of July Lord Beaverbrook paid his last visit to Paris before the war began, en route to the Riviera in the company of his close friend and employee, Viscount Castlerosse. It was to give me my friendliest contact with him in this pre-war period. I had expected it to be otherwise, for I had turned down as worthless a story which he had brought to the paper's attention. A titled English lady in Monte Carlo was gaining fame locally as a faith healer, claiming to be able to cure by laying on of hands. The fame may have been genuine, but our local correspondent could find no evidence of its being based on any genuine cures. The *Sunday Express*, however, thought otherwise. A few days after I had rejected the story, they sent a special correspondent down from London who found it all very true and very wonderful.

When I entered Beaverbrook's suite at the Ritz the *Sunday Express* lay prominently displayed. 'I see you were scooped yesterday,' said his lordship. Not so, I countered, the *Sunday Express* had got it wrong.

To my surprise, Beaverbrook did not show annoyance. Instead, he turned to Castlerosse. It was the first time I had met this Irish peer whom Beaverbrook ranked not only amongst his leading columnists, but amongst his closest friends. A tall, sleek, pear-shaped figure, superbly dressed in a dove-grey morning suit and black cravat, in which shone a jewelled tie pin, with shrewd eyes alert above long, close-shaven jowls, he allowed himself a slight smile as Beaverbrook said:

'We have an independent witness here. Lord Castlerosse knows the lady well. Tell me, Valentine, could Lady X cure you by laying on of hands?'

'It all depends where she laid them on,' came the Viscount's swift reply.

The main reason why Beaverbrook had summoned me proved to be more serious. With the threat of war ever closer, he wanted a candid survey made of the attitude towards a possible war of the ordinary people of France and Germany. This, he claimed, needed a fresher eye than a resident correspondent could bring to bear. Therefore, instead of my reporting on how the French felt, I was to go to Germany and find an answer to the question 'Will Germany fight for Danzig?' Castlerosse would do the same in France. We would meet in three days' time, here at the Ritz, to report our findings.

To assess accurately in three days the feelings of a nation living under a dictatorship, with security already tightened as it mobilised for war, verged on the absurd. I decided the best thing was to call on the British consuls in Düsseldorf, Essen and Cologne. If there was hostility to Hitler, it would be in this traditional working class heartland, the Ruhr. All three consuls proved to be sensible and helpful. They were unanimous that not only would the Germans fight, albeit reluctantly, but that they would go on fighting so long as they were called to do so. The anti-Nazi Right were powerless so long as Hitler was successful. The Left was smashed to smithereens and could be revived only in a defeated Germany. I supplemented this with more direct research, chatting to workmen in small taverns close to the railway station in each of these cities, and in talks with a correspondent of the *Kölnischer Zeitung* I had come to know in Prague. Though there was no sign of the elation with which Germany had gone to war in 1914, and everywhere a sense of concern and apprehension, there was no sign either of opposition to Hitler. To the traditional German sense of discipline had been added both the constraints of Nazi terror and an unmistakable trust still widespread in Hitler as the Führer.

Three days later I reported at the Ritz at noon. As I waited in an anteroom Castlerosse arrived. 'I've a message to be here by twelve,' he said. 'Do you know what it's for?' I reminded him of our assignments. 'Hell!' he commented. 'I had completely forgotten about it. I've made no enquiries at all.'

I thought my findings would be unpalatable to Beaverbrook, as I expected him to be hoping for signs of anti-Nazi feeling in Germany which could curb Hitler. But he nodded his agreement. 'The German sense of discipline is bound to assert itself at a time like this.' Then he turned to Castlerosse. 'Now, Valentine,' he said, 'tell me of your findings. Will the French fight for Danzig?'

Castlerosse relied on candour. 'Max,' he replied, 'I haven't got much further in my enquiries than the bar of Fouquet's. But I can tell you one thing for sure. No one in the bar of Fouquet's is going to fight for Danzig.'

It was to prove a shrewder assessment than appeared at the time. For the rich who drank in Fouquet's, many of them very much the *nouveaux riches*, reflected accurately the views of their fellows who, when the crunch came in the summer of 1940, preferred to surrender to the Nazis than to continue a fight which could put their wealth and power at risk.

Early in August the old Adam of Beaverbrook's appeasement reasserted itself. He got Christiansen to conduct a poll of *Daily Express* correspondents in Europe on whether there would be war in Europe in 1939. I was convinced that the French would do everything possible to avoid fighting for Danzig and Poland, and that when the crunch came Chamberlain would find some means of doing a Munich on the Poles – as indeed he would have done had Hitler been prepared to accept a Polish surrender instead of yielding to the temptation to launch the first blitzkrieg. So I replied, 'The odds are now in favour of there being no war this summer and autumn – but only just.'

It was a view which, even as late as 15 August, was shared by the well-placed Canadian diplomat Charles Ritchie, later to be Canadian High Commissioner in London. He noted in his diary for that day: 'We are to sell out the Poles apparently . . . the advice going out to them from the Foreign Office over Danzig is just what we told the Czechs this time last year over the Sudeten crisis.' What neither Ritchie nor I foresaw was how the odds would be abruptly swung on 23 August, when Stalin entered into his pact with Hitler, the deal which enabled the Nazis not only to attack Poland without fear of Russian intervention, but to share the spoils with them.

Of the fourteen *Daily Express* correspondents in Europe (how many popular papers today have four, let alone fourteen correspondents in Europe?) twelve opted clearly for no war in 1939, whilst two hedged their bets. Beaverbrook had these findings triumphantly blazoned across the front page of the *Express* on 7 August. He was later to make much play of this poll. On it he justified the repeated use in the paper of the slogan 'There will be no war this year or next year either'. This was nonsense. The slogan had been in use by the *Daily Express* for fifteen months, ever since its first appearance in May 1938, before this poll of correspondents was conducted. The attitude it expressed had been implicit, and often explicit, in a multitude of leading articles and feature pieces

from early 1937 onwards. It was Beaverbrook's view long before any
of his correspondents were asked to give theirs. In the event, the 'No
War This Year' slogan was used only once more in the *Daily Express*,
on 11 August. By this time, in any case, it was too late for public
opinion to be affected. What had mattered was Beaverbrook's
appeasement stance over Czechoslovakia, when a tough stand might
have prevented war, and even earlier, when the seizure of Austria
made plain that Nazism was on the march. Even so, it stung when,
the opening sequence of Noël Coward's film *In Which We Serve*
showed the front page of 7 August 1939. I was thankful that when
I first saw this film, it was in an open-air cinema behind the front
line in Italy, and I wore the khaki of a serving soldier.

This was not the first time Lord Beaverbrook had canvassed the
views of his staff. In the summer of 1938 all the main members of
the editorial staff were asked to state their political views. These
would, it was stressed, be kept in the strictest confidence. I replied
that I belonged to no political party, but had voted Labour at the
1935 General Election. Alan Moorehead thought this was a good
formula, and recorded that he too had never belonged to a political
party, but had voted Conservative in 1935.

The findings of this poll, held now in the Beaverbrook Library,
show that Tom Driberg had answered without hesitation, 'I am a
member of the Communist Party of Great Britain.' At a time when
Communists working in Fleet Stret were usually anxious –
presumably on Party instructions – to keep their membership
quiet, this was a surprising admission. The most likely explanation
for it became clear only after Driberg's death, when it became
known that he had been a member of MI5 throughout the thirties.
Indeed he remained one until Anthony Blunt in his own MI5 role
discovered the fact during the war, with the result that Driberg was
abruptly expelled from the Communist Party in 1942. It is likely
that Beaverbrook knew of Driberg's link with MI5, providing a
good reason – and a good excuse – for him to keep this brilliant
journalist in his team despite his Communist associations.

CHAPTER FIFTEEN

Towards the Precipice

By mid-August events began to move at a pace which made fore-casting superfluous. From Danzig, from the Polish frontiers, and from Berlin appeared the signs we had come to recognise that Hitler was about to move against yet another country. Arms, including even armoured cars, were being smuggled into Danzig for the use of local Nazis. At border stations disputes began to erupt between Polish and German guards. The Swiss Dr Carl Burckhardt, who ruled Danzig as the League of Nations High Commissioner, was invited to Berchtesgaden and subjected to a tirade from the Führer. German press and radio each day printed more and more stories of alleged Polish atrocities against Germans living in Poland.

Then just before midnight on 21 August came the news which made war seem a virtual certainty. I learnt of it in the strident setting of the Café Coliseé, the biggest and brashest of the cafés of the Champs Elysées. We often dined or drank there now in the evenings, because it had a Havas ticker tape machine in its basement on which we could check on developments. It was this machine on which, amidst the perfumed and noisy setting of Parisians and Parisiennes making telephone calls and chatting, the news was spelt out just before midnight on 21 August that the Soviet Union and Nazi Germany had agreed to sign a non-aggression pact. Unbelievingly, I twice read through these few words, set out in the bright blue type of the Havas machine, my mind yielding only slowly to the knowledge that this meant only one thing – war.

I was thankful that Cecily and our two boys were at this time on holiday in England, with her mother in Sussex. I arranged for her to stay there until the Polish crisis either blew over or became war. I locked up the St Cloud flat, and moved into a small hotel near the office, the Hôtel St Romain in the Rue Saint Roch. It was in a pleasantly historic quarter. The walls of the church of St Roch still bore the marks left by the 'whiff of grapeshot' which Napoleon had fired from two 8-pounder cannons to disperse the last counter-revolutionary attack and consolidate the grip of the Convention on

post-revolutionary France in 1795. The Palace of the Bourbons
which the mob had stormed in 1789 had stood just across the way,
on the far side of the Rue de Rivoli. The Tuileries Gardens, with
their formal flower beds and gravel walks now occupied the site.
They provided a perfect place on which to read the papers on a
sunny day, with before one the finest city view in the world, the long
sweep of the Champs Elysées rising towards the Arc de Triomphe
on the sky line.

The St Romain had no bar, and provided no meals beyond coffee
and rolls for breakfast, but its small rooms were scrupulously clean,
and its proprietors, Monsieur and Madame Lamartine, came to be
my friends, a friendship which was cemented in the next summer
when the St Romain was my base during the Battle of France.

Paris in the closing weeks of August saw a strange pilgrimage, as
those who loved it, particularly Britons and Americans, sought a
final taste of its life before the deluge engulfed us all. Claud
Cockburn was in the Dome, as ill-shaven and sardonically ebullient
as ever, with a lithe young woman with a small head of jet black
hair, who looked like a figure from a Scott Fitzgerald novel, and
spoke with the most cut-glass English accent I had ever heard. As
we came near to war, I thought, we all revert to type, and Claud's
type, whatever his Communist beliefs, was that of a ruling class.
Dan Davin, who had come to Oxford as a Rhodes Scholar in 1936,
was in the Deux Magots, a first in Greats from Balliol under his belt,
and a pile of saucers on the table in front of him proclaiming that
war or no war there was always time for a drink and a debate with
friends. John Mulgan and Jack Bennet from Auckland arrived in
time for us to fit in a few days at a small riverside hotel on the bank
of the Seine, west of Paris. John had with him the typescript of *Man
Alone*, the only novel fate was to permit him to write. I read it in a
small bedroom overlooking the village square, whilst in the café
below the juke box thumped out the hit song of the moment:

Jeepers, creepers, where did ya get those peepers?
Jeepers, creepers, where did ya get those eyes?

and the reservists in cheap khaki uniforms danced the Lambeth
Walk with girls in dresses of imitation silk and satin.

We talked of the trench warfare we assumed would be our lot, and
of how well or badly we would face up to the moment when we in

our turn, like the men buried at Verdun, would have to stand in a trench at zero hour ready to move out across a bullet-strewn no-man's-land. John's comment reflected the good humoured good sense which was his strength. In our time at university, boxing in the annual inter-university tournaments in New Zealand had been dominated by a middleweight from Fiji called Tom Dovi, a smiling, frizzy-haired man who seemed to be carved from granite. John brushed aside the debate about whether we would be afraid. 'I don't think that anything else could ever be as frightening as finding oneself alone in the ring with Tom Dovi after the gong had gone,' was his estimate.

As war came nearer, those who had served in the last war could at times be persuaded to talk of their experience. Tom Cadett, the *Times* correspondent, had found himself within a few days of arriving in France as an eighteen-year-old lieutenant in the Argyll and Sutherland Highlanders, in charge of a platoon sent out in the darkness into no-man's-land to repair a barbed wire entanglement damaged by enemy shelling. It had to be repaired before daylight when a German attack was expected. The enemy had been using gas shells, and gas still lingered in hollows and shell holes. But in their gas masks the men could make only slow progress. The only way to get the job done was to order them to remove their masks. One man refused to do so, and defied Cadett's repeated order.

'I took out my revolver, thrust it into his stomach, and gave him one further order. He still refused, saying he would sooner die than risk breathing gas. Then the very seasoned sergeant-major who was with us took a hand. He clenched his fist and said to the man, "If you don't take off your bloody mask and get on with the job, I'll knock your bloody head off." That threat was far more effective than mine. The man complied, and we got the job done just in time.'

Not all recollections of these veterans were gloomy. Martin Herlihy, head of Reuters' office in Paris, told me that what stayed most clearly in his mind was not the mud and strain of the trenches, but the pleasure of marching, in a column of well-trained troops, with larks in the fields beyond the poplars. 'Memory seems to blot out the awful bits,' he said, 'and leave the pleasant ones.'

By the last week in August huge placards, each with small crossed tricolours at the corners, had proclaimed the Mobilisation Generale, and throughout the day train after train of reservists pulled out from the Gare de l'Est for the frontiers and the Maginot Line. For the most part they went with dignity and sadness. *'Il faut en finir'* was

the tenor of this mood. They ranged from youngsters barely out of
their teens to grey-haired men who had been just old enough to serve
in the concluding stages of the last war, some carrying suitcases,
some with their belongings in a roll under one arm. Grimly they
parted from their tearful wives and mothers and fathers and sons
and clambered aboard the carriages marked Metz and Strasbourg.
One couple in particular caught my eye, a young wife and her
officer husband, locked in each other's arms at the barrier, standing
silent, a silence which said more than any words could have done,
until the officer tore himself away and strode off towards the train.
The woman, beautiful under her tears, her hand resting on a bunch
of violets pinned to her coat, watched until the last carriage of the
train disappeared on the eastward line of tracks.

An hour later I was sitting on the terrace of the Colisée on the
Champs Elysées when this woman appeared, easily recognisable
because the bunch of violets was still on her coat. Her face was set,
held high, almost as if in a trance. Once seated, she stared angrily
around the café, her glance resting defiantly on the men in civilian
clothes who crowded so many of the tables. Ten minutes later she
drained her cup of coffee, paid her bill, and with an almost elaborate
slowness moved towards the door. A man who had been seated a few
tables away from her followed her out. I saw them talking on the
pavement in front of the café, clearly two strangers making contact,
before they called a taxi and got in. Had I misread the sincerity of
that parting at the Gare de l'Est? Or are some partings so painful
that they call for more human opiates than are provided by alcohol
or drugs?

In the last week of August Otto Katz left for Mexico. He asked
me to dinner, in a small restaurant near the Opera, shortly before
he left. For the first time I met his wife, a small blonde woman with
a pinched and anxious expression. At the end of the meal Katz
stared across the table at me intently and said, 'During the next few
years events will take many strange turns. But if you want the key
to them, remember one thing – Stalin is always right.'

Thirteen years later Stalin had him hanged. As a key figure in the
Czechoslovak Communist Party, Katz was caught up in one of the
last of the Stalinist purges, and together with six other Ministers
went to the gallows in Prague, condemned as Trotskyist deviationist
and a spy.

CHAPTER SIXTEEN

War – and Phoney War

Came Friday, 1 September, and by breakfast time the agency tapes were clattering out the news that German forces were swarming across the frontiers into Poland and Danzig, and their bombers were striking at Polish towns. Widespread fighting was under way. Was France at war? The Quai d'Orsay could answer only that we must wait until the next afternoon, when Prime Minister Daladier would speak to the Chamber of Deputies. Was Britain at war? It seemed not. In the House of Commons Neville Chamberlain gave no indication that an ultimatum had been sent to Hitler. Only a warning message had been despatched. The smell of last-minute appeasement seemed to be in the air.

I got to the Chamber of Deputies only just in time to hear Daladier begin his speech. I had been held up by a phenomenon we were soon to become only too familiar with – the wartime queue. I had queued to get a gas mask from a stock made available by the Embassy for Britons living in Paris. Chief of the volunteer workers organising the distribution, in a hall near the Arc de Triomphe, was a cashier from the English bank where the *Express* kept its account. His manner at the bank counter had always verged on the obsequious. Now, dressed in the alas none too brief authority which war confers, he had great pleasure in ordering us all about.

In the lofty Chamber of the Palais de Bourbon the air seemed even staler than usual, as deputies packed the semi-circle of seats, and journalists and visitors crammed the galleries. In this atmosphere of weary strain Daladier spoke with effective, blunt, peasant eloquence, a lock of hair falling from time to time over his wide red forehead. France, he thundered, must honour her obligations. If France allowed German aggression against Poland to go unchecked, it would earn her contempt, isolation and discredit. 'At the price of our honour we would be purchasing a precarious and revokable peace, and when the time came for us to fight, having lost the esteem of our allies and of other nations we would be a wretched people, doomed to death and enslavement.'

Powerful words, but of action there was no sign. The French Prime Minister ended his speech without any word of an ultimatum to Germany, or of a French and British declaration of war. Once the Chamber realised this, there was tumult, with deputies from the left and centre booing and hissing, and with derisive cat calls and whistles from the French press gallery. For good measure I added the whistle I had learnt for controlling sheep dogs in New Zealand. Out in the lobby Emil Buré gave his summing up. 'They are talking to the Italians, and hope to get a conference tomorrow. We will yet see a sell-out.' With Chamberlain having made a similar stalling speech in the Commons, I went to bed convinced that my prediction that war would not come to us in 1939 was well on its way to fulfilment.

For all my keen sense of history, I cannot record that I learnt in any memorable manner the next day of either the British or the French declaration of war. Exhausted by the work and strain of recent weeks, I slept deeply, and woke late on the morning of 3 September. I was unaware of Chamberlain's broadcast when I joined Walter Kerr for coffee on the terrace of the Café Select on the Champs Elysées. Then I saw Edwin Hartrich, of the *Wall Street Journal*, running up the Rue du Berri. He had a piece of agency copy in his hand. 'You're at war, Geoffrey,' he said. 'A British ultimatum to Germany expired at eleven o'clock, without response.' I looked at my watch. It showed twenty past eleven. There was a chilling incongruity in finding oneself at war on this half-deserted boulevard in a foreign land. And though Kerr and Hartrich were my close friends, I felt suddenly a wide gap between us, the gap between those who are at war and those who are neutral.

France had also sent an ultimatum, due to expire at five that afternoon. I passed this news on to the driver of the taxi in which I was heading for our office in the Rue du Louvre. He reacted with fury, pouring out a stream of oaths and obscenities, and driving like a madman, weaving in and out of the traffic as if the Germans were already coming down the street in pursuit. 'Take it easy,' I pleaded. 'There are eighty million Germans trying to kill us now. There's no need for you to do the job for them.'

The moment of France's entry in the war passed for me even more anti-climactically. During the afternoon Alan Moorehead and I drove in his Ford V8 car up to the heights of Montmartre. Alan was in Paris on leave, to take a last look over a Paris which we believed could before the night was out be reduced to a shattered smoking ruin under the attacks of the Luftwaffe. It was a grey, overcast afternoon, warm and humid, with a break in the clouds away to the east, the direction from which the bombers would come. I thought of Madrid under its bombardment, and tried to envisage these close-packed roofs, broken here and there by the lines of green from boulevard trees, and by church steeples and the dome of the Opera, being ripped apart and burning as had been the Gran Via.

Down on the Boulevard Montmartre, as we drove back to the office, the crowds were as thick as on a normal Sunday, but now their faces were tense and their steps hurried. I was studying them when Moorehead's car spluttered and stopped. There was nothing for it but for us to get out and push. We were doing this, in a stream of horn-blaring traffic, when I glanced at my watch. It was just after five o'clock. France too was now at war.

As we expected, the air-raid sirens began to wail that evening just before midnight. To be close to the *New York Herald Tribune*'s offices, now the most reliable news source, I had moved into the Hôtel California in the Rue de Berri. Walter Kerr and I made our way to the shelter in the cellars with the rest of the guests, and I braced myself for the shriek and crash of bombs. But none fell that night, or the next, or the next — and none were to fall on Paris until June 1940. After three such uncomfortable and broken nights, I never again left my bed in Paris during an alert, however many sirens went. We were indeed engaged in what the French were soon to call '*cette drôle de guerre*'.

Discomfort, inefficiency, muddle and France's uniquely exasperating type of bureaucracy were to mark the opening weeks of the war in Paris. Central Paris adopted a very severe form of blackout and at night the Champs Elysées rang with the crash of colliding cars, the shriek of police whistles and the shouts of angry drivers. Within a week most of the traffic bollards in the middle of the avenue were damaged or destroyed. Gradually too realisation dawned that not only was there no war in the air over France, but very little war on the ground either. During those first few days of the war we of the foreign press had thronged to the Ministry of War in the Rue Dominique, on the Left Bank, and to the new Ministre d'Information established in the Hôtel Continentale in the Rue Castiglione down the road — and very much down market — from the Ritz. We had expected to hear of offensives launched against the unfinished sections of the Siegfried Line, and of the advance of French divisions, which greatly outnumbered those of the Reichswehr opposing them, into Germany. No official word came of any such, though the military correspondents of several Paris papers, particularly of *Le Petit Parisien*, had accounts of heavy fighting which we duly relayed. But after a few days these too died away, and we had virtually no news of any value to send to Britain about the activities of their ally in this life and death struggle.

If news was difficult to get, it was equally difficult to transmit. Some genius in the French High Command had decided that the moment war broke out all telephonic and telegraphic communications between France and Britain, except for official traffic, should be cut off. But to avoid antagonising the Americans, the lines to the United States were kept open, though liable to censorship. This produced the absurd situation that the journalists of two countries allied in a common struggle could not communicate directly with their offices, but had to do so via a third neutral country – the United States – many of whose citizens (and presumably of its telephone and telegraph operators) were hostile to the Allies. Instead of being able to write a story out fully, and telephoning it, down to the last comma, to London, we now had to resort to the cruder method of cables, and send messages via Cable and Wireless to our offices in New York, for relay to London.

In these circumstances I was surprised – and pleased – to find myself able to secure two major scoops, giving the *Express* – and the British people – the first eyewitness account of the arrival of British troops in France and, even more importantly, the first description of the scenes on the inactive Western front. I owed the story about the British troops partly to the arrival of a new assistant in the Paris office, George Millar. Moorehead had gone on to Rome; Robertson had been withdrawn to London. To replace them Christiansen sent George Millar, the rising star of the home reporting staff.

Millar was in his late twenties, an upright, Bonnie Prince Charlie Scot, strikingly handsome, with fair hair, wide-set blue eyes, full lips, and with a steely self-confidence hidden under a quiet, self-mocking modesty. His wife Netty was an equally striking redhead, forthright and charming. I sensed quickly that Millar was a man of exceptional calibre, whom I would be able to lead if I made plain that my leadership rested not just on my position as head of the office, but on my ability. To do this the best way was to tackle a major story which remained uncovered – that of the arrival of British troops in France. All our requests for permission to go to the disembarkation areas had been refused. I decided to act without permission, and set out by car for Brittany with Eric Sevareid and Walter Kerr.

Sevareid was a tall, handsome mid-Westerner of Norwegian stock, in his late twenties, who could well have been cast for the film role of Abraham Lincoln when young. He had come to Paris a year earlier, to be a reporter on the Paris edition of the *New York Herald Tribune*, the journal of the considerable American expatriate community in France, and had been recruited for the Columbia Broadcasting System by Ed Murrow. Eric Sevareid was to come through quickly not only as one of the greatest of radio reporters, but was also one of the few in time to make the transition from radio to television news. His broadcasting skill rested on his ability to write, which not only enabled him to produce scripts of depth as well as vividness, but was also to make his book *Not So Wild a Dream* a classic of this period – and a best-seller when it was published in 1946.

On the outskirts of Cherbourg we found what we sought. In columns of threes (a formation which surprised me, as when I had done my territorial training in New Zealand eight years earlier British troops had still formed fours) a company of the Black Watch were striding up the hill from the port, their tartan kilts replaced by khaki, but their cap badges unmistakable. Down in the port Bren carriers and trucks were being swung ashore and other Tommies – the World War I word was in vogue again in the French papers – were stacking supplies on the quayside. When the port authorities discovered we were journalists, they hastily hunted us out of the place. But we had seen British fighting troops back again on French soil, and we hastened back to Paris to write our stories.

The French censor passed them, but in London the War Office banned my piece peremptorily. A few days later chance gave me another glimpse of the BEF. I had gone back to the riverside hotel where John Mulgan and I had stayed, to collect some shirts I had left there. I was standing on the station platform at Villennes when a long troop train came rumbling through. Leaning out of the vans portrayed in so many World War I photographs with their labels of '*8 chevaux ou 40 hommes*', were British Tommies, in the new battledress khaki, waving to the crowds on the roadside and singing, in poignant imitation of 1914, 'It's a Long Way to Tipperary'. From a carriage at the rear two British officers saluted. The station master saluted back, tears pouring down his cheeks.

This story too I sent to London. It arrived on Christiansen's desk at the same time as an official ruling from the War Office that British newspapers might now, after nine days of war, make public the fact that British troops had arrived in France. The other papers had no eyewitness material to add to the official statement, but Christiansen had my pieces from Cherbourg and Villennes. He made the most of them in a story which covered the whole of the front page.

This proved too much for the censors, who took the view that only the bald official communiqué should be published. The first edition presses were rolling when a police inspector, wearing a World War I DCM ribbon, and carrying a tin hat and gas mask, arrived in Fleet Street with an order for them to be halted. Chris raised hell with the War Office, who at 3 a.m. changed their minds, and let the edition go, with one excision. Any reference to '*8 chevaux ou 40 hommes*' had to come out. The halting of the presses led to a furious debate in the Commons about censorship, skilfully fuelled by Christiansen, who relished the publicity for this, the first scoop of the war.

I was able a few days later to provide him with a second one. Encouraged by the success of our Cherbourg venture, Sevareid, Kerr and I decided to make another excursion, this time towards the east, to the areas where the French and British armies were deploying. Chuck Findlay, a newsreel cameraman, came along with us, but just for the ride, as we thought the presence of his camera would be a certain way of our being turned back. We set out on a Sunday morning, expecting at the most to get no further eastward than Rheims, or perhaps Verdun.

We had no passes, other than our French police cards – those highly distinctive thin metallic cards, very aptly called *coupe file* – which could cut their way through red tape as well as the more literal white tapes with which the French police loved to bar access to areas where anything newsworthy was happening. Yet we found no difficulty at checkpoints along the way. Often we were waved on without even being stopped, perhaps because Sevareid and I, in the front seats, were both wearing brown belted raincoats which had a military look, perhaps because the Peugeot was of a near khaki colour. In any event military convoys of the time were full of requisitioned civilian cars and vans, still in their original colours. For kilometre after kilometre we passed the signs of the Allied forces deploying. Near Rheims RAF aircraftmen were setting up tents alongside a temporary airfield, with Gloster Gladiator fighters already hidden among cornstacks and barns. We drove into one village just as a bus full of RAF men arrived there. The men disembarked on the green in front of the church. Villagers pressed eagerly forward to see these men who had come to fight on their soil again. Soon they were talking to each other in broken French and English, exchanging cigarettes, and soon making their way to the small café on the corner, beyond which stretched the airfield.

Near Verdun columns of lorries carrying shining-faced Senegalese infantry bumped over the cobbled roads, along the Voie Sacrée of 1917. We still expected to be stopped, but even when we entered the clearly marked Zone Militaire around Metz, our passes were only casually scrutinised, and we were waved on. In the dusk we drove on through Thionville and out towards the frontier, our ears cocked for the sound of gunfire. Though we could not be far from the front, there was none of the crack of rifle shots which had marked even the quietest nights in Madrid, or of the staccato sound of machine-gun fire, or the flat crump of mortars, let alone the thump and thud of artillery fire. It was quiet – so quiet that at one stage we argued whether a sound we had heard had been a rifle shot, or the bark of a dog. Of the constant frontier skirmishes, let alone the raging battles featured by *Le Petit Parisien* there was no sign.

At the village of Sierck, only two kilometres from the German frontier, we finally caught up with the war. Down a lane came some thirty or forty Moroccan infantrymen, their khaki uniforms mudstained, their faces under the steel helmets weary and fringed with a dark growth of beard – the growth which brought French troops the name of *poilus*, the hairy ones. Their long bayonets were still fixed to their rifles, and behind them rolled two tanks, muddy also. It had every appearance of a fighting patrol returning from a stint in the no-man's-land between the two armies.

At the edge of the village the patrol came abreast of a column of fresh troops, with their own two tanks, waiting to take their turn on patrol. Men lay by the roadside amidst stacks of new haversacks and rifles. Some talked with a farmer and his wife at the door of their farmhouse. Others filled their waterbottles at the village well. On an order they formed up and swung forward into the growing darkness, followed by calls of '*bonne chance*' from the men who had returned.

When they had gone it was very quiet, except for the distant clanging of a church bell. Suddenly across the sound of the bell came a deep thump, thump from under the black hill which was Germany. I knew from my days in Madrid that it was the sound of artillery fire. But it died away as abruptly as it had begun. We turned round the car and made our way back to Metz.

We spent the night in an hotel there. The city was half evacuated, with little but military traffic in the streets. No one challenged our bona fides, and the next day we drove back to Paris. I was working on my story when the telephone rang, and a Frenchman, identifying himself as an official of Quai d'Orsay, told me that he knew of our trip, and warned me that we would all be expelled from France if we sent our stories. The threat was one Sevareid and Kerr could readily defy, as correspondents for the great neutral power whom the French were anxious to win over. But as a reporter for a country at war I could not afford lightly to disregard such a warning. I rang Sevareid, told him of the call, and arranged to meet him in half an hour's time outside his hotel, where we could talk without risk of being overheard. I was about to leave for this meeting when the telephone rang again. This time it was Ken Downs, head of the Hearst International News Service in Paris. He explained, with many chuckles, that the call had been a hoax. He had heard of our expedition to the front, and had set a Frenchman who worked in his office to the task of acting as the bogus official. What Downs claimed as a practical joke virtually killed my story. The delay caused by the first call meant that the story reached London in time to make only the very last and smallest edition of the paper.

Sevareid's broadcast, and Walter Kerr's story were, because of the time difference, unaffected by the delay. Yet the story had one further twist. Three days later another group of American journalists including Ken Downs followed in our tracks. By one of the quirks of fate, their exploit caught the attention of *Time* magazine in a way ours had not, and they were acclaimed as daring defiers of red tape, and as the first journalists to visit the Western Front. But it was Kerr's report which was to prove the most durable. He commented that this looked like being 'a pretty phoney type of war' – a phrase which was to pass into history.

The French authorities were infuriated by our stories, both because these showed how lax were their controls behind the lines, and how inactive were their forces on the front. They were unwilling to act against the Americans, but as a correspondent from a co-belligerent I was more vulnerable. I was berated by an army officer in the censor's department, and told that no official credentials to cover the front would be extended to me. The British Embassy also made a fuss, so Christiansen decided to move me to Brussels, and there I went late in September.

Neutral Belgium was drenched in highly effective German propaganda, including dramatic newsreel material showing the swift – and by now completed – blitzkrieg against Poland. Shot on 16mm film, using the lightweight Arriflex cameras which were still in use when we set up ITN fifteen years later, and obtained by daring cameramen up with the foremost troops (twenty-three of them were killed or wounded covering the Polish campaign) it was a revelation of the power of the moving picture. British propaganda was by comparison feeble, concentrating not on proving that we were winning – which was what the neutrals wanted to know – but on why we should win, because of the virtue of our democracy. Helped by Maurice Fast, a Brussels newspaper editor who was the *Daily Express* local correspondent, I wrote an article which began 'One German army has already invaded Belgium, an army of propagandists and they are achieving victories because they have the field almost entirely to themselves'. It seemed to have impressed Lord Reith, then Minister of Information, because he called me in when I at last got back to London, and questioned me at length in his room at the top of the University of London building in Bloomsbury.

From Belgium I went on to Holland, which throughout the rest of the autumn was to be the most newsworthy part of Western Europe. Holland provided the first major spy story of the war. On 8 November two leading members of the British Secret Service, Major H. R. Stevens and Captain S. Payne Best, were lured by the Germans to Venlo on the Dutch border, seized there, and taken off to Berlin to be interrogated and imprisoned. It was a coup which smashed the British Intelligence network in Western Europe. The Venlo frontier post was ideally suited for such a kidnapping. It was on a stretch of open heathland, with about five hundred yards separating the Dutch and German frontier posts. The only building on the road between the two was a restaurant and café, still formally on Dutch soil. It was here that the two British agents had agreed to meet what they thought were dissident SS and army officers prepared to mount a putsch against Hitler. It had been a matter only of a few minutes for the waiting Gestapo, once they had seen the two Britons arrive at the café, to raise the frontier barrier and send a truck full of soldiers to surround the building, make the arrests, and rush their captives back into Germany. The Dutch authorities, in their post two hundred yards to the west, had no time in which to react, even if they had been prepared to risk a border incident by doing so.

Two days later, when I visited the café to talk to the waitress who had witnessed the kidnapping, the place seemed very exposed, and I had a wary eye on the nearby German frontier guards throughout the interview. They left us alone, but another British correspondent had a narrow escape. German troops did surround the café whilst Ralph Izzard of the *Daily Mail* and a Dutch journalist were there. Izzard hid in the lavatory, ready to drop his British passport down the pan should he be found. But the Dutch waitress insisted to the Germans so vehemently that only one man, the Dutch journalist, was on the premises that they left without a full search.

The main and continuing story from Holland throughout that autumn, and into January, was the possibility of a German invasion. The Dutch plan to deal with this was to open key dykes and river locks, to form a series of water lines, flooded areas two or three miles wide, which would form huge moats, barring the way to German tanks and lorries and guns. It was a costly scheme, for it involved flooding valuable farming land, and the Dutch were not anxious to give the signal for it until danger seemed to be genuinely imminent. Yet on a number of occasions in November they were on the point of doing so, as information reached them from their agents in Germany of signs that Hitler was preparing to move against Holland.

From Amsterdam and the Hague we reported these fears, and the Dutch state of readiness, and we frequently drove out towards the German frontier to check for any signs of the water lines being flooded. Most military experts in Britain and France could not believe that Hitler would do anything so rash as to attack at a time of the year when bad weather could impede not only his troops on the ground, but above all the Luftwaffe, which had shown itself so deadly against Poland. We were in consequence accused of scare-mongering and exaggeration. I felt confident of what I was writing, however, because my information came chiefly from the head of the Dutch Military Intelligence in the Hague, who adopted an unusual policy for a military man, that of trying to tell the press all that he could, within reasonable bounds of security.

The German archives captured at the end of the war have revealed that Hitler not only did plan an invasion, at first of

Holland, and then, under a later scheme, of Holland and Belgium, but issued specific dates on which Operation Yellow, as it was code-named, was to begin. It was set first for 25 November. This was later brought forward to 12 November, and cancelled only after a furious row between Hitler and the Commander-in-Chief of the Reichswehr, General Brauchitsch. During December four more dates were set, but each had to be cancelled because of the terrible conditions of snow, ice and fog which settled over Western Europe. Even so, when fine weather brought clear blue skies in the New Year, 17 January was set as a new D-Day for an attack which was to be launched against both Holland and Belgium. This was cancelled only after an extraordinary stroke of fortune. At Mechelen, just across the Belgian frontier from Aachen, a light plane carrying two Luftwaffe majors to a conference lost its way in mist, and crashed. The majors had with them detailed plans for the invasion, part of which they were able to destroy, but part of which safely reached Belgian Intelligence. Fearing that all surprise had been lost, Hitler hesitated, and then, as the weather closed in again, abandoned the attack until the spring.

In one story about developments in the Luftwaffe, I went direct to the source – in Germany itself. Towards the end of November rumours spread that Professor Messerschmitt, designer of the fighter aircraft which were, in the Battle of Britain, to become as well known as Hurricanes and Spitfires, had fled the Reich and taken refuge in Holland. The French and American papers made such play with these that Radio Berlin was driven to issue a formal denial, and added, 'Those who disbelieve our report can telephone the Professor at his Augsburg works.'

This seemed to me an invitation which should be taken up, so I placed a call from Amsterdam to the Professor, allowing myself the gloss of saying merely that it was 'from a journalist in Amsterdam'. To my astonishment I was put through immediately to his office. 'Hier Messerschmitt in Augsburg,' stated his brisk voice. After he had denied the rumours of his defection, I put to him a query about the Me109. In the few aerial encounters which had taken place along the Western Front, the French had claimed to have destroyed several of these. 'Is it not true,' I asked, 'that the French have shot down a number of Me109s, and that they are not manoeuvrable enough?'

'I have heard rumours like that, but I have other information on the subject,' was his dry response. But when I pressed on with further questions about his new plane, the Me110, either he, or some security check, became suspicious, and I was cut off with an abrupt '*Gute Nacht*'. It cannot be said have been a very productive interview, but *Time* magazine liked it, and gave me a chuckling pat on the back for the manner of my getting it.

CHAPTER SEVENTEEN

Real War in Finland

Holland proved to be a stepping stone for me to another war – and very much a shooting war. The Dutch airline KLM still maintained a service to Scandinavia, its new DC3 airliners – the first civilian version of the Dakota – flying across the North Sea, parallel to the German coast, to Copenhagen. When therefore at the end of November the Soviet Union began to issue threats against the Finns, it was logical for the *Daily Express* to move me from Amsterdam to Helsinki, to cover what looked to be a brief war of nerves, in which tiny Finland would surely yield without a struggle to their giant of a neighbour.

That Amsterdam–Copenhagen flight, which I was to make four times in the next three months, was a strain, for it would have been very easy for the Germans to have sent up fighters to intercept the KLM plane and divert it to a German airport. I was thankful when, on 29 November, I saw the flat coast of Denmark moving towards us, under the wings of the Douglas. I had no wish to spend the war in a German internment camp.

The Russians had already drawn the Baltic states of Estonia, Latvia and Lithuania into their orbit through a series of mutual assistance pacts negotiated after they had overrun their share of Poland. Their demands on Finland were stringent, involving a rolling back of the Finnish frontier for some thirty miles to protect approaches to Leningrad, the leasing by the Russians of the Finnish naval base of Hango, and of the ice-free port of Petsamo in the north. The Finns refused, but did not break off negotiations. To their astonishment, and to that of the outside world, Stalin did not continue the negotiations. Instead on 30 November he launched the Red Army and the Red Air Force against Finland, and set up a puppet government under a Finnish exile, Otto Kuusinen, who had long been resident in Moscow, where he had been General Secretary of the Comintern. The Russian view was simple. Khruschev, who was present when Stalin took the final decision, set it out in his memoirs. 'All we had to do was to raise our voice a little bit, and

139

the Finns would obey. If that did not work, we could fire one shot and the Finns would put their hands up and surrender – or so we thought.'[1]

Stalin's one shot took the form of an all-out invasion of Finland. When I reached Helsinki on the evening of 30 November the red glow of burning buildings glowered against the thick darkness of the Arctic night. Black clouds of smoke were shot through by sudden spurts of red which could only come from some great fire. They came, I was to learn, from the Technical High School and two nearby apartment buildings which had been hit by high explosive and incendiary bombs that afternoon, in raids which, the Finns claimed, killed 61 people and wounded 120.

These raids had been launched by the Soviet Union without warning, and without any ultimatum having been issued to the Finns. They were attacks on the capital city of a country with which Russia was still formally at peace. No last-minute chance had been given to the Finnish Government to yield to the Soviet demands, if they knew that the alternative was war. Even when, on the night of 30 November, the Finns made a further bid for the reopening of talks, the Russians would not listen. The Soviet Government's reply, sent through the Swedes on 2 December, was that it recognised only the 'People's Front' Government of Otto Kuusinen as the true government of Finland. Not even Hitler, in his onslaught on Poland, had shown such a degree of callous cynicism.

The political as well as the military implications of this attack came home to me vividly when, on my second day in Finland, after a further nine Soviet bombers had attacked the centre of Helsinki, I tracked down the wreckage of one bomber which had been shot down by Finnish anti-aircraft guns. In a patch of pines on the western suburbs of the city the smashed remains of a two-engined medium bomber were on fire. The tail section, with the letters 'S.B.' and a huge dull red Soviet star, lay against a tree. Near by was a bloody, tangled mess which had been the pilot's head, and his khaki-clad torso. His hands were tightly clenched. I noticed they were surprisingly small. His uniform was the same drab khaki I had seen worn by the tank crews at the Hill of the Angels before Madrid, those grave-faced young men who had stood then as the defenders of a democracy, and of a small nation battling against the power of Hitler and Mussolini. These same red stars had been on

[1] *Khruschev Remembers*, André Deutsch, 1971.

the snub-nosed Soviet fighter planes I had seen swoop across the roofs of Madrid, cheered as deliverers by the people in the battered streets. This was the air force which only a little over a year earlier had seemed to us in Prague one reassuring final guard against a Nazi invasion. Now this boy had been sent to his death hurling bombs against a small people defending its own freedom.

The Finns had built a defensive line across the narrow strip of territory, south of the huge Lake Ladoga, which provided the main route from the Soviet Union into southern Finland. It had been given the name of the Mannerheim Line, after Field Marshal Mannerheim, who had led Finland in its struggles against the Bolsheviks in 1918–21, and had been recalled to take command in this war. True to the prevalent military theory of the time, we assumed that this line, like the Maginot Line in France, would be virtually impregnable to direct attack by any but overwhelming forces. This view seemed to be borne out by the events of the opening weeks of what came to be called The Winter War. The Russians launched massive attacks of infantry supported by tanks and guns against the Mannerheim Line, and were repulsed.

Other attacks launched in the heavily forested country north of Lake Ladoga, on all the seven main roads leading westwards from their frontier, were equally frustrated. So too was an attack from Murmansk towards Petsamo, in the very north. All these attacks were halted by fierce resistance by the highly trained and determined Finnish Army. In several instances Soviet formations, unable to move off the narrow, tree-lined and snow-bound forest roads, were cut off and annihilated. In the intense cold, the dead were frozen where they fell, sprawling or lying like waxworks in a staged spectacle of warfare. Photographs of these scenes were to provide a powerful visual impression of a Russian defeat, an impression which, as the weeks went by, was to give rise in Britain and France for demands not merely for assistance to the Finns, but for a declaration of war against the Soviet Union.

I was the first correspondent from Britain or America to witness these forest battle scenes. I did so by adopting the methods we had employed in France; that of not waiting for official permission, but instead of moving directly towards the front, of marching towards the sound of gunfire. The Finns had from the outset clamped strict controls on all foreign journalists. They would at first allow none of us to visit the front. When they relented, it was to allow only four agency reporters to make a one-day visit to the area behind the

Mannerheim Line. The rest of us had to subsist on a diet of stale communiqués, or on what gossip we could pick up in the gloomy hall of the Hotel Kamp in Helsinki.

After a few days of this I decided to try the fronts further north. I teamed up with a Swedish woman correspondent, Babro Alving, who had been in Madrid during the siege. Without informing the Press Office in Helsinki and armed only with a letter of credentials from the Finnish Foreign Office, Babro Alving and I and a Finnish girl interpreter took the train north from Helsinki. Fuelled only by wood, the train moved northwards with excruciating slowness. After a journey of a full day and night, we reached Oulu, where – so a young officer travelling on the train had told us – there was a military base. The general in command was a sensible man. Instead of making a fuss about red tape, he had us escorted to the front in the forests of Kuhmo. Only patrol activity was in progress, but we had our first sight of the ski troops, moving almost invisibly in their white snow capes in the half light of the few brief daylight hours.

It was at Kemijarvi, further north, just above the Arctic Circle, that we encountered the first of the astonishing battle scenes of this war in the frozen snow. A Russian column of some six thousand men and twenty tanks had thrust across the narrow waist of this part of Finland, aiming for the top of the Gulf of Bothnia, hoping to cut Finland in two. They were met by Finnish troops under a tough, seasoned commander, General Wallenius. A former Chief of the Finnish General Staff, he had turned politician, and had tried to mount a military coup in 1932. Virtually exiled, he had worked as a war correspondent in Spain, and had reported the Nazi invasion of Poland. Recalled now to the army, he had been given command – though in his early sixties – of this crucial northern front. Half way across the country, on the frozen River Kemi, the Russians were stopped and then counter-attacked on the narrow, snow-covered roadway where they had halted for the night. Within a few hours half the Soviet force had been destroyed. The rest retreated.

It was just beyond the village of Kemijarvi, where the open fields suddenly narrowed down to one road edged with pines, that we found the first twisted corpses. Scattered in the ditches, or on the road itself, they were a ghastly trail that led us to the low cliff above the River Kemi. Here the fight had been around a group of farm buildings. The log walls were shattered like the skeletons, where shells had smashed through. Horses, smashed wagons, and more dead lay twisted beside the road. The horses, their coarse blood spilled among the snow, seemed almost more tragic than the men. They had certainly had no hand in this ghastly business, yet here they lay.

On the ice-covered river itself a lorry stood where the Russians had left it, right in mid-stream. Beside it lay the bodies of two men. Farther off, half-way to the shelter of the pines on the bank, was another crumpled figure, killed by some Finnish sniper's bullet as he ran. We drove on across the ice to the narrow entry of the Salla road that dropped, still and white, to the edge of the river.

The ruins of the column lay three-quarters of a mile farther on. We scraped past another great van, loaded with more bodies of the Finnish dead, being gathered up to take home to their families. For in Finland till the end all dead were sent home for burial. Then ahead I saw a line of what looked like junk cars drawn up in some empty allotment on the edge of a city. At the head was a staff car; behind it three tanks; then lorries, some straight on the road, others swung into the ditches.

Still gripping the wheel of the staff car was the driver, his forehead smashed by a bullet. Alongside lay the body of a Russian officer – the first of the dead who were strewn everywhere. How strange were these bodies, on this road where it was already so cold that if I took my glove off to write I could keep my hand in the air only a minute. The cold had frozen them into the positions in which they fell. It had, too, slightly shrunken their bodies and features, giving them an artificial, waxen appearance. The whole road was like some huge waxwork representation of a battle scene, carefully staged. Even the dark brown-red stain that was split on uniforms and on the snow was paint rather than blood. Dead that I had seen in Spain had usually been slumped, shapeless bundles of clothes and flesh, that still had about them the horror of decay as well as death. But this scene here struck in me, I found, no horror. It was hard to believe that these figures had ever been men. Yet men lay with hand grenades in their hands, poised to throw; one man leant against a wagon wheel with a length of wire still in his hands; another was fitting a clip of cartridges into a rifle. Until you got right up to him you could not tell that he was not still living. Others had spun into ditches, and fell there, still giving an impression of movement. It was this incredible effect of the cold which gave the Finnish battlefields their fake appearance, for the very action seemed to be frozen into stillness. It was as if in one moment of the battle time had suddenly stopped on this road near Kemi, halting the scene for all time.

There was a line of thirty-eight trucks, all Fords made in Russia,

with hinged sides. The tyres, with chains on one rear wheel, looked
of poor-quality rubber. They lay amid the spilled gear, the endless
gear of war. Gas masks, telephone wires, machine-gun belts,
sausages tied together like ropes, a spilled barrel of frozen fish, a pile
of old leather shoes, a poster of a girl advertising a Red Cross fund,
two curved swords, and amidst this, the dead, like so much more
gear. Here a shattered arm; there a leg covered with snow. Wooden
boxes that had held ammunition lay everywhere; horses, their guts
smashed and open, artificially pink, lay under the high wooden arch
of the sledges.

The Russians had apparently cleaned out anything left by the
Finns in evacuated houses along the way. I saw an ancient sewing
machine, a butter churn, even a bundle of silk stockings, two silver
teapots and some girls' underclothes – the rather pathetic looting
of men who have few consumer goods in their lives. Some of the
Russian dead wore steel helmets; some peaked caps. They all had
heel-less felt boots, which are wonderfully warm when the snow is
dry, but hopeless if it is wet. Some had overcoats that were
adequately thick; others had thin coats, and I saw that their padded
uniforms were rotted. Few looked adequately clothed for this terrible
temperature.

You could follow the course of the battle as you walked from man
to man. Here three men had spun and fallen as they charged for a
machine-gun pit; there the horses were piled in one great hillock of
flesh where they had been mown down, farther on half a dozen
lorries were half turned, as their drivers had tried to get them round
and move off. Other lorries were on their side. And everywhere I
turned back from the material to the men. Russian dead lying face
down, as if weeping, in the snow; curled on their backs, eyes closed,
as if asleep; clutching stomachs, sides, heads; gripping the sides of
lorries; stumbling forward, gun in hand; running back, gun thrown
away; everywhere the dead. In one place two men, Russian and
Finn, lay frozen together in their final death struggle. Over most of
the bodies frost and light snow had already put a faint hoary coating.

The Finns were easy to distinguish. They all had white snow
clothes over their grey uniforms, and their boots were of new, yellow
leather. Every man's face had been covered by his comrades with
a piece of cloth or a fir branch. I drew away the branch from the face
of one man, huge in his grey uniform. It was a typical Finnish
peasant face, rounded, with almost slit eyes and strong, curving
sweep of jaw. In his death he looked very young – just in this

BLACK-OUT
ZERO HOUR
TO-NIGHT

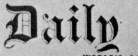# Daily Express

WORLD'S LARGEST DAILY SALE

No. 12,265   Tuesday, September 12, 1939   One Penny

Men in khaki lean from a train as it rumbles through a village, revealing to the world—

BRITISH TROOPS IN FRANCE

'rench folk run to heer the Tommies

'OGETHER IN MAGINOT'

From GEOFFREY COX
Daily Express Staff Reporter

PARIS, Monday.

A FRENCH VILLAGE THIS MORNING I WATCHED A LONG RITISH TROOP TRAIN RUMBLE THROUGH. THE VILLAGERS ED TO THE STATION AS A FEW WATCHERS ON THE FORM SHOUTED "LES ANGLAIS!"

Infantrymen in khaki leaned from the carriages, waved cheerily houted to the French people. From the compartments at the of the train officers saluted smilingly.

The grey-haired stationmaster turned to me, saying, "I fought the British at the Somme, "My son has already gone to the not. He'll be with them now."

NO FLOWERS, BY REQUEST

NO flowers may be thrown at Hitler during his visits to the front, says an order from the "Fuehrer's headquarters," quoted by the German radio yesterday afternoon. The order added: "Flowers should be handed to the troops."

U-boat sinkings: A row in the Nazi command

From SELKIRK PANTON
Daily Express Staff Reporter

COPENHAGEN, Monday.

JUST as Grand Admiral von Tirpitz the

50,00
German killed

IT was reported night on the h est authority German casualt until Saturday day—after a week war — were 50, killed and 170, wounded.

WHY TH ADVANC STOPPE

Daily Express Milita Correspondent

THE Germans have drawn from Warsaw to the south-west of the

The author's story which led to the seizure of the *Daily Express* by the police.

The author with Finnish ski troops, December 1939.

The battlefield of Soumussalmi.

twenties. I had seen enough of this uniform now, in my three weeks in Finland, to realise what this death was going to mean when word of it got back to some red-painted peasant shack in the forests of the south.

And the Russians? I went from body to body, staring at the faces of these men fallen here, in their peaked Soviet caps with the dull red star on their front. The faces underneath were Oriental, simple, a little brutish, those of peasants from southern Russia. One man, a huge fair figure, had completely Mongoloid features; another the dark, sharp look of a Tartar. But the mass had the broad nose, narrow forehead and wide dark eyes of the peasant.

I tried to think of what this slaughter would mean to their families and lovers in the collective farms and the dusty peasant villages from which they had come. But, though I had visited Russia, I found this difficult, for these people and their lives were, I realised, strange to me. Then, fallen across the body of a dead horse, I saw one man who brought it home to me abruptly. He clutched still in his hand a doll and two pairs of children's black gym shoes, and a child's frock. He had clearly picked them up from a Finnish peasant's house. The man was young. You could see how carefully he had gathered these things, thinking of the day when he would be able to go back to his home, and his daughter would run out to meet him, and he would give her this doll, and these precious clothes. Now here he lay, outstretched on this forest road in Finland, beside a horse with its entrails scattered in the snow.

The sun was already almost gone, and the sky behind the pines was a brilliant, lovely yellow that made the scene more fantastic than ever. Through the small pine trees on either side of the road patrols moved looking for survivors. A band of peasants were piling saddles, rifles and other gear together, and carrying corpses to the huge yellow wagon that had returned for yet another load.

In his nearby headquarters General Wallenius readily explained to me, in German, the course of the battle. A stocky man with greying hair, a deeply lined face, small blue eyes, a scarred nose and curiously bony handshake, he responded with remarkable frankness to my queries about his methods and his tactics. This may have resulted from his belief, which I was never able to shake, that I was not just a reporter, but a British officer in disguise. At times, in an effort to catch me out, he would suddenly address me as '*Herr Hauptmann*', and then chuckle loudly with disbelief when I would disavow the title. 'Now, now, *Herr Hauptmann*,' he would say. 'You

British are our friends. It is good that the British Army should learn all about us.'

The *Express* made the most of my story from Kemijarvi, and within a few days many of the correspondents in Helsinki had made their way northwards to Rovaniemi. Amongst them was Edward Ward, the first BBC reporter I had encountered on a news story. Ward, who in time was to inherit the title of Viscount Bangor, was to pioneer with skill and success the new art of on-the-spot radio reporting. He had an easy, relaxed style, an eye for significant detail, and a command of clear and often vivid English. He sensibly decided to concentrate on providing eyewitness material of the scenes of battle, leaving the day-to-day progress of the war to be dealt with by the agencies. He faced formidable practical difficulties. He had no recording gear and his talks had to be delivered live from the nearest radio station.

At Rovaniemi we lived in considerable comfort in a modern two-storied hotel, the Pojanhovi, half of which had been turned into a military hospital. Rovaniemi was almost exactly on the Arctic Circle, a fact which enabled me to use a phrase which had been on the tip of my tongue ever since I got to Finland, 'It is reported in Arctic circles'. The only discomfort we endured was when we were from time to time hustled out of the hotel, into an eighteen foot deep trench in the grounds which served as an air raid shelter, and which proved necessary when Russian planes ultimately raided and damaged the town. From Rovaniemi the foreign press, now numbering a score or more, were taken on long bus or car drives to the widely scattered forest battle fronts. On one of these, at Suomussalmi, the Finns repeated the Kemijarvi victory on an even larger scale. Two Russian divisions, the 163rd and the 44th, were almost completely wiped out by Finnish ski troops, moving like shadows in the forests. The scenes at Suomussalmi, much photographed and much written about, brought home most vividly to the outside world the extent of the Russian defeat in the north. There was one significant difference from the scenes I had witnessed at Kemijarvi. There the Finnish dead had been still on the battlefield. At Suomussalmi they had all been removed before the press arrived. Only the Russians, in their peaked caps and thin uniforms, frozen in the lifelike or terrible contortions of sudden death, appeared on the pages of the newspapers and on the cinema screens of the outside world.

Rovaniemi was a small town, not much more than a village,

almost entirely of single-storied wooden buildings. Even its sauna was no more than a hut in which an aged peasant woman poured water on to hot stones, and where the only way of taking a cold plunge was to leap into the snowdrifts outside. This smallness brought the advantage that in the weeks we were based in Rovaniemi we were able to meet and get some idea of the attitude of ordinary Finnish people caught up in this struggle. Since many of them spoke German, language was not an impenetrable barrier. This experience left met in no doubt that the Finnish people fought this war with unity and a deep-rooted patriotism. I felt this particularly strongly one day when I climbed to the top of the two hundred-foot wooden ski jump, which stood like some strange mechanical toy on the edge of a wood four miles from the town. A seventeen-year-old girl, her cheeks flushed with the wind, her fair hair thrust under a grey fur hat, stood wrapped in a great Robinson Crusoe goatskin coat. A refugee from the frontier city of Viipuri, she did eight hours' plane spotting a day, two hours on, two hours off, warming up in a hut at the foot of the structure. The top platform swayed in an icy, whistling wind which felt as if a fully grown man were tugging at your sleeve. A fourteen-year-old boy with a rifle stood by her, the only protection against a machine-gunning Soviet plane. Yet the two of them laughed and joked with the guide who was with us, and shouted a cheerful '*Huyva paivaa*' – 'Good-bye' – to us as we climbed down. I was to think often of that pair when later pro-Soviet propagandists assured me that the Russian army came to Finland as liberators of an oppressed people.

*

Early in February I returned to England for a spell of leave from what seemed likely to be a long war, with the Russians halted at the Mannerheim Line and blocked in the northern forests. I was astonished to find in Britain a considerable degree of acceptance of the Soviet case that the Red Army was intervening to rescue the Finnish people from an oppressive, white Fascist Government. In the train up from Dover a well-dressed man, learning that I had just come from Finland, assured me knowingly that he was not taken in by all this anti-Russian propaganda being written from Helsinki. Letter writers to *Picture Post* took the same view. A. J. Cummings, much cultivated by Maisky, the astute Soviet Ambassador in

London, lent his influential pen to throw doubts on the bona fides of the Finnish Government. D. N. Pritt went off to Finland to write a Penguin special strongly slanted against the Finns.

Left-wing friends sought me out, some to berate me for what they saw as deliberate anti-Soviet bias, others – who had made, or were about to make – a break with Communism, to question me about what I had seen and experienced. For many British Communists, and particularly many fellow travellers, the invasion of Finland was a final blow to a faith which had become interwoven with every aspect of their lives, in which not only beliefs but friendships, contacts, even jobs were put at risk by their change of mind. Other people, more to the right, wanted to probe my views about the chances of continued Finnish resistance once the snows melted, and General Winter, the Finns' best (and only) ally, was no longer in the battle. The Finnish defensive victories had encouraged a number of politicians and military writers, particularly in France, to develop what was surely the maddest of all the strategic ideas which were to emerge in World War II – that France and Britain should use the war in Finland as an excuse to attack the Soviet Union, widening the struggle into one not only against Hitler but against Stalin. Since we had stalemate in the West, this argument ran, and since neither the Maginot Line nor the Siegfried Line could be breached, we should hit at Germany through the Soviet oilfields of Baku. By capturing them, and moving on to capture the Rumanian oil fields as well, we would then cut off Hitler's oil supplies and bring Germany to her knees.

This rested on one key assumption – that the Russian defeats in Finland showed that the Red Army was rotten through and through, its officer corps ruined by Stalin's purges, and that therefore it could not withstand attack from France and Britain. This seemed to me a very dubious deduction, given the degree to which the exceptionally hard and early winter had aided the Finns, and I threw my weight against any such idea of extending the war wherever I could. The most we could do for Finland – and this was a position I did support – was to help the Finns secure a stalemate, and so protect their independence, by supplying them with the fighter aircraft, field and anti-tank guns and ammunition which, we were assured, both Britain and France now possessed in abundance.

Even that policy depended, however, on the assumption that the Mannerheim Line, like the Maginot and Siegfried Lines, could withstand direct attack. By the time I returned to Finland late in

February, this faith in prepared positions, so deeply rooted in the military theories of the thirties, was being overthrown by events. Frustrated in the forests in the north, the Red Army had opted for a massive onslaught on the Mannerheim Line, an onslaught which was to go on continually for forty-six days. They ultimately smashed their way through the Line, but the decisive move was a daring flanking movement in which armoured formations were sent across the frozen waters of the Gulf of Viipuri, and seized positions on the shoreline to the rear of the main Finnish line. The Finns had to sue for peace – and to buy it by conceding all Stalin's demands. At eleven on the morning of 13 March the fighting stopped.

The Finns, with their difficult language, their reticence and their pride, are not an easy people to get to know. Yet they showed in those three months of the Winter War that even when the odds seem to be stacked adamantly against you, it pays to fight. Their resistance between November 1939 and March 1940 cost them 27,000 dead – a high figure for a country which, with its two million people, was no bigger than New Zealand. They had not only bared their teeth but sunk them in so fiercely that the Soviet Union took care not to try any offensives against them when, in 1941, the Finnish Government sought the recapture of its lost territories by coming into the war on Germany's side. When Germany lost that war, the Finns could have faced a terrible retribution from the Russians. That nothing of the kind was exacted – except in terms of draconic reparations – must owe much to the reluctance of the Soviet High Command to get caught up in any more military operations in such terrain, and against such people.

It was not, of course, only their freedom as a nation which the Finns had protected in the fierce fighting in those bitter snows. It was their freedom as individuals, a freedom which today may have some limitations on it, but which is incomparably greater than that of any other people within the aegis of the Soviet Union.

When I left Finland in mid-March to return to Britain, Giles Romilly took over the Scandinavian coverage from me. He and his younger brother Esmond were celebrated figures of their time. Nephews of Winston Churchill, cousins of the Mitfords, they had, as schoolboys, started an anti-war, anti-Establishment magazine called *Out of Bounds*. Both had enlisted in the International Brigade, and had fought in battles around Madrid. That war over, Esmond had married Jessica Mitford and gone to the United States. Giles had joined the *Daily Express*. We had worked together during the final stage of the Finnish war in an easy partnership. He had a Churchillian courage and gaiety and forthrightness. His courage was indeed to prove his undoing. A month later, when the Germans invaded Norway, he was in Narvik, in the far north of the country. The Germans had sent marines into the Narvik in advance, hidden in the hold of a merchant ship. When these stormed ashore to seize the town, the porter at the hotel where Romilly was staying woke him and told him there was just time to get to the Swedish frontier, a mile away, before the Germans reached it. Romilly was half way to the border when he realised that he had left his overcoat behind in the hotel. 'I thought,' he told me after the war, 'why the hell should the Germans have that good woollen overcoat of mine? So I went back to the hotel, got the coat and was just walking out through the front entrance when a squad of marines arrived and arrested me.'

As Churchill's nephew, Romilly was deemed by the Germans to be a prize catch. He was imprisoned for much of the war in Colditz. When I saw him again in 1945 he looked much older, and battered – though the Germans had not used force against him. The loss of those years, made the harder because he felt he had contributed to his own capture, drained some of the vitality out of him, and he died when still in his early thirties.

When I arrived back in England in mid-March, President Roosevelt's Assistant Secretary for State, Mr Sumner Welles, was touring Europe exploring the possibility of a negotiated peace. Beaverbrook was taken with the idea, and invited me to a dinner at Stornaway House, at which the Welles tour was the main topic under discussion. It was not the only bid for peace which had interested Beaverbrook since war broke out. He had given some encouragement to the Clydeside ILP leaders, James Maxton and John McGovern, and to the Labour MP Richard Stokes, in campaigns they had mounted for peace by negotiation. Indeed McGovern even declared that Beaverbrook had offered them £500 to fight a by-election on the issue – a claim which Churchill had in 1941 to deny on behalf of Beaverbrook, who was by then Minister of Production.

The guest list of the dinner at Stornaway House in mid-March survives amongst Beaverbrook's papers. It was:

> Mr Christiansen
> The Duchess of Westminster
> Mr McCloughly (a Canadian businessman)
> Mr and Mrs Frank Owen
> Mr Cox

We wore dinner jackets, with the stiff shirts of the time, a practice still usual in many homes and restaurants, war or no war, in London's West End. After the meal, as we sat over coffee and port at the dinner table, Beaverbrook canvassed our views on the Sumner Welles mission. He posed the question in his own probing way. 'Are you for peace?' he asked his neighbour, and then went round the table asking each of us in turn. Most echoed our host's manifest preference for negotiation. But when he came to where Frank Owen and I sat he said, 'I'm not going to ask you. I know your views. You are both for war.'

Beaverbrook's appointments diary for that day gives not only the names of his dinner guests, but of the man with whom he lunched – Maisky, the Russian Ambassador. He is not likely to have got much encouragement from Maisky for a negotiated peace, for the last thing the Soviet Union wanted at this stage was for Germany to make peace in the west, and be free to turn east.

Hitler, in any event, soon demonstrated his reaction to talks about such negotiations. On 9 April, only a few days after Neville Chamberlain had assured a Conservative rally that Hitler 'had missed the bus', German forces invaded Norway and Denmark. I learnt this news in the Buckinghamshire countryside, near Princes Risborough, where Cecily had leased a house. In an upper room there, with a view stretching away from the Chilterns, where the white Whiteleaf Cross, cut into the chalk, was now covered with turf to lessen its value as a marker to German aircraft, I set about writing a book on the Winter War in Finland. I was determined to get on the record events as I had seen them, and probed them. This I did, though I finally had to complete the work in the barrack room of an Officer Cadet Training Unit in Droitwich six months later. It was published by Victor Gollancz in May 1941, was well reviewed and sold all that were printed in those days of paper rationing. I had sought another publisher, to be free of the propagandist stamp associated with Gollancz, but those to whom I submitted it rejected it, some in terms which made it plain that I was up against the network of fellow travellers within the publishing world, who were not going to bring into the bookshops a book recording this deed by the Soviet Union. A similar attitude within the New York publishing world could account for the fact that it was not published there. Gollancz had, however, now broken decisively with the Communist and fellow-travelling Left, particularly once they opposed the war against Hitler, and willingly devoted a considerable part of his quota of scarce paper to *The Red Army Moves* – not an ideal title, but the best we could devise to give the book timeliness in the swiftly changing pattern of events.

I had completed only the first couple of chapters when the Germans launched their invasion of Norway and Denmark. Christiansen recalled me to London, and asked me to go to Norway as the *Express* war correspondent – the proposal which triggered off our discussion about Beaverbrook's memorandum in 1938. I had long been clear in my mind that I would not become a war correspondent in my own country's war. In other people's war, the correspondent role was undoubtedly journalistic. Your task was to discover and tell the truth about what was happening. In your own country's war, your task was bound to be largely that of the propagandist, writing material which should sustain and encourage the war effort. You could still execute, to a considerable degree, the role of instant historian, by careful observation and clear portrayal of the scene and atmosphere of battle – a role which Alan Moorehead was to fulfil superbly, as were, in the new field of radio, men like Eddie Ward, Richard Dimbleby, and Robert Reid. But at the end of the day what you wrote or said had to be subordinated to the more immediate task of winning the war. This was a perfectly reputable role and one which, God knows, was to involve war correspondents in much danger. But it was not one I wanted to execute.

There were deeper reasons, too. In my reporting throughout the past four years there had been the message, implicit or explicit, that we should stand up to Hitler. Now that we were doing so, it seemed to me only right that I should carry my share of that task, that now that war was here I should fight in it, not just write about it. The time had come to fulfil the pledge I had made to myself on that September day in Prague. Perhaps, indeed, it was even simpler than that. Perhaps I just wanted to be able to look in the eye those veterans beside whom we had paraded, as school cadets, on Anzac Day in Invercargill.

I could not set all this out to Christiansen. Nor was it a simple matter, in that early spring of 1940, to become a soldier. New Zealanders in Britain who had volunteered at the outbreak of war had been formed into an anti-tank battalion, which was already completing its training on Salisbury Plain, and had no scope for new recruits. For the British army, I was told to wait until my time for call-up came, which – since I was now thirty years old – might not be until much later in the war. Nor did those of my friends who had joined the British army seem to have fulfilling tasks. John Mulgan, commissioned into the Oxford and Bucks Light Infantry, was guarding arms dumps in Northern Ireland. Dan Davin, a private in the Warwickshires, was in a training camp on Salisbury Plain. Bill Williams had had the best break. He was in an armoured car regiment with a prospect of action – if any came. In these circumstances I accepted, as the best interim alternative, Christiansen's decision to send me to Brussels, even though he – and I – both saw it as banishment to an apparent backwater.

CHAPTER EIGHTEEN

Belgium on the Eve

Beyond the frontier bridge on the road to Aachen the jagged concrete teeth of the anti-tank barriers of the Siegfried Line curved away like the Great Wall of China across the swelling, smiling, green slopes to the north and into the depths of a wood to the south, white dragon's teeth of a modern sowing. Behind them, scarped white amidst the golden clay, were the turrets and loopholes of strong points. One, built beside a cottage, covered the road and the bridge.

With a Belgian frontier guard I walked down to the stone barricade which the Belgians had put across the road just this side of the border. A German sentry in grey-green uniform and cowled steel helmet walked to his edge of the bridge and stared at me. From a window of the German Customs Station an official photographed me. Out of the other windows leant young soldiers off guard, brown-skinned, laughing boys. Their voices and laughter rang in the still air of this April evening. Someone was playing an accordion. The Aachen tram clanged to its terminus by the bridge and a group of Belgians, girls and men, passed into the German Customs House, had their passports stamped, and came on towards Belgium. Two of them laughed back to shouts from the soldiers, who, stripped to the waist, called to them from the windows overlooking the road along which, three weeks later, the German tank columns were to roar into Belgium. When later in the Western Desert and in Italy I was to hear the refrain of 'Lili Marlene' from the Soldaten-sender in Belgrade, with its evocation of the scene 'underneath the lantern, by the barracks gate', this moment of early spring 1940 by the Aachen bridge would recur to my mind.

In a field only a few kilometres back the young grass was still scarred and rutted where the small plane carrying the two Luftwaffe majors had crashed in fog on the morning of 9 January. Scorched stems of bushes showed where they had tried to burn the documents they carried, detailing the German plan to invade Holland, Belgium and France. Enough of their papers had fallen intact into the hands of the Belgians to set their forces, and those of the French and British

154

on the alert. The Allied armies in Northern France closed up to the Belgian frontier, ready to counter-attack. When German reconnaissance planes appeared overhead, photographing these movements, it was widely assumed that the crash had been a fake, skilfully organised to force the Allies to show their hands. I recorded in my notes at the time that it was probably 'a beautifully organised plant'.

Brussels, into which I had flown the day before, was garishly but attractively bright after the drab, blacked-out streets of London, Paris and Helsinki. On the Place de Brouchère, outside the Metropole Hotel, yellow letters twenty feet high burned in the darkness, calling upon Brussels to buy Cresta Spaghetti. Next to them a bunch of grapes, looking rather like a pineapple, gave another electric message for someone's port wine. Above Maxim's bar three neon chorus girls tossed a ball again and again above their heads, and moved shining feet in a flicker which lit up the ceiling of my hotel room. In the hall of the hotel, where ochre-coloured marble pillars rose towards a glass church-like dome, plump women in black satin and shining hats gathered in the afternoons to drink coffee or sweet liqueurs, and await the massive men who came in from the Bourse, smoking cigars and spilling provincial prosperity. One corner table was occupied regularly by a Spanish actress who claimed to be a refugee, but whom I overheard speaking excellent German to a man and a young woman who visited her every afternoon. I put her down as doing a watching job for the Reich, just as I assumed that a charming grey-haired English couple, he claiming to be a retired businessman, were doing the same job for the British.

The Metropole was a centre for the British, Americans and French. The Germans, dozens of them, journalists and Gestapo agents, were in hotels close to the railway station. Amongst them was the correspondent I had visited in Cologne nine months before. We passed one another in the street one evening, each restraining a half grin of recognition before we averted our gaze, and hurried on our ways.

The first clear sign of what was to hit us came less than a week ahead of the invasion. On Sunday 5 May, Maurice Fast, who had been so helpful to me in the autumn, asked me to come to his office. He told me that he had information direct from King Leopold's private secretary that Hitler had informed Mussolini that he had plans to make a simultaneous attack on Holland, Belgium,

Luxembourg and France. Mussolini wanted to bring the Italians in on this but the Italian royal family were against it. The king of Italy decided, however, to inform the Belgian king of what was about to happen.

The information rang true to me. Fast, as the editor of a small but influential newspaper was in too exposed a position to risk exaggeration on a story of this kind. He would not have trusted me with knowledge of his source unless he was anxious to underline its reliability. Moreover a simultaneous attack against all four western countries along his border was the type of audacious move which Hitler had a genius for. Until now the military experts in Britain and France had been busy arguing which of these countries Hitler would attack. Few if any had predicted an attack all along the line. On the other hand, if the story was untrue, or a plant, I would be guilty of crying wolf, and so not only of giving a false alarm to the British public, but of weakening my voice when the real thing occurred.

I tried to check the story with the British Embassy, without disclosing my source. They knew nothing which could confirm it. At a lunch at the Brussels Chamber of Commerce I managed to get a word with the American Ambassador, Cudahay. He said he had seen the king within the last week, and nothing of the sort had been mentioned. Even so, I decided to back my instinct, and wrote the story.

The *Express* published it, but in an obscure place on the back page – in sharp contrast to the lavish front-page presentation of a recent interview with General Ironside, who had said 'Come on Hitler. We are ready!' Even though mine was an exclusive report I could not altogether blame them, as I had not been able to disclose my source. I suspected, too, that the policy line coming from Stornaway House was that if we did not predict a flare-up in the fighting all might settle down again to stalemate. But *Newsweek* in the United States were less inhibited. I had been cabling them material, on a freelance basis, since the previous summer. They ran my story with a flourish.

Next day provided some confirmation, with reports of pontoon bridges being assembled near the German frontier, and of big troop moves around Hannover. I decided that this was the real thing, and for the first time, in all the invasion scares since the war began, I wrote a further strong red light warning that a German D-Day was near. I held to this even though by Wednesday, 8 May the alarm, which by now was filling the Belgian newspapers, seemed to be lessening. I recorded in my notes that the British Embassy 'believed it was blowing over'. Marcel Fodor, who had been the astute and very well informed correspondent of the *Manchester Guardian* in Vienna, was now representing that paper in Brussels. He was convinced that I was wrong. He saw the reports of German troop movements as a bluff to distract attention from a German thrust into the Balkans. From Amsterdam my colleague Morley Richards telephoned to say that the Dutch too thought the crisis was past.

Thursday, 9 May was clear, blue, sunny. The morning BBC news reported that in the Commons the night before thirty-three Conservatives had voted against the Government. In the cautious fashion of the day, it did not however predict that this would bring down Chamberlain and pave the way for Churchill. In the afternoon I drove northwards through Antwerp towards the Dutch border to see what signs there might be of extra preparedness against invasion. I went with Bob Okin, of the Associated Press of America, and his lovely Spanish wife Pepita. He had married her during the Civil War, and was deeply worried for her safety, should the Germans overrun Europe, for she had been ardently anti-Franco.

It was an afternoon of complete spring beauty. In the big parks on the edge of Antwerp women wheeled children in the sunshine, pausing to watch, on one big open sports field, troops training to meet air attack. Belgian biplanes swooped, and the khaki-clad soldiers scattered and went through the motions of firing back. The old city forts loomed behind new barbed wire barricades, the forts of which Winston Churchill, even though he was First Lord of the Admiralty, had impetuously taken command in 1914, with a young Lieutenant Freyberg among his officers.

When we reached the wide, straight line of the Albert Canal, which ran, a sixty-foot-wide natural anti-tank barrier, from Antwerp to the Meuse and the German frontier, the sentries were strict, noting details of our passports, our passes, our identity cards. It was the same at the forward defensive line north of the canal, where iron rails, set as an anti-tank obstacle, and a series of trenches stretched across the dead flat plain towards Holland and the Ruhr. The trenches were solidly built, with revetted sides and in places strengthened with concrete. There was no sign of any special alert. When I had driven through here in October the trench lines had been manned. Now they were untenanted. In front of the barracks in one village three men raked a flower bed, bright with early pansies. Others strolled about the street in the sun, exuding

boredom. Along the Canal, when we passed back southwards over
it, anti-tank guns were in position, but were unmanned. So, too,
were the weapon pits on the canal bank. Groups of troops,
unarmed, waited by the roadside to hitch-hike into Antwerp on
leave. Reliefs for sentries sunbathed beside the sentry boxes. It
looked as if I had indeed fallen for an invasion scare. But I could
check the situation at a high level the next day, for I was due to
lunch with General Badoux, the Belgian general who had designed
for Finland the Mannerheim Line defences.

On that grey gold spring evening I dined with the assistant press
attaché of the British Embassy, a man who before the war had had
the tough task of selling British beer in a country which could boast
twenty-eight different brands of excellent beer of its own. He had,
as an artillery officer, been a member of the first British party to
enter Brussels after the Armistice. 'The Metropole had been a
German officers' centre, and we ate in its dining room with officers
in field grey all around us.' On our way up the hill to the little
restaurant where we ate roast chicken and drank red wine he showed
me the bullet marks on two houses where the Reichswehr had
turned their machine guns in 1918 on Bolshevik mutineers in the
Germany army.

I went on to have a drink with Okin and his wife at Le Boeuf sur
le Toit, where the small dance floor was a crowded, bobbing,
turning mass of young Belgians, very much the *jeunesse dorée* of this
wealthy city, the girls wearing wide short skirts in what was then
deemed the American style. They were dancing to '*Sur le Pont
d'Avignon*', adapted as a swing tune by Marius B. Winter and his
British band. I had a final coffee with Marcel Fodor in a café
opposite the Opera. He had already established there a *Stammtisch*
like that over which he had presided in the Café Louvre in Vienna,
where friends came to hear him talk and tipsters came to give him
information. He smiled knowingly and relievedly behind his big
spectacles when I told him of the peaceful scenes along the Albert
Canal. 'The attack will come in the Balkans, not there. You will
see,' he assured me.

I was in my pyjamas, writing a letter to Cecily in my room in the
hotel, when the phone went, and the bottom dropped out of the
world as we had known it. It was Fast's voice. 'You had better come
round. They are on the move. This time it is the real thing.'

CHAPTER NINETEEN

Attack in the West

I hurried into my clothes, and round to Fast's office. In the streets it was just another Brussels night. Outside the night clubs touts and commissionaires waited for any late pleasure seekers. Couples still strolled home slowly from the cinema. Waiters were cleaning up the cafés around the Opera, and taxi drivers stood by their cars, chatting. I found Fast, and his military correspondent, Colonel Piquard, and a group of sub-editors in the paper's newsroom.

'The Belgium secret service has been informed that German columns are now moving towards the frontiers of Belgium and Holland. All Belgian army leave has been cancelled, and the General Staff is leaving Brussels shortly.' I thought of grey-green tanks I had seen massed along the roadside outside Karlsbad, of the lorried infantry moving into Innsbruck, and envisaged them moving now through the villages of Western Germany, and the streets of Aachen and a score of other frontier towns, no doubt watched excitedly and apprehensively by people from their doorways and windows. Yet one thing seemed inexplicable. Why was Hitler, shrewd and successful as he had always been until now, hurling his army against the bastions of the west which, if not impregnable, were strong?

We tried the radio. From Europe, silence. From America, a mid-Western news announcer was summarising events of the day in Europe. Of Belgium he said, 'The Nazi invasion scare has died away. Every report from Brussels and Amsterdam shows that tension is easing there.'

I ran back to the Metropole, and got the old, old man who was night porter to put in a call to London, to the Ministry of Information through which all wartime press calls had to pass. The call was refused. The Ministry of Information censors went home at twelve o'clock, so no further press calls were accepted after that hour. It did not matter that the world was cracking under our feet, that I had information which could prepare the public for the shock which was to come the next day. Censors were respectable fellows who lived in Ealing, and had to take up their bowler hats and get the last tube home.

More news. A call from General Badoux's ADC. The General would not be able to keep our lunch date. He was leaving town. So it was definite that the General Staff was moving.

Hugh Greene of the *Daily Telegraph* hurried into the hall. His local correspondent had just rung with news that Pierlot the Prime Minister, and Spaak the Foreign Minister had hurried from a dinner party at eleven o'clock to the Foreign Office, and that a Cabinet meeting was going on there. I got a taxi and drove to the Foreign Office. Its lights were ablaze.

It was now close on one-thirty. As I got back to the hotel a police car drove up, and a constable came to the desk. Any army officers staying in the hotel, he told the porter, were to be woken up and told to rejoin their units at once. Other police cars were racing through the streets, their tyres screeching, on their way to wake up air-raid wardens.

But nothing else gave any sign of war – no black out, no guards. In the small, all-night café on the far side of the square two girls and two men in flashy striped suits were eating and laughing. On the pavement in front of the hotel a small man came up to me, 'Like a nice American girl, mister? First class American girl, just round the corner from here.'

No, I didn't want an American girl. Why not? Well, if you really want to know, because there is going to be a war. He shrugged his shoulders. Of course there was going to be a war. But you couldn't hold up all life just because one day there might be a war, his manner implied.

I said, 'I mean it. I am a foreign newspaperman, and I tell you that at this moment the Germans are crossing the Belgian frontier. You will be at war in a few minutes.'

His face changed. The wheedling look of the pimp vanished and alarm took its place. 'No, not war,' he said. 'I've had enough of war. I was in the last one.' He pulled open his coat and showed me the medal ribbons on his waistcoat. 'You are fooling, eh?'

'Fooling? Wait till dawn,' I said abruptly.

The alarm on his face grew. He ran across to the concrete benches in the middle of the square, and shook awake a man stretched out sleeping on them. I could see the tout gesticulating, talking rapidly. The man on the seat was unconvinced. He waved his arm in scorn, and turned over to sleep again. The tout returned. 'My mate

Edward Ward, BBC war
correspondent in Finland,
1939.

George Millar, newly
commissioned in the Rifle
Brigade, 1940.

The 2ⁿᵈ Malplaon of Belgium ─ Tournai

The hus passes ─ A Belgian town behind the lines after an intensive bombing. Bomb holes in streets ─ Fires from incendiary bombs ─ dead horses ─ wrecked motorcars ─ people flying dug out from their houses which have collapsed +

(*Above*) The bombing of Tournai, from a drawing by Captain Brian de Grineau.

(*Right*) Premier Paul Reynard (centre right) with General Weygand (left) and Marshal Pétain (right).

doesn't believe you,' he said. 'And anyway' – this part with a smile – 'what about that nice American girl?'

I went back and rang Fast. There was still no definite news that the invasion had begun. His paper was going to press with 'Serious New Crisis' as its headlines. But in the hotel army officers were now clattering downstairs and driving off in taxis. Two agitated businessmen, who must have been telephoned by someone in the know, appeared with their bags, paid their bills, and went off.

Into the midst of all this walked a tall, beautiful, dark girl, very well dressed, and a tall young man. The man asked the agitated night porter for a room. As he did so the girl slipped her hand into his. On her face was a look of shining contentment. They went off upstairs, key in hand. Did they know nothing of what was happening or perhaps did they know a great deal?

I decided I must try to get some sleep, and lay fully dressed on my bed. I slept and then suddenly I was awake, and guns were booming. I tried to reassure myself that perhaps after all these were just Belgian guns firing at British or German planes flying high overhead. They often did. Perhaps it had all been just one more crisis, one more huge false alarm.

But the scene outside my window destroyed these last illusions. It was dawn. The sky was clear, a pale bluish grey. Away in the distance, where the airport lay, heavy clouds of black smoke were rising. Above them, like minnows in a pool, long dark bombers were circling. Then the guns started again, and streaks of golden sparks crossed the cloudless, delicate sky. Ack-ack tracer shells. The roar of engines grew and grew. There must have been scores of planes about. Seven biplanes, which I knew to be Belgian fighters, rose in formation behind the towers of the cathedral, climbing steadily. A bomber, moving high above the roofs, climbed swiftly away from them. The chatter of machine guns broke through the flatter crump of the anti-aircraft fire. Belgium was at war. We were all now truly at war.

Down on the ground floor two charwomen, half cowering, half curious, stood by the glass fish tank at the dining-room door, staring out into the street as the guns thumped and as glass fell on the pavement. The glass dome of the hotel lounge looked suddenly lethal. Whistles and sirens sounded, and a small man in a bowler hat ran in through the swing doors shouting, 'Take cover, take cover. I am an air-raid warden.'

The lift buzzer went incessantly, and the night porter, too old to show his fears or his weariness, set about bringing down the baggage of those wanting to leave. Fat Jewish businessmen from Amsterdam, fat Belgian businessmen from Liège and Bruges milled around the desk, paying bills, shouting for taxis, whilst their wives, hastily dressed, cried to them, or rushed for luggage. At windows all round the square outside pyjamaed people, nightdressed people stared skywards. Was a great city ever awakened into war in this way?

Down the stairs, down the lift people still poured. Into the middle of this uproar walked the two who had booked in the early hours, the tall beautiful girl and the tall young man. Quietly they went to the desk, he paid his bill, she smiled at him, and they walked out hand in hand. In the midst of the crowd battling for timetables and taxis another young man and his girl wife stood, his arms around her, lips to lips, for seconds, minutes, long minutes. Then the porter called, '*Votre taxi, monsieur*', and she turned, with tears over her face like rain, as he moved towards the swing door, outside which the guns had taken up their thumping again.

In the streets Brussels was going to work, as if nothing had been changed. Sturdy workmen, hurrying charwomen and shop assistants moved along the pavement in droves. A boy was cleaning the windows of a shop at the corner whilst the guns went on roaring, and a plane darted across a corner of the sky. There was one macabre touch. Through the crowds darted a woman, her face deeply rouged, her stockings cheap, her eyes glazed. An old, old tart. She grabbed at the hands of workmen carrying their lunch boxes, at the hands of businessmen seeking taxis. They brushed her away, and she darted on through the crowd, her white handbag swinging.

I drove to the Foreign Office as the sirens wailed, and bursts of shrapnel showed like white roses in the pale blue sky, just as I had seen it above Madrid. With me was Mike O'Leary, correspondent of a group of mid-western papers, and very different from the other American correspondents I had known, who were either ardently liberal, like Mowrer or Gunther, or shrewdly sceptical, like Walter Kerr. O'Leary was anti-British to every corner of his Irish soul. 'Oh boy, this is the works, this is the works. I've seen what those monkeys did to Poland, and believe me they know their business. Those monkeys don't mess about once they've begun. You've really got it coming to you now.'

Guards stood outside the Foreign Office, big Flemish peasants who looked bewilderedly at our passes, and whose hands seemed too

big for the light machine guns set up on the pavement. Iwens
D'Eickhoute, head of the Press Bureau, told us that the German
Minister in Brussels had called on Spaak at five in the morning and
told him Germany was moving into Belgium to anticipate an Anglo-
French invasion of the country. The king had issued an appeal to
the nation, and had gone to take command of the army; the Dutch
were resisting; there was no word from the fronts. Appeals had gone
out to the Allies who were sending help at once.

At midday the first sign of that help appeared. Up the Rue de la
Loi raced a khaki-coloured car, with a white-helmeted Belgian
policeman standing up through the open sunshine roof, his whistle
going like a fire-engine siren. Behind came a British military
policeman on a motor cycle, the scarlet top of his flat cap brilliant,
his steel helmet slung across his shoulder. He led another car in
which sat four British officers, steel-helmeted, their scarlet staff tabs
bright within the shadow of the car. The first part of the British
Expeditionary Force was in the Belgian capital, on their way to plan
the move through the capital of the British divisions which were to
take up a position along the River Dyle, south of Louvain.

On the pavements the Belgians stared and clapped. I clapped with
them – proudly. This was at last no Spain from which we had
averted our gaze, no Czechoslovakia which we had betrayed, no
Poland we were unable to help in time. This time we were meeting
Hitler with the one argument he understood – force.

The BEF was part of a wide Allied sweep forward. The plan was
that, like a great steel door hinged on Sedan, three French armies,
with the BEF in their centre, would swing round to form a
barrier, stretching from where the Dutch stood behind their water
lines, covering the great port of Antwerp and across Belgium east of
Brussels, lining up with the River Meuse, which in turn would link
up with the Maginot Line.

Throughout this Friday, 10 May, the Allied armies poured into
Belgium. On the frontier the customs barriers were cut down to let
the tanks pass, and crowds waited in every village, hurling lilac at the
troops in their lorries. By nightfall, when the sirens, which had
wailed all day as the airfields around the capital were steadily
bombed, were still going, the advance guard of the BEF rolled along
the Chaussée de Mons, and made its way across Brussels towards the
great avenue which led out of the city towards Louvain. In the dusk
the Belgians stood cheering and the men in the trucks and Bren
carriers and cars waved back. Every man was wearing lilac, purple

on his steel helmet, in the barrel of his rifle, stuck in his web equipment. They smiled and saluted with thumbs up – a gesture which at first shocked the Belgians, to whom it had a very rude significance, but which they soon recognised as a sign of cheerful confidence, a thumbs up in the tradition of ancient Rome. Soon the children who ran or cycled beside the British columns were giving it in return. It was a great sight, one to bring tears to the eyes, as this military machine moved forward in all its strength, efficiently, quietly, with the British military police guiding it on at every crossroads as if they were dealing with rush-hour London. It was to prove itself a good fighting machine, too, whenever it was given the chance to fight during the next few weeks.

When dark fell I came out of the hotel with Okin to get dinner at a nearby restaurant. As we came into the Place de Brouchère I stared around, for the moment puzzled. It seemed completely changed. Then I realised that the spaghetti advertisement and the girls above Maxims and the bunch of grapes were gone, and in their place was just the grey cliff wall of the buildings, with a few pale searchlights beyond. It was like being suddenly thrust into a dark, narrow canyon. In one more country in Europe the lights had gone out.

All through that warm night the sirens kept up their noise, and over the radio came incessant alerts. 'Enemy planes are moving over Anderlecht and Molembeek and Koekelberg. Parachutists are believed to have been dropped near the Jardin Botanique. Police cars take note.' The guns continued their clamour, planes droned overhead, and from time to time came the distant crump of bombs – but chiefly on the outskirts, where the airfields lay. Few fell in the city itself, though one did hit a building thirty yards from the American Embassy, sweeping the inside out of an old five-storied building as if with a great hand. There was no fire, and the debris looked old and dusty when we saw it half an hour later.

Parachutists was a word on everyone's lips. Though the Germans had used them only to seize specific strategic targets, chiefly bridges across the Meuse, and though their military achievements were considerable – perhaps even decisive – the indirect blow they dealt to morale was equally important. In Holland, on Hitler's own orders, some parachutists had been dropped in Dutch army uniforms. Other German troops on the ground had dressed in Dutch police uniforms, to seize a key bridge. From this tiny seed of fact a monstrous growth of rumours spread – and endured.

Parachutists, it was said, had descended dressed as nuns, though given away by their hob-nailed boots; as commercial travellers with explosives rather than samples in their bag. Poisoned chocolates were being dropped from the air for children. Fifth columnists were signalling, it was reported, from attic windows. On that Friday afternoon I had seen Belgian troops rushing to surround a block of buildings close to the British Embassy where parachutists were reported to have been seen. British Field Security troops raced round the block on their motor cycles, keeping watch.

The first round-up of German civilians in the city had taken place on Friday morning. Outside the Metropole a crowd gathered round a large covered van. In a corner of the lounge a group of men and two women were guarded by half a dozen plain clothes policemen and other helmeted police in uniform. Two of the men I had seen daily in the hotel for weeks.

At a signal from the door four police gathered round one man and hurried him to the van. The crowd were at first silent, and then, with cries of '*Les salots*' a group of men and women tried to get at the prisoner. Police bundled him into the van, and two stayed to guard him whilst others went back for the next man.

With each prisoner the cries grew louder, mixed with laughter and shouts of sheer excitement until it formed a harsh, baying noise. It was ugly, and somehow artificial. The Belgians, were, heaven knows, soon to have reason enough to hate the Germans and their Gestapo. But at this moment some of the crowd gave the impression that they were showing a hostility they did not really feel, but which, from books and pictures of the last war, they felt they ought to feel. We had all in 1940 read of war so long, imagined it so long, that now that it had come it had an air of unreality. It was as if we were watching others looking like ourselves, and dressed like ourselves, playing parts in a film which would suddenly flicker to a close, and the cinema organ would strike up 'God Save the King' and we would come out into the open air of reality again. But this was the reality, as on this Brussels pavement yet another generation learnt to hate.

On Saturday, the second day of the invasion, Hugh Greene and I drove out towards Louvain. Through the streets the British infantry were now moving. Brought up by rail, they marched through in platoons – bigger formations could have been more vulnerable to air attack – to their billets in schools, parks and big houses on the city's eastern edge. They were small compact units of men burnt brick red by the sun, a boy officer in front, stick under his arm, map case at his side, moving along at a steady, swinging pace from corner to corner where the military police, rifles slung over their shoulders, directed them on. The troops were bedecked with lilac. The military police drank glasses of beer which people brought out from the cafés.

Under the trees of the big avenue leading towards Louvain line upon line of lorries and of twenty-five-pounder guns, with their tractors and their ammunition trailers, were drawn up, utilising the camouflage of the thick green chestnut leaves. They must have formed a tempting target to the Luftwaffe. Yet they went unbombed – as indeed had been virtually all the long British and French columns which had crowded the roads from the frontier since Friday morning. For the first time the thought occurred to me that perhaps this was not where Hitler's main blow was going to fall, that the spearhead of his thrust might be elsewhere, that the bulk of French and British armies were being manoeuvred on to the wrong foot. 'When I fight France,' Hitler had told the German writer Hermann Rauschning,[1] 'I will lure their armies out from behind the Maginot Line and destroy them in the field.' British censorship would not allow any such speculation in British papers, but I could, and did set out, in my weekly cable to *Newsweek*, a warning that we might be being lured into a trap.

Louvain was a name which, to my generation, spelt the 'Hun frightfulness' proclaimed by the propagandists of World War I, when newspapers and magazines had been filled with drawings depicting German troops burning the historic library of Louvain, with its irreplaceable ancient volumes, and stabling their horses in the city churches. The road to it this afternoon lay through countryside of great beauty, with the pale green of meadows, the dark green of forest, and the bright green of young corn stretching away under an arching blue sky. Convoys of lorries, some Belgian, some British, moved under the young chestnuts still decked with their soft maroon candles. A Belgian biplane fighter rose from behind a wood, and soared away eastwards, and in the roadside fields British gunners were setting up Bofors and Brens.

In this setting we came suddenly face to face with a tragic procession, a long column of refugees making their way to Brussels,

[1] *Hitler Speaks*, Rauschning, 1939.

the first I had seen in this war. Cars, farm carts, even hand barrows
were laden with baggage, mattresses, household gear, crates of fowls
and ducks. Set-faced men, harassed and weeping women,
bewildered or weary or excited children stared from vehicles or
trudged in the dust. In this rich land this seemed an even uglier sight
than the similar columns I had seen set against the background of
the poverty of Spain or the austerity of Finland.

We could explain this exodus as that of peasants fleeing from
fighting zones along the Albert Canal. What was harder to account
for was the steadily increasing number of Belgian troops who
intermingled with these civilians. Some were on foot, some on
bicycles, others in lorries and carts. There were staff officers in cars,
and lorries where troops in ribbed Belgian steel helmets held
machine guns, or sat amidst piled crates of ammunition. There
seemed to be no units, no set order, just a great stream of troops
which thickened steadily, jamming the roads against the advancing
British convoys. These were unmistakably Belgians in retreat, an
ominous sign in a battle not yet forty-eight hours old.

From a ridge outside Louvain we had a view across the city roofs
and the spire of the church. From a wood some ten miles further east
a column of black smoke rose, the only clear sign of war in this
sunny countryside. Then steadily the air filled with the sound of
planes. I could pick out, black gnats against the blue, seven bombers
circling high above the countryside.

Suddenly one fell, dropping like a stone thrown from a cliff top,
its engine wailing, wailing. 'Good God, what a shot,' I said to
Greene. 'The ack-ack guns must have got a direct hit on it.'

I looked for the smoke which must come from its crash. Smoke
there was from the ground, and a sudden roar, but the plane had
not crashed. Steadily it was climbing up to rejoin the others, and
another was diving down behind it towards the smoke marked
target. The roar of the bombs came, heavy, clear. 'Stukas,' said
Greene abruptly, drawing on his experience of the Polish campaign.

It was my first sight of dive-bombing, the tactic which was to
prove so devastating in this campaign. All the bombing I had seen
in Spain and Finland had come from bombers following a steady
level course above their targets. This was a new method, in which
the bombers were put into a steep dive aiming the plane towards the
target before releasing its bomb, with a siren wailing to intensify the
shriek of the falling bomb. Throughout that long afternoon we
watched relays of planes circle, dive, bomb and soar away again,

in attacks on what we later learnt were positions the BEF had taken up. The Germans had the air to themselves. Not an Allied plane appeared to tackle them. We drove back in sombre mood towards Brussels. The same mood had spread to the British troops in their lorries. They were no longer the smiling men who had shouted and waved to the crowds in the city streets. Set-faced, they were picking the lilacs out of their rifle barrels and throwing them away from their gear. The men at the Bren and Bofors guns stared keenly skywards.

The next morning there was at last news from the front – and it was bad news, shockingly bad. Not only had the Germans seized two bridges across the Albert Canal, but the mighty fort of Eban Emael, the most powerful in Western Europe, had been captured. Eban Emael had been built into the bank of a 300-foot-high terrace which ran above the River Meuse. One sunny Sunday afternoon in October Eric Sevareid and I had stood on that terrace close to the fort, and had looked out at the perfect field of fire its guns had, covering the flat land below which stretched to the Albert Canal, and to the Meuse with its mined bridges, and to the outskirts of Liège, with its black pyramids of coal debris. Eban Emael had seemed impregnable – and so it had been to everything except attack from the one direction in which it was unguarded – from the air. At dawn German sappers had landed on the unguarded top of the fort. At the time they had been described as parachutists, but they had come silently by glider – yet another new technique of war introduced by Hitler's Reichswehr. With new powerful hollow charge high explosives they had swiftly knocked out the gun turrets, even destroying the largest guns by thrusting high explosives down their barrels. The troops inside, with the ventilation system damaged, could offer little resistance, and by midday on Friday, 10 May Eban Emael surrendered.

Its loss had not been announced when, at one o'clock on Sunday, 12 May, Paul Henri Spaak held a press conference at the Foreign Office. His plump young face was lined with weariness and worry. Most of the journalists present were Belgians, and it was to them Spaak spoke, 'I appeal to you, gentlemen, to help us support public morale. I assure you news from the front is not as bad as you hear, but these rumours flying round must be checked. Write that the situation is all right.'

This brought a white-haired journalist, whom Spaak addressed as colonel, on to his feet, his face white with fury. 'You ask us to support morale, M le Ministre, but what are you doing? Are you doing anything to stop desertion? Are you telling the public anything definite, to replace the rumours? Aren't you making all the same mistakes as the Government made in 1914?'

Back in the Hôtel Metropole many of the official war correspondents with the BEF had arrived. Among them was William Forrest, arrayed now in khaki, with war correspondent tabs, and J. L. Hodson, a World War I veteran whose novel *Jonathan North*, with its searing account of life in the trenches, had become a best-seller just before this new war was declared. Kim Philby represented *The Times*. It was another *Times* man, however, whom I remember most clearly from that day. I was about to take the vacant place at the table where they were lunching when someone pointed out that I would bring their total to thirteen. I am not usually superstitious, and more in jest than in seriousness I sat down at a table near by. A few minutes later Jerome Caminada of *The Times* took the place I had avoided. A few days later he was captured by the Germans in Ostend and interned in a German camp near the Polish border, from which he ultimately escaped.

To my delight that evening Edward Ward arrived at the hotel, the first time we had seen each other since we went our separate ways after reporting the battle of Suomussalmi. Not only was Eddie a good man to work with, but a man of nerve and judgement, qualities which, I suspected, were going to be needed in the days ahead. For I was about to face one of the most difficult choices which civilians confront in war – that of deciding when to leave a threatened city or country. For the military, that choice is made for them by their superiors. But civilians caught up in an invasion have to decide, usually on very little information, for themselves, whether they are being courageous, or rash, to stay at their posts a little longer, or prudent – or cowardly – to leave while the going is good. This dilemma, facing expatriate Britons first in Rumania and then Greece provides the dramatic tension in Olivia Manning's marvellous *Balkan Trilogy*. Sefton Delmer had confronted the same problem in Warsaw in September 1939 – and, as he later made plain in his *Trail Sinister*, felt he had made the wrong choice, and left too early. I sensed, after Spaak's press conference, that I might soon have to make this choice myself.

I had arranged with Cecil de Sausmarez, the British Press Attaché, that if the Embassy decided to leave at short notice, he would alert me. In order not to alarm the hotel staff, we agreed on a form of code. A message saying that he wanted to see urgently at his office would be the signal that the Embassy was off. To my surprise, a message in exactly these terms reached me that Sunday lunchtime at the Metropole. I could not believe that events had worsened so dramatically, so I decided to check with de Sausmarez. I found him in the luxury flat which had been turned into a wartime press office. There was no sign of any urgent departure. No, the Embassy was not leaving, but the Ambassador had given instructions that all non-essential British residents should be got out of Belgium. Courtenay Young, Reuters correspondent, was with me, as was O'Leary, who had been drinking harder than ever since the German attack began, and who, with the cunning of the drunken, had followed us to see what was amiss. When I objected to de Sausmarez that our task of keeping the British public informed of what was happening hardly rated as non-essential, he was dismissive. 'They don't need the newspapers in a crisis. They can take their news from the BBC,' was his evaluation.

'But where,' I asked him, 'do you think the BBC get their news from?'

He pondered that a moment. 'That's an interesting question,' he said. 'I had never thought of it. Where do the BBC get their news from?'

It was clear the Foreign Office did not deem it necessary for their Press Attachés to be familiar with the workings of the press and broadcasting in Britain. When I explained that it came mostly from Reuters and similar agencies, he agreed we might have a case for staying longer, though he could no longer undertake to warn us if the Embassy left abruptly.

My advocacy of the importance of the press was not helped by O'Leary. During this talk he had disappeared, and we ultimately found him asleep in the flat's opulent black marble bath. War, I had already discovered, is often shot through with farce, but I had not expected to find myself in the third day of the Nazi blitzkrieg in the West engaged in hauling a drunken Irish American out of a millionaire's bath tub.

Signs of mounting chaos multiplied that afternoon, even in the heart of Brussels. On the pavement in front of the Metropole a small crowd gathered round a young Belgian soldier, who was talking excitedly about '*les Boches*', and their terrible tanks and bombers. A Belgian officer, realising the dangers of such wild talk, asked Edward Ward, and a British officer from the Intelligence Corps who had come to Brussels with him, to drive the man home in his car. I went with them.

In the back of the car the soldier poured out his story. 'We were in reserve behind the Albert Canal last night and suddenly a motor cyclist came down the road shouting that the Germans were coming. They were only three miles away, and they were racing on, and we were only in reserve and our officers got up and grabbed a car and went off, so, *tiens*, we went off too. It was only reasonable, wasn't it, to go off if the officers went? We had been bombed all day. God, what bombs, all day. No man wants more than one day of that.'

His young, beardless face was tense. Reddened eyes showed that he had been weeping.

We dropped him outside an old apartment house close to the Midi station. An old man rushed out from a tobacconist's shop on the corner to greet him. The boy saluted us as we drove away, and then stood out on the roadway shouting to an upstairs window, '*Maman, maman, c'est moi, c'est Jean.*'

Maman. It was heart-rending, the cry of that frightened boy. But, as the intelligence officer commented, you don't win wars by calling on *Maman.*

That night we dined at the Savoy restaurant. With its oaken walls, its big mirrors, its massed flowers, it was one of the pleasantest restaurants of pre-war Europe. When I had been there four nights before, it had been crowded with women in evening dress and men in uniform. No doubt in just such places Wellington's officers had dined in the weeks before Waterloo. This night we were the only guests. The cloakroom attendant was in tears. 'Is it true that the Chasseurs Ardennes have been almost wiped out, that the Germans are right through the Ardennes? My husband is there, and my boys, both my boys, are on the Canal Albert.' All of which was true, though we did not know it until two days later.

Pierlot, the Belgian premier, had spoken on the radio at six o'clock in an attempt to check the flood of rumour. He said the Germans had penetrated some distance into the Belgian first line of defence, but were being held on the main positions. Which was as good a half truth as any, but it was not going to halt the flood of refugees from the north and east. They were still streaming along the boulevards as we drove back to the hotel that night, with the sirens wailing again, and the street lights dim spots of blue in the warm spring darkness.

All the next day, Monday, 13 May, this flood poured on into the city. It was now a vast column, streaming along all the by-roads and main roads from Louvain, through the outer suburbs, and the parks on the city edge, on to the inner boulevards. They walked, they rode in cars and carts or on donkeys, were pushed in bathchairs, even in wheelbarrows. There were youths on bicycles, old men, old women, babies, peasant women, kerchiefs covering their heads, riding on farm carts piled with mattresses, furniture, pots. A long line of nuns, their faces red with perspiration under their coifs, stirred the dust with their long grey robes. Under a tree at the city's edge an old man sat, staring exhaustedly, as an equally old woman gathered sticks for a fire. A village priest in a black cassock and high black hat strode beside a donkey piled high with church gear. There were old creaking cars jammed with peasant women and children, and modern limousines, one with an anxious plump man and his anxious plump wife on the front seat, and the back seat and the roof loaded with their luggage.

Many headed for the railway stations, hoping for trains to take them southwards. The stations were like drawings from those of Russia during the Revolution, with people sleeping on the floor, huddled against the walls, women with weeping babies, men pale and exhausted. You had only to glance at such scenes to know that Belgium could not long hold out, with this huge extra problem – unexpected and unprovided for – on its hands.

The Germans soon realised what a bonus these refugees were to their strategy, and from time to time machine-gunned or bombed the refugee columns to add to the chaos. Already on Saturday evening a young girl had been brought in to the Metropole, wounded in the head by a machine-gun bullet. We drove towards the front that Monday morning, past mile upon mile of these columns, until I found my feelings becoming deadened by the sheer size of the tragedy, and I felt myself running out of pity, and instead, perhaps to maintain some sanity, I began to dwell on the military problem it presented, on the way it must clog up the roads for the troops.

Just beyond the edge of Brussels, on a ridge to the north of Waterloo, we caught up with the BEF. Gunners were placing their 25-pounders in orchards and farm yards, whilst officers with range finders worked out targets on maps spread on the ground amid the young corn. British voices rang strangely amongst the grey barn walls and the muck-smelling farmyards. Ahead the guns were roaring steadily, where battle had been joined along the line of the River Lyle. Planes moved constantly overhead, hard to detect or identify in the hazy blue sky. It looked as if the settled phase of the battle, which we had for so long been told to expect, was beginning.

The reality was very different. In ferocious fighting further to the south, near Dinant, a hitherto obscure German general called Erwin Rommel had forced a crossing of the Meuse. Even more significantly, under intensive bombardment by Stukas, the Germans had secured a bridgehead across the river at Sedan. In Holland German tanks had reached the outskirts of Rotterdam, cutting off the Dutch armies from the advancing French. The Allied front in front of Brussels was soon to become untenable.

CHAPTER TWENTY

Collapse Under Blitzkrieg

Tuesday came and went swiftly, another sunny day with the sirens wailing, police on motor cycles dashing after parachutists, and everywhere the refugees. It was ideal bombing weather, and eighty miles to the north of us the Luftwaffe used it to deadly effect. Within twenty minutes, beginning at two o'clock in the afternoon, German bombers smashed to ruins the old centre of Rotterdam, even though the Dutch were at that time negotiating for peace. Working in relays from captured airfields on the outskirts of the city, Heinkel bombers pattern bombed the crowded and defenceless city, as they had learnt to do at Guernica. That evening the Dutch Foreign Minister announced that 30,000 people had been killed or wounded in the raid. These figures were to prove wildly exaggerated. The actual total of dead was 900. Even so it was the most terrible air raid in history up to that time. It dealt a final blow to any chance of Dutch resistance, and by ten o'clock that evening the radio from the Hague announced that Holland had capitulated.

Even more ominous were the German news bulletins the next morning, with their cold, triumphant, curt communiqué, announcing not only the Dutch capitulation, but that the Belgians had been pushed back, the French lines broken at Dinant, and the Meuse crossed above Sedan. How on earth had the Germans got through the Ardennes, that 'one great minefield' which the experts had told us was impassable to tanks? It was clear to me that I must now prepare my own lines of retreat.

I had arranged with our driver that he would hold himself ready at any time to take us to Ostend, where we believed the Belgian Government would go. An ex-soldier, of steady nerve, he had agreed. He was making a fortune, working by day for us, and running refugees to the French border at night. He usually reported at the hotel at seven-thirty in the morning. But by nine there was no sign of him. I went across to his garage. It was closed, and the man in the shop next door told me that the driver had gathered up his family, locked up his premises, and moved off early that day to Ostend 'for the duration'.

To hire another car, or even to buy one, was impossible. The wealthier refugees had taken the lot. In the centre of the Place de Brouchère a white-helmeted policeman had blown his whistle and was shouting to the crowd around him. 'Every man between the ages of eighteen and forty who has not been specially told to stay in the city must make his way as best he can to Ypres.'

Evacuation of all men of military age. The Belgians had at least learnt one lesson from the last war, when thousands of their men were taken off to work in Germany. This move showed foresight – but also that things were now very serious.

My search for transport was interrupted by a call from London, asking me to do an urgent task for John Fitzwilliam. He was a middle-aged freelance journalist who had appeared in Paris shortly before the war began and had later stationed himself in Brussels. He mixed little with the regular press corps, eschewing the comforts of the Metropole for a small hotel near the railway station.

London told me that John Fitzwilliam had left Brussels just before the attack, could not get back, and wanted me to go to his hotel and get hold of money and documents he had left in a deposit box there. It was not an easy task. All I had by way of credentials were the number of the deposit box, and my own press card and passport. The hotel manager at first refused point blank to give a stranger access to any deposit box without written authorisation. I argued and pleaded as outside the sirens wailed, and police continued to blow their whistles and shout orders for the evacuation. In the end I discovered a way. Had Mr Fitzwilliam paid his bill? No, he owed a substantial sum, as he had expected to be away for only one night. I offered to pay with the money I knew was in the box. This – and perhaps the general sense that the world was cracking beneath our feet, that the Germans might well be in Brussels that night – did the trick. The manager produced the key. In the box I discovered well over a thousand pounds worth of Belgian francs, a very big amount for those days. Beside it was a list of names of Belgian people, each with a sum set against it. One name I recognised as that of an official in the Belgian Foreign Office whom I had often met: two others were Belgian journalists; yet another a retired army officer. It did not take any profound act of judgement to realise that John Fitzwilliam had had other tasks than those of a freelance journalist, and that this was the payroll of Belgians helping British intelligence. I felt incensed at the utter incompetence this revealed. Had I not been able to talk the manager into letting me open the box, this list would have remained, almost certainly to fall into the hands of the Gestapo. Every man on it would have been lucky if he ever reached a concentration camp alive, after monstrous torture. I took the money, paid the bill, and on the pavement outside burnt the list and dropped the ashes down a grating in the gutter.

It was now early afternoon. Eddie Ward and I were debating on the pavement outside the Metropole whether we should try to buy bicycles, and make for the French border, since we could not get a car, when fate intervened. Up to the hotel drove a van, camouflaged in khaki and green, belonging to the official French radio. In it was M Masson, correspondent of Radio Diffusion Française. More realistic than the BBC, the French broadcasting authorities had provided their reporter with his own transport. Masson was very ready to offer a lift to his *cher collègue* from the BBC, and to that *cher collègue's* friends. We could squeeze seven in all into the van. But Masson must leave by five that evening for Lille, in order to send off his report.

We had feared that might be too early for us, that after all the fighting front might yet stabilise, that we should not quit our posts too soon. At the headquarters of the Belgian Broadcasting Corporation, in an old red-brick château on the edge of the city, it was difficult to feel that matters were urgent. Its French windows looked over a garden which had been allowed to run wild, with untrimmed grass, and lilac and rhododendron bushes banked around great beech trees. Troops, mostly big Flemish boys, lounged under the trees. To the north-east the roll of guns from Louvain sounded almost reassuring, like breakers on a distant shore. On a poplar in a corner of the garden a thrush sang, its notes rising above the gunfire. Even when three Dornier bombers moved across the sky and a lone fighter soared towards them, its machine guns rattling, they were all soon out of sight behind the trees, and the springtime peace returned.

But this was a false oasis. Elsewhere there was ample evidence that it was time to go. At the French Embassy the grates were black with the charred remains of burnt papers. All over the diplomatic quarter scraps of blackened papers drifted down from the chimneys, falling over the long queues outside the banks. Fast had gone. At the War Ministry Colonel Piquard, now a member of the army press department, was hastily stuffing papers into a rucksack. 'Still here?' he queried. 'Get out as quickly as you can. We are going this afternoon, so too are the censors. The Government moves this evening. Head for Ostend.'

I asked him what had happened at the front. *'Mon vieux,'* he replied, *'c'est bien simple, et bien tragique.* We have simply come up against a new type of war, one we cannot deal with. These dive bombers, these heavy tanks have changed warfare. We Belgians could not cope with it. But we do not matter. What matters is that you and the French cannot cope with it either. You are preparing to retreat. Worse still, it seems that at Dinant and Sedan a thousand tanks are across the Meuse, inside France. That's why we are going and why you had better go.'

The Metropole Hotel was now almost empty, except for the correspondents, and a few others. The staff watched us closely. These journalists know what is going on, their manner seemed to imply, and so long as they are here, things can't be too bad.

The lift man had lost an arm in the last war. His chest was covered with war medals. 'Tell me,' he said. 'Is it true that they have crossed the Albert Canal already? It can't be true, surely? The line there is so strong. They have always told us so. My boy is up there. It can't be true,' he said, pleadingly, as if after all he had known and suffered in the last war it could not be true that there would be Germans in Brussels again, that all the efforts of 1914–18 were to prove meaningless and in vain.

I reassured him. 'We have no exact news, but we will hold. Remember, our armies are big, and strong.'

I could not have told him the truth, for the life of me.

In the hall a woman, her face pale with agitation, came up to me. She was Dutch, but married to an Englishman, with an English passport. Could we help her to get out? The consul had told her he could do nothing. The last parties of Britons had left two days ago. 'I should have gone with them, I should have gone with them,' she said, her voice near to a shriek.

There was nothing we could do for her. We had no room in the van. I felt sorry for her, but also angry. She was only too typical of hundreds of people who have no direct concern with the waging of a war, but who stay out of foolhardiness, or out of excitement, or out of sheer inertia, despite all the urgings of consulates and embassies, until it is too late. We had to tell her that her only chance was go up by train, and that in fact she would take less risk by staying. Better be caught than take her two children out on the roads in their present state.

When we told the hotel to bring down our bags it was as if someone had fired off a revolver in the lounge. The cashier and the manager both paled. The porter, another old soldier, stared blankly, and the liftman looked at me with disbelief. The old luggage man went off muttering. Two businessmen in the lounge got up and asked for their bills too. Almost ashamedly we piled our luggage into the van.

We prised O'Leary out of a small bar round the corner, on the ground floor of a bordello. With the infuriating calm of the not-quite-drunk he insisted on finishing his half bottle of champagne. The young blonde madame sought my reassurance that she was right not to flee. 'My girls are frightened we will be bombed as Rotterdam was bombed. I tell them, go if you wish. I will stay. I am not going to start rushing madly all over the countryside.'

For the last time we drove up the big boulevards towards the Foreign Office. Under the trees lorries of Belgian soldiers waited, sad-faced in the sun. Lines of BEF trucks still moved through, the troops singing, waving cheerfully, unaware of the atmosphere that was steadily gripping the hearts of all the people who stared at them, silently now, from the street corners. The refugees still poured in in their ghastly stream. An old man sat calmly on a seat in the sun, watching it all. A boy and a girl on another seat had their arms around each other and their cheeks touching. They too seemed indifferent enough. Then out through the suburbs, with sirens going and ack-ack bursting to the south, on to the Mons road.

A Scots sentry at the main crossroads stopped us. '*Pas passer*,' he said, adding a Glasgow accent to the French. When he heard the English voices he grinned. 'All right, go on then. But ye'll have to tak' your chance. I canna guarantee anything further than yon corner.'

'Yon corner' was a mile further down the road. Here we were stopped again by a British patrol, but Masson produced a document hung with diplomatic seals and army stamps and we were allowed through on to the Tournai road, the one main road the army was keeping clear from the frontier to Brussels. The refugees were diverted on to side roads where they trudged now, one long cavalcade staring at us enviously as we entered the wide, empty highway.

It was not empty long. Soon we began to pass supply columns moving up, line after line of British trucks, camouflaged, with Bren guns mounted on top. A Lysander swooped low over us to see what we were doing and, uncertain of its markings, we stopped and dived for the ditch. O'Leary, suddenly waking to life, scrambled with astonishing agility up the roadside bank, and crouched in the hedge, his lips moving rapidly. His words were in a foreign tongue which seemed to me both familiar and yet unfamiliar. It took me a moment to realise that, for the first time in my fairly frequent experience of taking cover, I was hearing the Deity's aid being invoked in Latin. Then in the evening sunlight we moved on.

Luck was with us. Though the air-raid sirens were wailing in each of the three towns through whose narrow, jammed streets we had to make our way, no bombs fell whilst we were there, and we got to Tournai, seven miles north of the French frontier, just after dark. Here the four Britons – Ward, Hugh Greene, Courtenay Young and I – got out and gave our baggage to Masson to take on to Lille. We got beds in an hotel opposite the great jagged mass of the cathedral, and slept like children.

We were to need that sleep, for there was to be none for us the next night.

*

We woke to find Tournai full of refugees. They were massed on the railway station. They covered every inch of the huge square outside. They lined every street, and filled the Grande Place, with its gold-fronted Flanders houses and its great stone bell tower, till it was like the slopes of Tattenham Corner on Derby Day. Every café, every restaurant was jammed. Along the main streets, over the canal bridges, round the bell tower and on the road towards the frontier went one endless stream which never halted and yet which never seemed to ease the congestion in Tournai itself.

On to this town at three o'clock that afternoon the Germans launched their bombers. I heard planes and saw, behind the massive, pointed bulk of the stone medieval bell tower, line upon line of bombers, black against the blue sky. I ran for the doorway of the tower, which looked the solidest place in the city. But it was an ARP post, already jammed full. So I lay down at the foot of the tower, on the side furthest from the bombers, and pressed myself against the stonework. Ward and Courtenay Young did the same.

On the pavement corner opposite a Belgian soldier watched us, a sneering grin forming on his face. At that moment the first salvo of bombs sounded from the far side of the town, and his expression changed to sheer incredulous fear. In the square there were shouts, and a panic rush for shelter. As wave after wave of bombers came over they dropped their bombs in rows across the town, thudding, roaring, smashing their way closer, closer, until one line crashed just behind us and then another smashed into the square itself. A pause, and then another wave would start up on the far side of the town again, closer and closer, until the final salvo felt as if a bit of the sky itself was falling on us. The air was filled with dust and the stink of explosive and the sound of bricks and beams hurtling and breaking.

Then silence, except for the sound of falling beams, the crackle of flames, and cries. The Grande Place was hidden in a cloud of dust through which showed golden, leaping flames. Out of this a woman came running, blood streaming from her face, a baby clasped in her arms.

Gradually the dust cleared. Three cars were burning in the centre of the square. Two of the golden-fronted houses were on fire. Bodies lay strewn on the cobbles. From a café opposite the belfry they were helping out people covered with blood. There was glass everywhere.

The café had not been completely cleared of its wounded when the sirens went again. This time we dived for a cellar. There the explosions sounded less terrifying, and most of the bombs seemed to fall on the far side of the town, by the railway station. When again there was a pause we hurried round to our hotel. In one corner of the lobby a young Belgian soldier sat sobbing in a chair.

Again the sound of bombs. Hugh Greene had now joined us, and we went down to the wine cellar. It was crowded with the proprietor and his family. When at last the bombing had died away the proprietor blocked the doorway, 'I intend to have you arrested,' he said. Why? Because we were suspicious foreigners. Tournai had never been bombed until we arrived. We must come with him to the British headquarters in the town.

Ward had the most sensible response. He suggested that the proprietor might at least sell us a bottle of champagne to settle our nerves. The proprietor did this – and called the police while we were drinking it. A gendarme and the proprietor then escorted us to the office of the British Town Major, the army officer set up to liaise with the local authorities. A small crowd began to gather round us as we made our way through the bombed streets, their attitude increasingly ugly. I could hear mutterings of *'espions'* and *'parachutistes'*.

We got clear of these troubles by a coincidence no novelist would have dared to invent. The Town Major had been at Harrow with

Edward Ward. They greeted each other by their school nicknames. The Town Major vouched for us, and the crowd dispersed – rather sadly. He was indeed delighted to find himself with fellow Britons. He had been badly shaken up in the bombing. His car was one of those we had seen blazing in the square. He had leapt out of it, and flung himself on the ground just in time. The Duke of Gloucester, who had been in another army car just outside the city, had had his wrist cut when he too jumped for safety. Already eighty civilians had been brought in dead.

As we talked a BEF truck drove up, its sides splintered and torn by bomb fragments. A corporal stepped out and saluted.

'All OK?' asked the Town Major.

'OK, sir, but the sergeant stopped one in the neck. We picked a six inch strip of shrapnel out of his neck. But it went in just under the skin, and he seems all right.'

Self-possessed, alert, disciplined, that corporal made me feel good to be British – and stirred my feelings that it was high time I too was in uniform.

We made a quick tour of the town. One street, near the entrance, was smashed flat, its buildings burning. Smoke rose from a score or more other places. The big square before the station was cratered. But the bridges across the canals were intact, and the refugees were on the move again.

In the evening sun we sat on the terrace of the bombed café. The glass had been swept away. The burnt-out hulks of the cars stood in the square. A patch of blood was drying brown on the paving. Yet the evening sky was serene with yellow and turquoise, and the sun warm. It seemed as peaceful as if we were sipping drinks beside a beach in New Zealand, watching the late sun glint on the long Pacific rollers.

The hotel proprietor came hurrying up. He had an air of grievance, as if he resented being denied the satisfaction of capturing a nest of spies. He went into a long discussion with the Town Major, who turned to us. 'Here is your chance to get a lift to Lille. Our boy friend here wants to get his wife away to France. She has two women friends with a car, but no one to drive it. If you offer to drive it to Lille you could all cram in.'

Outside the hotel stood a five-seater Chevrolet. Inside were three Belgian women, massive, fleshy figures, and a great heap of luggage. The proprietor explained his plan. His wife began to weep. She didn't want to leave. One of the huge women said that with the luggage they could take only two of us, but not all three. The Town Major acted with admirable decision. In a heavy English accent he explained they would have to take us all. '*C'est votre bagage ou votre vie, Madame,*' he declared. Even there, in the dark, with the flames from the burning buildings behind us, it sounded so corny as to be comic. But it worked. Madame decided to sacrifice her *bagage* and save her *vie*. So we piled in, with Ward driving, and Greene and the least bulky of the women in front. Young and I settled into the back, each with one of the huge women on our knees. Even before we started I felt as if I had cramp, with every leg muscle being crushed. I did not know how long I could take it, but at least we were on our way. The Town Major told us to make for France, and give up any idea of getting to Ostend. The game was up around Brussels, the BEF was preparing to pull back, and the Belgian Government had gone.

The frontier was six miles ahead, a darkened roadside building with a gendarme who suddenly loomed up to halt us. We got out and looked round. Heavy clouds now covered the sky. Roaming them, brushing against them in pools of light, were searchlight around Lille. On the northern horizon guns flashed and from above came the steady drone of planes. Moving along the road, past the frontier post, on into Belgium was a long line of BEF lorries, their lights blue, shaded. They went on and on quietly, in the dark.

The frontier guards took little persuading to let us pass. Our journalists' passes were enough. As we turned to clamber back into the car, I looked back towards Tournai. Suddenly great flashes leapt into the air from where the town lay, followed by the glow of flames reflected against the sky. A few seconds later came the roar of explosions. The bombers were back.

At noon the next day we were in Paris. Between the frontier and Lille we had argued it out and decided to push right on to Amiens. We had a car now, and God knows when we would get another. There was an air raid on when we got to Lille, and the military picket was perfectly willing to let us go ahead. We drove out on the Arras road with the ack-ack lighting up the night. The clouds had gone now, and it was a clear pale green moonlit night. After many errors we found our way out of Arras on to Bapaume, where we stopped briefly. My legs were almost paralysed with the strain of our Belgian hostesses. One of them kept complaining bitterly that she would have done better to have stayed; she would lose all her furniture, and it was wonderful oak, genuine oak. Another was being noticeably, consciously calm and brave, with a soothing insistence that all would be well. She was very responsible and concerned. 'Are you on the right road, monsieur?' 'Ah, yes, monsieur, but I too am a driver and I know how easy it is to be on the wrong road. You are sure, yes?' Was the back tyre not flat? and the petrol, were we sure there would be petrol enough, and 'Oh, that back tyre, it felt so strange and my husband had always said, now you be careful of the back tyre when you drive. But monsieur was an experienced driver, wasn't he?' And monsieur, alias Edward Ward, hung on in silence cursing under his breath, and drove like mad. By two o'clock we were again able to call a halt, and I walked up and down the road getting some circulation back into my legs.

We went on, driving towards Amiens over the road which a week later was to be the main line for the German armoured columns' advance on their way to the coast. Here and there an occasional barricade of carts held us up, and peasants with shotguns looked at our papers.

We had just petrol enough to get to the railway station at Amiens. We were luckier than most. The last ten miles of the way into Amiens the roadside had been dotted with dark shapes of cars around which people slept, exhausted. They were refugees who had driven till their petrol ran out.

At Amiens we left our hostesses and their car at an hotel opposite the railway station. The next day they were to go on to Normandy. They felt sure they could manage the driving now they were out of the danger zone. We got a cup of coffee and at five o'clock climbed aboard a train that, jammed with refugees, limped towards Paris. The three-hour journey took more than twice that time. On the way we passed a few trucks carrying tanks. Then the white shape of Sacré Coeur showed above Montmartre, and we were in Paris again.

I had seen it last in early February, on my way back from Finland. Then it had been a grey, wintry Paris, but still cocksure, cheerful enough despite the blackout. Now, in this same spring sun that lay over Flanders, it was a city terribly afraid. It had reason to be. Twenty-four hours earlier General Gamelin had told Daladier and Reynaud that between Verdun and Paris not a single corps of French troops stood in the Germans' path. What had saved the city – for the time being – was that Hitler was aiming first at the Channel ports, before he turned south towards Paris and central France.

George Millar, in a well-cut khaki uniform of a war correspondent with the French army, and looking like a boy of eighteen rather than the very experienced 29-year-old he was, had just got back from Sedan. We drove up to the Champs Elysées and sat in a café in the sun and talked. He had been with a party of correspondents up behind Corap's army, at Vervins, close to Sedan, on the fateful Tuesday. They were waiting in a village close behind the lines unaware that the Germans were anywhere near, when suddenly stragglers began to pour in, filling the cafés, ordering pernods, standing talking in the square. They all told the same story – of terrible bombing by planes against which they had no guns, of tanks from whose armour the French anti-tank shells bounced off *'comme les balles de tennis'*.

The village had been bombed, and bombed again, and then the press officers had hurried up and rushed them away from the front and back to Verdun. What was happening was something the French army was not anxious to have seen or written. In the streets of Verdun they watched the French infantry being thrown in to stop the gap. Boys with rifles and bayonets and grenades, sitting silent, set-faced in the long clumsily camouflaged Paris buses, going out to face the thirty-five-ton tanks and the dive bombers. 'And when we bought the Continental *Daily Mail* that morning the headlines told of the "Steel Ring Being Drawn Round the German Advance,"' said George bitterly.

As I listened to him I stared round the café. Here, as in Brussels in the last days, you could smell fear, alarm. A journalist can acquire an instinct for sensing a situation almost unconsciously, an ability to 'smell' confidence or defeatism or danger. All that weekend in Paris fear hung in the air. Many factors went to make it apparent – there were fewer taxis about and the streets were emptier and bleaker, because the taxis were being used to rush troops to the front and refugees to the rear; people talked tensely, their faces concerned, leaning over tables; you noticed, curiously enough, the whites of their eyes more. Perhaps these dilate with fear. They were more impatient, more nervy.

I had noticed it first when I drove to the Hôtel Saint Romain. When I had reached there in February from Finland, in the middle of the night, the proprietor, since the war his own night porter, had carried up my bags and got me supper, talking cheerfully all the time. Now he forced a smile for my welcome, worriedly said, yes, he thought he had a room, hurried down as soon as he had shown me to it, and contented himself, when he saw from my police form that I came from Belgium, with saying, '*Alors, c'est bien fini la bas, eh?*' instead of breaking into his usual flow of questions.

This atmosphere was a shock. In our two days on the way from Brussels we had had no outside news. I had regarded Paris as well away from the war zone, a safe base city from which I could make my way back at my leisure to the Belgians at Ostend. Yet here it was, grim if not determined, manifestly in danger.

CHAPTER TWENTY-ONE

Maytime in Paris

Paris had three weeks more of freedom before she began to serve her term of bitter imprisonment under the Nazis, years which were to leave scars which still remain. She had three weeks during which the Reichswehr was fighting its way to Dunkirk, and then reorganising and driving south across the Somme, until the French Government were to flee to Tours, leaving the capital to fall into the hands of Hitler. It was an extraordinary period to experience. Out there in Flanders, and to the north, the greatest battle the world had ever known was raging, with this beautiful city as one of its main prizes. Yet here inside Paris itself there was hardly a sign that this was different from any other spring. Like a beautiful woman, Paris waited, delicate, lovely, to see who should conquer, who should possess her. Not until the end was very near were there any signs of war in the city itself, and even then they were few – an occasional barricade, the thunder of guns at night, tanks in the streets at dawn.

Never was Paris so beautiful as in those last days of May and early June. Dawn came clear, tinted, gentle behind Notre Dame; midday was a blaze of sunshine on the chestnuts along the Champs Elysées, on the red umbrellas on the café terraces; in the evening the sun went down behind the Arc de Triomphe and the soft spring night came slowly over the boulevards. We walked across the Tuileries, where children played on the unscythed grass, to conferences at the War Ministry, where we heard of more German advances towards '*Le camp entranché de Dunquerque*' – Dunkirk, an inferno of fires and corpses rotting in the sand and long lines of men waiting under the bombers, and here the birds singing in the limes of the little square beyond the red, white and blue striped sentry box in the Rue Saint Dominique. We lunched in the shade at the Racing Club in the heart of the Bois, while overhead tiny white specks turned and fought for the possession of the sky above Paris, and the radio told of heavy counterattacks '*pour le saillant d'Amiens*', Amiens where men were being crushed under the caterpillars of the German tanks and where shells burst all day in the streets where the refugees

186

cowered. We walked back from the evening conference, with its same tale of blood and steel and the ghastly noise of battle transformed and hidden behind brief words of *combats locales*, and the Seine shone like silk beneath the bridges and the old men sat and fished from the quays under the Concorde Bridge where Daladier's police had fired on the rioters in 1934.

I had taken charge of the *Daily Express* Paris office again, even though Sefton Delmer was now also based on Paris. Tom Delmer, as he was known to his colleagues and friends, was at that time one of the half-dozen best known figures in British journalism. A big, stout man in his early thirties, he was a blend of Friar Tuck and Prince Hal, with a commanding presence, a sharp eye for his own (and his paper's) advantage, and yet with a merry, boyish manner, in which there was even a hint of diffidence. The son of an Australian-born professor of English in Berlin, he had spent the First World War as a schoolboy partly at a German Gymnasium and partly at St Paul's in London, at both of which he had suffered because he did not fit the accepted norm. He spoke perfect German, a quality which had made him an outstanding correspondent in Berlin for the *Daily Express* – he had walked through the burning Reichstag with Hitler – and was to make him a formidable head of Black Propaganda in World War II.

In Paris this May Delmer had opted for the role of war correspondent with the Allied armies awaiting the German attack along the line of the Somme. George Millar, also in war correspondent's uniform, was ready to report from the French army's fronts. With the blind hopefulness without which wars could not be endured, I allowed myself a faint belief that a line might yet be stabilised along the Somme, linking up with the still intact Maginot Line, that we might still get to the more static warfare for which our armies were trained. And with every day that passed I got increasingly restless, increasingly anxious to get back to Britain and to get some role, however minor, in which I could take a direct part in fighting this monstrous force. It was no longer a question of freeing other countries from Nazism. It was a now a question of preventing it over-running our own country – and installing in its wake a British version of itself.

I scanned the British papers for signs that Britain was aware of the danger which faced it. They seemed disturbingly few. The papers were worried about the right name for what was to become the Home Guard. Should they be called 'parashots', or 'anti-parachutists' or 'paracops'? 'Vicar joins the parashots' ran one headline. Anyone would have thought it was a clay pigeon shoot. What we wanted, I felt, was a million tough, armed, determined men to back up the fighting forces. We were to get them, but in those lotus-eating days in Paris the chances seemed remote.

I was, at this distance, misreading the British mood, and I was underestimating what Churchill would do. He seemed to me too old for the task, however valiant his spirit. Old men like Gamelin had failed France. Even older men, like the 84-year-old Pétain and the 73-year-old Weygand were about to surrender her. I had shocked Mara Scherbatoff by declaring, when Pétain was appointed Deputy Prime Minister, that he was the one man famous enough to sack Gamelin and make peace with Hitler. That forecast was to prove true. But it was only when Churchill's first great speech to the House of Commons was printed in the Paris *New York Herald Tribune* that I realised that he was someone very, very different, someone at last who understood the nature of the enemy we were up against. One passage in particular caught my eye. In it he spoke of the 'dull, plodding masses of the German infantry, ever ready to stamp out with their jackboots the freedoms which they have long surrendered in their own land'. For the first time I became aware of the way in which, as Edward R. Murrow was to put it, Churchill 'mobilised the English language and sent it into battle to fight for democracy'.

The sense that Britain was not only in the struggle, but likely to become the next front line, subtly modified my relationship with the American correspondents with whom I had so long worked, and at least two of whom, Eric Sevareid and Walter Kerr, were close friends. Though I continued to work closely with them, I felt myself now increasingly in a world apart. They felt the tragedy of these defeats, they were heart and soul on our side, but they were not yet in the battle. They had another chance. If Europe fell, they could return to America, and prepare to fight on there. But for us this battle of France, and the battle of Britain which loomed ahead, were the last chance. The Americans could, however deeply they felt, watch this fighting as a spectacle, something to be reported in the coolly objective terms demanded by the American networks. I could not do that. Increasingly I found myself feeling as I was sure the Czechs and the Poles and the Finns had felt towards us: 'However much you sympathise with us, and want us to win, you are not caught up in it as we are, it's not quite your war – yet.'

I felt this keenly on Sunday, 19 May, two days after I had reached

Paris, when Vincent Sheean took me to see Claire Both Luce. I noted my reactions at the time in the diary notes I kept intermittently.

I had been to see Jimmy Sheean at the Crillon, and he said, 'Come across to the Ritz and meet the loveliest woman in France – the loveliest woman you ever saw. Haven't you met Claire Booth? But Geoffrey, she's the loveliest and wittiest creature you ever saw, and you must meet her. I'll take you over now.'

Behind the Louvre the sky was pale primrose and children played in the Tuileries around the half-finished ARP trenches. In the Place Vendôme sandbags had burst around the foot of Napoleon's Column. 'It's instinct that Hitler's got. He's got the most phenomenal instinct of anyone of our time,' said Jimmy. 'Not brains. Just instinct.'

We went in through the narrow doors of the Ritz, the doorway which never looked as if it led to an hotel, let alone to the grandest of hotels, and up in a gilded lift cage, where the liftman was dressed like a footman in livery, and along the shell pink corridor.

Claire Booth was indeed lovely, in her late thirties or early forties, with fair hair and a slightly worn, well pressed, well dry-cleaned American face, a little lined but still beautiful. There was no doubt about the sharpness of her mind. With her was a General in British uniform with red tabs. He was Lindemann, brother of the Professor I had met at Oxford. 'Jimmy, they're in Amiens and the advance guard is in Abbeville, and it's all up,' was her greeting. 'They're in Abbeville and the Channel ports will go.' Her voice was full of brave tones, as if to say 'I'll face the worst. No need to hide anything from me, even though it hurts me to hear it.' I felt suddenly savage, and cursed her, sitting there with a clipper ticket in her pocket, knowing you can get out when you want to, and it's all a great experience and good copy. But it's not your war, and it doesn't go right inside you as it does us. I know now what the Czechs felt about us, and why the porter in the Ambassador in Prague was so savage on the night of Munich, and said, 'You go away, but we have to stay here and live with it.' I knew that Claire Booth felt it deeply all right, but it was her playground which was broken up, not her life.

Lindemann was talking of the German tank columns. 'They spend the nights in a sort of korral with their transport in the middle. I can't understand why we don't take a few bombers and smash them at any cost. I'd take a bomber and crash it down on them if they would let me', and I knew he would, and felt better.

The sunshine streamed across the ironwork on the balcony and into the room with its pale green furnishings. A cool wind stirred the curtains but I felt suddenly stifled, and said I must get away to the office. Outside in the Place Vendôme the pigeons wheeled around Napoleon's Column. In Schiaparelli's window three gold ornaments and a black handbag lay on the silk display cases. In the background was the flat where Noël

Coward had carried out the hush hush mission which everyone seemed
to know about, in those first foolish days of the war.

*

One evening a few days after my return to Paris Charles Gombaux
of the *Paris Soir* took me to visit Paul Reynaud in his flat on the Left
Bank near the Chamber of Deputies. It was a small, compact place,
reached up a narrow flight of stairs, but Reynaud preferred it to the
official residence of the Prime Minister in the Hôtel Matignon.

Reynaud was sitting in an arm chair by a low table covered with
documents. It was the first time I had seen him since the war. He
looked pale, his face puffy with fatigue, which made his high,
arching eyebrows seem almost artificially black. But he radiated a
quiet defiance, and was confident that under Weygand the Germans
would be halted when they thrust south. Hélène de Portes came and
went from time to time, as we talked. I knew of her as Reynaud's
mistress, but had no idea at this stage of the power she was
exercising both in the choice of ministers and in the conduct of
affairs, and I have to admit that I did not study her closely. I carried
away only an impression of an active woman, expensively dressed,
with an unusually athletic build for a Parisienne and with dark hair
brushed into curls, giving an impression of tousled, restless energy.

Reynaud was Minister of Defence as well as Prime Minister, and
meetings of his War Cabinet were held in the War Ministry in the
Rue St Dominique, a five-minute walk from his flat. In the same
building conferences to brief the French and the foreign press were
held each morning and evening. We would gather in a long room
frowsty with ornamented chairs, and with walls hung with suits of
armour. They were wonderful suits of armour, chain and mail and
sheet, with spears and lances and pikes underneath them, and they
gave an appropriate touch of irony to the scene they looked down
on. For they seemed only a little more out of date than the rifles and
light anti-tank guns and inferior planes with which the French army
was opposing the highly mechanised, highly trained Reichswehr.
This lovely old rambling building, with its creamy walls, its
courtyard peaceful as an Oxford college quadrangle, its red, white
and blue sentry box that looked like something out of a comic opera
set, was in atmosphere a building of another era, not of the twentieth
century. This era, this war called for rooms with great businesslike

desks and lines of telephones and swift lifts and radios and speed and machinery. The Third Republic, someone has pointed out, never succeeded in evolving its own style of architecture. It took over all the fripperies and ornateness of the Third Empire, as if it lacked confidence in itself. Now, like the Third Empire, it was crumbling to ruins.

So in the fresh morning sunshine, and in the warm evening sunshine, George Millar, Eric Sevareid, Walter Kerr and I would walk down the narrow Rue St Dominique, show our passes to the Gardes Mobiles in their shining black steel helmets at the iron gates of the War Ministry, and cross the wide hallway to the conference room. Often in that hallway we would pass the men who were ruling France – Weygand, striding up the stairs two at a time; Daladier, red-faced, glowering; de Gaulle, tall, stiff; Blum, grey, gentle, yet surprisingly robust in figure; shaggy-moustached Louis Marin; the sly Bonnet; the thin-lipped pale figure of Georges Mandel, who had been secretary in World War I to Clemenceau – 'The Tiger' – and was now Minister of the Interior.

In the conference room the grey-haired old men of the French press and the younger British and American correspondents would gather. Everything had its set routine. On my first visit I sat on a chair near the door. But some old French correspondent had sat on it every day since the war began, and he raised as much fuss as if I had shouted, 'Heil Hitler'. There was Charles Maurice, pompous as ever, getting together a few scraps of fact for his long-winded articles in the *Petit Parisien*. There was de Caux of *The Times*, with whom I had spent so many vigils in the Telefonica in Madrid, watching and listening with a calm I envied and admired. A liaison officer in the Great War with the British army, he sat now, tall and erect and quiet, recording philosophically the breakdown of this world which he knew and loved.

A stir by the doorway, and Colonel Thomas, the official spokesman, would stride in. A tall Norman with dark hair *en brosse*, pince-nez and a sense of confidence and strength, he was an excellent man for this job. True, he told us very little, but that was what the French High Command wanted. In a few incisive sentences he would outline the main shape of the struggle, answer or not answer a few questions, and the conference would be over, with the Germans a few score miles more across France, more towns bombed, the end a little nearer.

In the last week of May the Dunkirk evacuation was drawing to its close and our eyes and the eyes of all the world turned on the battle of France. On the line of the Somme, the Aisne Canal and Aisne the French at last had a front on which to stand. Here, Colonel Thomas told us, strongpoints, villages and woods defended with artillery and anti-tank guns, were being organised in depth. New tactics were to be employed. The tank columns would be allowed to pass, but these strong points, *points d'appui*, would hold up the infantry. The High Command were 'cautiously optimistic'. At Reithel, at the western end of the Maginot Line, the Germans had been attacking in old style, with infantry unsupported by tanks following an artillery barrage, and the French had held them easily. Once the speed of the war slowed down, all would be well.

But the main *point d'appui*, Paris, was not being put in a state of defence. Would Paris be defended, we asked? Of course, we were told. But there were few signs of it. Sevareid and Kerr and I drove out north eastwards, past Le Bourget Airport. Here and there on the roads that ran across the open country a tank waited by the roadside, a few troops guarding a barricade near by. They might have been some protection against parachutists or spies, but no more. Inside the city itself we had seen a few small sandbagged pillboxes being set up at the Rond Point, but in the outskirts there was nothing, no real barricades, no tank traps, no last-line defences such as Madrid built, such as England was to be covered with by late August.

The long, white French road, lined with poplars, wound over the plain. Paris, close at hand, was hidden by a curve in the ground. Then we came over the rise and there was Montmartre, with Sacré Coeur white and glowing on the top, and the tiny Meccano toy of the Eiffel Tower. How long would it be before the German tank crews were staring at it from this point? What a sight they would have of it, just as the Moors of Franco's army had when they first climbed the Hill of the Angels on the Castilian Plain and saw ahead the roofs of Madrid. In silence we drove on back to the city, past the old forts that had held the Prussians in 1870, which could help to hold them again if men with weapons were put along their ramparts. There were men there in plenty in those Paris streets, but they had no weapons.

On Monday, 3 June, I lunched with de Caux and his wife in a flat they had leased on the Place de la Madeleine. It was brilliantly sunny outside, with a whitish haze above the great squat mass of the Madeleine. Tom Cadett of *The Times* and I stood with the de Cauxs on their balcony and drank sherry before lunch. The room behind, the sitting room of the flat, was a museum piece. The woman who owned it was the daughter of a friend of Zola, and photographs of the writer and scores of knick-knacks and bits of bric-à-brac covered the walls and the tables.

Half-way through lunch the sirens went. We had had them often enough at night and morning recently, but this was the first daylight warning for a long time. In the streets the police whistles blew and the Place steadily emptied. We heard guns in the distance.

Throughout the meal we could hear overhead, distant, very high, the drone of planes, and roars that might have been bombs but might equally well have been guns. It kept up for a full hour. The All Clear had only just gone when I left just after two o'clock and went round to Pierre Lazareff's flat in the Palais Royale. His wife, Hélène Gordon, was there.

'What news have you?' she asked me. 'Of the raid, of course.'

Before I could reply the phone rang. Pierre was speaking from his office. I could hear Hélène repeating, 'Citroën works, Boulevard Souchet, Air Ministry.' So it had been the real thing – a full-scale bombing raid, the first Paris had ever known. I grabbed a taxi outside the door and rushed off.

We had had many *alertes* in Paris in the early days of the war, and some raiding on the outskirts this spring, but there had been no real attempt to hit the centre of the city. I drove along the quays to the Citroën works. A huge crowd blocked the last half mile. I went through on foot. Firemen were hosing a part of the factory that was blazing fiercely. Cars, half finished, were being dragged out on to the pavement; wounded were being carried from houses and cafés smashed near by. A line of bomb craters ran up the street towards the new, brick-red Air Ministry. All the windows were out of the main building. One bomb had gone through the wall, another had gone clean through the Minister's study next door. Bullitt, the American Ambassador, who had been lunching there with the Air Minister, had missed death by feet.

I drove across towards the Porte de Versailles. Bombs had fallen haphazardly, tearing the innards out of flats and houses. It was the first bombing I had seen of an area I had known well in peace time. One bomb had fallen in the roadway outside the Auteuil flat where we lived in our first days in Paris. Houses along the street where Cecily had taken Peter for his morning walk were one line of destruction. One big crater lay in the Boulevard Suchet, five hundred yards from the house the Duke and Duchess of Windsor had lived in till the invasion began and – under advice from London – they had moved off abruptly to Biarritz. The French had not liked that move, though enough of them had already gone to Biarritz themselves. 'Gone with the Windsors,' they used to say in Paris. It gaped now in front of the flats where the pick of the Hundred Families used to live, and maids and butlers in livery came out and emptied dust trays of broken glass into the gutter.

The main damage was on the outskirts. The railway junctions at Versailles and St Oye had been badly smashed. At Surennes the hospital was hit. One bomb at Versailles went through the roof of the courtroom where Weidemann, the German who had murdered six people in France in 1937, had been condemned to death in the last April before the war. It passed clean through the dock where he had sat. In all over eight hundred people were killed and injured in this raid.

The bombing of Paris had been the first move in the final battle of France. At the rail centres through which the French reserves and supplies would be moved, at the airfields from which the scanty French air force would work, the Germans had struck heavily. The next night, the night of 4 June, they made their final preparations. With incredible speed they had turned their armies southwards from Dunkirk towards the Somme and the Aisne. At dawn on Wednesday 5 June they began their attack. That morning when we went to the War Ministry Colonel Thomas came in, his face grave, and said simply, *'Alors, messieurs, ça commence.'*

The attack came all along the line, but developed chiefly at two points. From their bridgehead across the Somme at Amiens one gigantic tank column thrust forward, trying to get to the lower stretches of the Seine and cut off Paris from Brittany and the part of the coast through which British aid could still come. Another hit down towards Rheims, to cut down behind the Maginot Line and isolate the troops there. Stubbornly in their positions the French resisted, but they had not the organisation or the armament for this moving war. The break came more rapidly than we expected. By Friday the French were moving back. By Saturday June 6 they were at Rouen, on the Seine, to the west of Paris.

I was determined that this time I would have my lines of retreat prepared, and not left to chance, as in Brussels. My luck had held there, but I was not going to rely on it again. So I laid plans carefully, helped by George Millar, who showed at this time that capacity for thinking ahead, and planning ahead, which was to make him a highly successful Maquis leader in the Besançon area four years later.

The *Daily Express* already had one car, a Renault convertible, which could seat three people. Sefton Delmer, who was determined to wait until the last minute and cover the fall of the city, needed this. For the rest of us I bought a big Renault limousine which could, at a pinch, carry seven people. My Belgian experience had convinced me that we must carry our own reserves of petrol. I secured a hundred-litre drum, a *bidon*, which I managed to get filled from a special pump run by the American Legion, the veterans association of World War I. We hid the car and the *bidon*, in a locked garage. All over Paris people were making similar plans, storing petrol in cans in attics, in gardens, even in their homes. If the Germans had dropped incendiary bombs on the city, it would have been an inferno within a few minutes. But they didn't. They didn't need to. They were going to get the place intact.

We bought, too, sleeping-bags, and maps of Southern France, and laid in a store of tinned meat and pâtés, and of wine and mineral water. All of these arrangements, simple enough in themselves, seemed extraordinarily difficult at the time. As the danger increased, so too did a strange sense of lassitude and fatalism. The immediate future was so ugly that you hated to think about it, let alone prepare for it. This lassitude took many forms. Some of those who refused to contemplate the future excused their attitude as being one of optimism and courage, and my insistence on these preparations could bring mutterings of 'defeatisme' or 'paniquards'. Others laughed confidently, reproached me for worrying too much, and then at the last minute rushed round to see if they could get in on the arrangements I had made. But I had my experience in Belgium to spur me on, to enable me to fight the waves of laziness and irresponsibility which swept over me. It was so much easier just to drop in at the Crillon Bar, and chat with the war correspondents with the RAF, who made it their base, and who were the best informed of us all, or with American diplomats who had strolled across from the Embassy, than to continue the search for petrol or maps.

My visits to the Crillon Bar led to me being caught up in a dawn sweep to gather in Fifth Columnists. Though later research has shown that the Germans had no Fifth Column in Paris and other parts of France, that the whole idea that they had a widespread net of sympathisers and agents spreading rumours and creating panic was a myth, it was a myth almost universally believed at the time. Early on Thursday, 4 June, the day after the final German attack had been launched, I was towelling myself down in my bedroom at the Hôtel St Romain, after taking a shower, when the door was suddenly flung open and a British military police officer, his uniform ablaze with red tabs, and a French officer with gleaming Sam Browne came into the room and demanded my papers. I had been reported as a suspicious foreigner constantly in the company of British officers in the Crillon. My papers were not in order, as I had entered France from Belgium without a permit, and the Frenchman was all for arresting me then and there. But the British officer, who was no less a figure than the Assistant Provost Marshal, gave me the all clear, and went off calming down his furiously protesting French colleague.

As soon as the German attack began I had sent Stephen Charing, the assistant correspondent in the *Express* office, ahead to Tours, which we believed would be the place to which the French Government would move. He secured rooms for us at the Hôtel de l'Univers and set up an office there. Swiftly the remainder of the week passed. George Millar and I would work in the morning and then drive out to swim in the Racing Club pool in the Bois. Suntanned Parisiennes lay on the grass at its edge, or bought drinks from the open-air bar, or flirted with the RAF pilots on sick leave, many with newly healed wound scars on their legs and backs. Next week, we used to say to each other, Hitler's SS will probably be swimming here. We may as well enjoy it while we can. The sunburnt girls were usually rather bitter, for their boys of our age were *quelque part sur le front* and why weren't we mobilised? They had a right to be bitter, though there were plenty of young Frenchmen too hanging round this pool, men employed in 'essential services' at the rear.

In the evenings, after we had sent off the news from the evening conference and while we waited for any later developments, we would go to the Café Flore, just down the Boulevard St Germain. Every night there would be a visit by police with their capes rolled under their arms, who examined everyone's papers. It did not take them long, because most of the people at the marble-topped tables were there night after night. In the Flore everyone knew everyone else. There was a floating population of girls, some mannequins, some shop girls, some typists, eating meals with anyone who had the money, having affairs with different people but always rather respectably and with a direct simplicity that came from their peasant origin. Lucienne, one of them, was typical. A Normandy blonde, she posed for magazine covers, laughed, ate when she had money or when her friends had, had a violent love affair with a young RAF pilot on seven days' leave, was heartbroken the day he left, and laughing and fatalistic the day after.

There was little wild living in this dying Paris, little of the reckless abandon, the last days of Babylon spirit that one thinks of in times of crisis. The police regulations were against this, for one thing. All the night clubs were closed, all dancing prohibited. Half the big hotels were shut. The cafes closed at ten-thirty. The city had already half emptied, and the restaurants were sparsely filled. Instead of wanting to live wildly, people seemed to desire to savour quietly the small things which they found enjoyable, like sipping an apéritif in a café in the sun, walking in the Bois, talking, taking a quiet meal in their favourite small restaurant. Troops back on leave took their girl friends to dinner, walked home with them in the warm black-out. The poet and novelist Antoine Saint Exupéry, who was one of my heroes, we found and interviewed one day on 48 hours' leave writing away at a new book in the corner of a Montparnasse café.

These last few days we paid our farewells to places we had loved. We drove up the Place du Théâtre in Montmartre and dined at the tables with their red and white check tablecloths in the open square, cheerful despite the black-out. A lone Russian violinist strolled round playing. Before the war he had had a mate, like himself a White Russian refugee, but when the Soviet-German pact was signed the mate had been badly beaten up by a drunken enthusiast who was looking for any Russian, of any type, to hit. We motored through the Bois, where I had often ridden in the mornings in those distant pre-war days, to Saint Cloud park where the goldfish swam in the pond around which my son had played, and near which the first great German concentration camp in Paris was to be set up. Much of the park was fenced off, for AA guns – mostly old French 75mm field guns with their barrels set skywards – were in position to guard the Renault works below.

By Saturday night, 8 June, the guns from the battlefield could be clearly heard in Paris. We had got used to the AA now, but behind their roar came a new sound – the growl of the artillery on the front, a sign that that front was dangerously close. One tank column was reported to be across the river at Rouen; others were in the forest of Chantilly to the north, where a stone monument by the roadside still marked the nearest point that the Kaiser's Uhlans had got to Paris in 1914. In the blackout I watched the big dust carts and farm wagons being trundled out on to the Champs Elysées and the other boulevards running down from the Etoile, placed there to prevent these splendid wide streets being used as landing grounds for gliders.

In the grey dawn, too, tanks now patrolled the main streets, and the Place de la Concorde was a camp for troops all night. One enthusiast used to drive a peculiarly noisy tank up and down the Rue Royale just outside my window. Every now and then a new ack-ack gun in the Tuileries would roar out, its flash lighting up the windows of the hotel. Yet the crowds still went quietly to the cafés, and quietly home in the blackout.

By Sunday it was clear the end was near. At the morning conference Colonel Thomas looked tired and anxious. One German column, he confirmed, was definitely across the Seine to the west of the city. Others were drawing closer.

For the last time we drove out to the swimming pool. I was dressing at lunchtime when Ken Downs arrived. 'The Germans are at Creil,' he said. That placed them only thirty miles from the centre of the city, a day's drive for a tank column.

That afternoon we made our final preparations to leave. From the *Paris Soir*, in whose offices we worked, we drew a stock of French francs; all spare papers we got ready to burn. M Prouvost, the millionaire proprietor of *Paris Soir*, was now Minister of Information. He had been put into the Cabinet when Reynaud made his last main reshuffle. We knew if we watched *Paris Soir*, and moved when they did, we would have a good idea of the Government's plans. And at mid-afternoon this Sunday *Paris Soir* started loading cars and vans to take staff and equipment to Central France, where they were to print on Laval's presses at Clermont Ferrand. They offered to take Mara Scherbatoff and her sisters with them to Clermont Ferrand, but Sherb would not go. Nor would she come with us to Tours. Her family would stick it out in Paris. I thought it a wise decision. As White Russians they would have nothing to fear from the Germans, and they would be spared the turmoil and upheaval of quitting their home.

At five o'clock the phone rang. M Prouvost would like to see the British correspondents immediately in his room at the Hôtel Continental, which served as the Ministry of Information. Prouvost, tall, dark, urbane, well dressed, looked more the businessman than the journalist. He was the representative of a rich northern textile trust which had put its money into *Paris Soir*. Largely owing to the genius of Pierre Lazareff, they had built the paper into the largest and by far the brightest journal in France, and had built up *Match*, a French copy – and a brilliant copy – of the American illustrated weekly *Life*, to a huge circulation.

Prouvost, it soon appeared, did not want to see us because the Government was about to leave. He was new in the job and wanted to meet us because of the hard days ahead. That was all, he explained.

'Gentlemen, I can assure you the news is better tonight. I have just seen the Generalissimo and I can give you that assurance. There is no question of the Government leaving Paris. When it does leave, I will let you know and you will follow my Ministry, attached to me. Now perhaps you would like a few details of the impression I have gained of my talk with the Generalissimo.'

In clipped sentences, as if he were writing one of the inside story articles *Match* ran every week, he went on to give a typical French journalist's picture of Weygand. 'One enters by a courtyard, along a passage, and *voilà*, a little room, quite simple, that is the work room of this man who controls the fate of France . . .'

So on, and so on. Very interesting background, but a sheer waste of time to journalists waiting for one item of news and one only – where had the Germans got to?

The phone interrupted him. 'A cabinet meeting at seven, certainly.' He hung up the ancient bedroom phone which was still in use in this gaudy old hotel, and turned back to urge us to tell England that the situation was far from desperate, that we should send all the material, all the planes we could.

At that moment two burly porters in blue workmen's blouses came into the room, picked up a filing cabinet, and carried it towards the door. 'What are you about?' demanded the Minister.

One porter shrugged his shoulders. '*On part*,' he said. '*On part pour Tours. Nous avons nos ordres.*' It was clear that the new Minister of Information was no better informed than his predecessors had been.

At the back of the Hôtel Continental big lorries were drawn up, being loaded with documents and furniture. At the Ministry of the Marine Sunday afternoon strollers were watching sailors carrying out bundles of documents and stacking them into lorries parked beside the wall of the Ministry on which was kept, glassed in as a souvenir, the mobilisation poster of 1914, with beside it now that of 1939. The military press conference we learnt would in future be held not at the Rue St Dominique, but at the Quai d'Orsay – a clear sign that the War Ministry was also on the move.

Prouvost was to play only a very brief, but a very important role on the French political stage. He owed his appointment to Hélène de Portes, who had been one of many elegant women whom he delighted to have at receptions in his magnificent apartment overlooking the Trocadero. She had exacted a price for the appointment. The letter inviting Prouvost to join the Cabinet was brought to him by hand by an ex-mistress of his, who was a close friend of the Comtesse de Portes. She had the satisfaction of seeing the man who had spurned her accept Cabinet rank from her own hand. Prouvost had never been a Deputy or a Senator, and was to be a Cabinet Minister for only a few weeks. Yet in that time he was to have a decisive influence on the course of French history, for he was one of the strongest peacemakers when the final decision to surrender or fight on came to be made at Bordeaux.

With the irony in which history delights, the final War Ministry conference in Paris was held that evening in the ornate conference room of the Quai d'Orsay in which eleven years earlier Germany and France had joined other countries in signing the Kellogg Pact, renouncing war as an instrument of national policy. Colonel Thomas was late, and all his news was bad. The Germans were already at Forges les Eaux, a popular bathing place twenty-five miles from Paris. Indignantly the French correspondents asked for definite news, particularly about the Government's plans to move, rumours of which were already sending people stampeding in their tens of thousands on the roads to the south.

That night I sent a description of Paris about to fall, with gun flashes lighting the horizon, and smoke drifting over from fires on the outskirts. The smoke was still there in the morning when I drove to the office. The advance party of the *Paris Soir* had left. At twelve o'clock we were rung up by American Press Wireless, the only reliable speedy method of getting our news out – it all went to London via New York at three shillings a word. They were moving to Tours that afternoon. The roads were already one great traffic jam. At three o'clock the censorship closed down. Reluctantly the Ministry of Information admitted that the Government might be moving – it was in fact already hot on its way to Tours. We decided the time had come to put our plan of evacuation into action.

We loaded up the big Renault, destroyed all our spare papers, collected the office files, put aboard the *bidon* of petrol, and set out.

At the St Romain, when I went to collect my bags, the proprietor and his wife were frantic with anxiety. They wanted someone to drive their two daughters, sixteen and fourteen, down to their parents' home in Central France. We tried by phone to find someone for them, but we could do nothing. Our route lay further east, and *Paris Soir* could not help. The younger daughter wept uncontrollably in the corner of the lounge, her sister trying to comfort her. The dry stench of defeat and fear was over everything.

Their quest had a tragic ending. When I returned to Paris for the first time after the war, in 1946, the proprietor and his wife broke into tears the moment they saw me. They told me the girls got away the next day with a friend, only for the older girl to be killed when a bridge south of Paris was hit by a German bomb.

We drove across the river and down the Boulevard St Germain. There was the Flore, with most of the regulars on the terrace. The blonde head of Lucienne gleamed in the sun. She recognised us and waved. Back up the Champs Elysées. Strange, there are those two refugee girls from Vienna who appeared just before the war and were always on the Champs Elysées in its first days, passing steadily from check tweed suits to prosperity and mink coats. There they sit, calmly waiting. Are they spies, or have they just good nerves?

We drove out by St Cloud, across the new bridge which I had watched being built, and which I had so often envisaged as the setting for this evacuation. The Seine, its water clean because there were few barges on it, gleamed under the willows. The tower on the Longchamps grandstand showed through the trees of the Bois, and the white walls of 32 Rue du Calvaire glowed in the sunlight. The café to which I had run to summon the taxi driver M Audet to take Cecily to hospital when Patrick was about to be born was closed. Its owners must have fled with the rest.

On the bend of the road curving up the St Cloud hill we were suddenly no longer one car, but a unit in the great column of refugee vehicles pouring out of the city. I looked back over Paris in the late afternoon sun, over the view I had looked out over so often, morning and evening, and I realised I was leaving not only Paris, but a whole period of life, a period in which there had been time to play.

CHAPTER TWENTY-TWO

Exodus

George Millar's war correspondent's uniform and passes won us access to a road set aside for military vehicles, and for a time we moved swiftly along a wide road through a forest, where tanks stood hidden under trees, their crews stripped to the waist to wash in the streams, and ambulances waited near by. But south of Versailles we were caught up again in the main refugee flood.

Unlike the evacuation from Barcelona, which had been mainly on foot, or that from Belgium, which had been largely by cart and by bicycle, the flight from Paris was predominately by car. Wide, low-slung family cars, bought to carry people fishing or camping or bathing, now crawled along with mattresses and luggage on the top, blankets and cooking gear crammed inside, sometimes with a pram, often with one or two bicycles strapped to the roof or the back. Every variety of motor vehicle was there. Sleek limousines with uniformed chauffeurs; great lorries loaded with machinery; a tractor hauling a high, curved Norman farm wagon packed with women and children; vans bearing the names of laundries, perfume makers, greengrocers, clothiers, each crammed with people and belongings; Paris taxis, and many, many old cars which looked as if they had been taken from junk heaps or dusted down from garages where they had lain unused for years. Hens, sheep and cats rode in trailers, and every car seemed to have its dog. In and out of this column moved an accompanying stream of people on cycles and on foot, the swish, swish of their tyres and the tramp of their feet sounding amidst the noise of car engines.

Frequently the column would halt – something which brought new problems. To save petrol, drivers would switch off their engines. But many of the cars did not have self starters. Each time we moved on, drivers had to crank their vehicles to get the engine running – a process which could take time, and sometimes failed. Then the stalled car, its occupants wide-eyed with anxiety, would be forced to the roadside, or even into the ditch, to let the rest crawl on.

For miles we jolted and crept along behind a lorry loaded with

machinery, where a sullen workman with tattooed arms caressed
two black retrievers, in the intervals at glaring at our efforts to pass
by. We crawled, stopped, crawled on again until dark came down.
We were now in open country, where wide unfenced fields stretched
away to the horizon. Every few yards now cars and lorries were
halted, with mothers feeding babies and putting children to sleep in
the fields. Just north of Chartres we turned into a field from which
the hay had recently been cut, took out our sleeping-bags, and dined
off crusty bread, sardines, cheese and red wine. It was a glorious
night, aglow with stars. Only the moving line of black shadows on
the roads, and the occasional glare of headlights told us that the
evacuation was going ceaselessly on, or even hinted at war.
Suddenly, an anti-aircraft gun boomed close by, a shell sang
through the air, and burst high above us. The drone of a plane
followed. Then the gun was silent again in the hay-scented night.
Across the field came the sounds of children crying.

By three in the morning we were on our way again, part of a line
of old cars and trucks which looked like the scene from the film of
Steinbeck's *Grapes of Wrath*, when the Okies fled from the dust bowl
of the Middle West to California. In every village, as the morning
light came, people stood in queues before bakers' shops, hoping to
buy something for their children to eat. Every good shop, be it a
bakers or grocers or butchers or greengrocers or general provision
sellers was stripped bare of produce, its windows empty. In
farmhouse courtyards exhausted children slept under haycarts,
whilst haggard women queued to get water from farm pumps. In
one village a group of soldiers were carrying in a blanket the body
of a seventy-year-old woman who had died of exposure when caught
in a thunderstorm during the night. The storms had missed us, but
had hit other regions, and continued throughout the next day,
soaking the trampling columns, drenching the mattresses and the
bags piled on the tops of cars.

The rest of the road to Tours was marked for me by dark-eyed,
tired children staring from the interior of darkened lorries and of
crowded cars as the line of traffic moved a few paces, and then
jerked to yet another stop. At one place a girl of nine was watching
over five other children in a broken-down car. Their mother had
gone off two hours before in search of food and help. Every half mile
broken-down cars had been tipped into ditches to clear the road. In
one village I met a journalist from *L'Ordre*. He told me that in the
wood where they had camped the night before they were awakened

by shrieks from a ten-year-old boy who rushed towards them shouting, 'Mama is dying; Mama is dying.' They found the mother twenty yards away, lying under a bush, beginning to give birth to a child. They had walked the two miles to this village in search, but no doctor was available, and only now, nine hours later, was a midwife on her way. The woman had lain in her suffering all the night, whilst one air-raid alarm followed another, and anti-aircraft shells burst overhead.

In another village I caught up with a big car in which were travelling a Belgian senator and his wife and his beautiful, dark-haired daughter. I had last seen him in Brussels in April, when he had given me a lift from the Senate in this same car. Now they had not eaten for forty-eight hours. When I gave them a tin of sardines and a loaf from our carefully hoarded stores they wept with gratitude.

As I spoke to them the column pressed on unceasingly past us, with the stench of petrol fumes filling the air, and the cries of whimpering children rising above the sound of the engines. Seen from the roadside, one aspect of it caught my eye. Many, if not most of the drivers were women. This was the women's evacuation. Their men were mobilised, and it was now the mothers and aunts and sisters who, set-faced and pale with exhaustion, tried to carry their families to safety. I began my story from Tours that evening – a story Christiansen, never one to underplay the work of his reporters, billed as 'the greatest and most moving of the war' – with the words, 'Through the green fields of the Loire and the Touraine today the mass evacuation from Paris produced scenes the world has not known since the days when Londoners fled the city at the time of the Great Plague, and roamed the countryside.' I concluded with this wording, 'When war hits England we must prepare schemes to avoid this evacuation ordeal for our people. For it is almost the ghastliest thing of modern war – worse certainly than any bombing I have seen.'

Tours was a madhouse. Into this provincial town, built beside the wide Loire, with its sandbanks and its brown swift waters and its narrow stone bridges, had poured – and continued to pour – hundreds of thousands of refugees. It seemed as if half of Paris had fled here. In the late morning we crawled, part of this endless procession, past the airfield where bomb holes showed in the nearby fields and as newly repaired patches on the field itself. We crept over the chief bridge, merely two traffic lanes wide, which spanned the

Loire into the city, and which bore the name of President Wilson, whose ramshackle handiwork at the end of World War I was now crashing about our ears. Along the narrow main street we inched our way to the Hôtel Univers, where our one precious room was being guarded by Stephen Charing. The hotel lobby was crowded with deputies and senators, many of them old, grey-haired men who had never known a day's discomfort in their lives, and who whimpered and growled because there were no rooms available, and because they had to queue to get into the restaurant.

On the wide pavement of the boulevard outside mothers with children wept because the bakers' shops were sold out, the *crêmeries* had no milk, their cars had no petrol. It was like a mad transformation of Derby Day, with people everywhere, jostling you, imploring you, harrying you, and always with their eyes on the sky beyond the rooftops in case the bombers should come. We hardly cared, in the midst of this, when we learnt that Italy too had declared war. Yet it was against this background of suffering and confusion that the Government was expecting to function, and the Cabinet to deliberate on the conduct of the war.

The censorship and Press Wireless were installed in the old telephone building, a ramshackle structure in a side street which would have been knocked over by one puff of bomb blast. Havas were already installed on the ground floor, with Reuters alongside them, and the Belgian Government censors, still eager to function. Here too gathered our colleagues. Edgar Mowrer, his hair as ever tousled, his eyes ablaze, aghast at the collapse of yet one more democracy; the red-haired H. R. Knickerbocker, with his pale horn rimmed spectacles, calm, judicial, efficient; Alexander Werth of the *Manchester Guardian*; Cadett; and William Forrest − the BEF had got him and the other war correspondents away safely from Belgium. He had flown in that morning from London along with the pregnant wife of a British consul in the south of France, whom the Foreign Office had assured that all was quiet, and that she would be quite safe to come.

Through the crowded, chaotic streets of Tours drove that afternoon a small procession which looked as if it had been introduced by a Hollywood director who was determined that his war picture was going to have a touch of glamour, however improbable or unrealistic it might seem. Up to the Univers came a line of ambulances and cars each driven by a cool and beautiful young woman, her carefully made up face all the more striking because of her superbly tailored khaki uniform and her elegant khaki cap. This was the Mechanised Transport Corps, a British volunteer unit into which fashionable young London had flocked. Their commander, Mrs MacDonald, had been publicity manager for Elizabeth Arden in South America. Now, with pale blue hair, self possessed and competent, she might have stepped from one of her own advertisements. George Millar's wife Netty had joined the MTC during the winter, and we searched the column for her, but she was with a separate unit which had moved south on another road.

We had been unable to find rooms in Tours for ourselves, but had secured three in a village on the outskirts. We gave up two of these to MTC drivers who themselves had no billet, and slept in the other ourselves. Jerome Willis was unlucky. He lost the toss and slept on the wire mattress. Millar and I had the two kapok mattresses on the floor.

We woke in the morning to find ourselves in a yellow stone village with green lime trees, and a Mairie where the town clerk tried to have us arrested because we had not had our identity cards signed by the police before we left Paris. But we left him expostulating by the kerbside, and drove back to Tours. The village was on the north bank, which meant we had to cross on one of the only two bridges. It took us half an hour to make our way yard by yard across the bridge, caught in a target exposed to the enemy planes which droned in the hazy sky above. In the city itself the refugees were everywhere – on pavements, in parks, in doorways, under the trees of the boulevards, more numerous, more exhausted, hungrier, more desperate than ever. Yet in the hall of the Univers Provoust was sitting, cool and confident, as if Tours had always been the capital, and the rest of us were all making a most unnecessary fuss.

We were falsely over-confident ourselves. On this Wednesday morning the Germans had not yet taken Paris, the Panzers were still one hundred and fifty miles to the north, and we assumed – as Churchill had done – that somewhere the French High Command still possessed reserves to throw into the battle, that *masse de manoeuvre* about which the British Prime Minister had queried Gamelin – only to meet the response '*Aucune*'. We had passed on our drive south British reinforcements, red-faced, confident boys, moving towards the Seine, and had seen reformed Belgian units waiting behind their Bofors guns by the roadside. So we settled down to write our stories at the desks provided for us in the shaky telephone building, and paperhangers came in and started to redecorate the walls.

Came Thursday, and the bombers, and Churchill. He and Halifax and Beaverbrook (transfigured now into the highly belligerent Minister of Aircraft Production) arrived during the morning at the bomb-pitted Tours airfield, and spent the afternoon in discussions with Reynaud and French Ministers in the city's Préfecture. Churchill, we learnt, had asked for an undertaking that the French would fight on. Fight on? Was there any doubt that they would? Had events reached that stage? I found it difficult to believe, until in a corner of the lounge of the Univers I came across an old French journalist with whom I had often talked in the lobby of the Chamber of Deputies. As a young infantryman, he had been one of those brought out by taxicab from Paris to be hurled against the flank of the German army advancing on the city in 1914. Now he suddenly clutched my arm, and with tears pouring from his eyes said, '*Ah, mon cher Cox, la France est finie, finie.*' Half an hour later he sought me out, and apologised, no doubt lest he be accused of defeatism. But his apology was mere form. If old Max felt like that, how much more sure would these doddering senators and their fussy, over-dressed wives and their scurrying secretaries be that France was finished?

And in the press room the first of the anecdotes about Hélène de Portes' malign influence was being recounted. She had, it was said, slammed the door of Reynaud's office in Halifax's face with the words, 'Come in only if you want to talk peace.' There is no proof that anything of the kind happened, yet the story, though untrue in itself, expressed a truth – that the Countess was now harrying Reynaud at every turn to make peace.

I had had to deal with these stories in the intervals of grappling with an exasperating administrative problem. That morning I had been standing in front of the Univers when a Paris taxi drew up. Its top was loaded with luggage, and through its windows peered the faces of Mara Scherbatoff and her sisters. All four of them and their old Swiss governess-nurse had at the last moment decided to flee. They were a heavy extra responsibility, made the less easy to bear because had they accepted the alternative plans I had made for them with *Paris Soir* they would now be in safety and comfort at Clermont Ferrand. There was nothing for it but for me to offload them into the Renault – the taxi driver was determined to return to Paris – battle my way across the bridge with them to our village billet, find rooms for them there, and make the slow, dangerous return journey into the city, along streets paralysed now by air raids. I was in no mood that evening to provide an audience for Delmer, who had arrived from Paris with an account of the superb lunch he and Eddie Ward had had in Maxims before, as the last British correspondents to leave the city, they had taken the road to Tours. The walls of the crowded hotel bar seemed paper thin as the bombers roared overhead, and the explosions from yet one more raid on the airport shook the town.

The first official confirmation of the seriousness was the situation that came late in the afternoon, when a new military spokesman, a young Chasseur Alpine officer, Major Vautrin, set out the facts with remarkable frankness. The reason, we later realised, was that Paul Reynaud had appealed to Roosevelt for help, and wanted France's danger to be made clear to the United States. The Germans, Vautrin told us, had flung over 110 divisions into this new battle. The French had less than half that number in the field. British forces were fighting stubbornly on the French left, along the Seine, German tanks outnumbered the French by three to one. Paris had been declared an open city, and was to be surrendered without resistance. On the Maginot Line the fighting was very heavy. At last we had something definite to write, and no longer to contrive to make our daily bricks without straw. How much more sensible it would have been had a comparable candour prevailed during the earlier days, when rumour and half truths had fed panic, and set the refugees stampeding from their homes.

On the morning of Friday the 14th Colonel Thomas turned up again and confirmed that the Germans had Paris and were advancing on Châtres. By midday the censors were packing, and Press Wireless was gathering together its gear, and everyone was off to Bordeaux. The Government had already moved there. Tours was too exposed, too full of refugees. The folly of not going from Paris to Bordeaux in one step was exposed. At Bordeaux the Cabinet would have had the navy at their back, and they would have been spared this endless, unnerving spectacle of the nation in flight, the endless weariness of waiting for meals in overcrowded restaurants, of the din and shoving and thrusting of crowds, and the cries of tired children and the faces of tired mothers.

I went to the telephone building at midday, in the hope of getting away a message to London. It was deserted except for the paper-hangers. Futility of futilities, they were still redecorating the walls.

We decided to leave for Bordeaux at seven that night. Delmer took his wife and Jerome Willis in the smaller car. George Millar and I and the four Scherbatoff sisters and their governess crowded into the big Renault, with their luggage tied on top and crammed into the boot.

This was a different type of withdrawal. We were no longer moving back to find a new base from which to cover the war. France, it was clear, would soon give up the fight, and we must now find a means of escape to Britain. It could only be by sea. Any other route except through Spain would be closed by the advancing Germans – and Franco's Spain would never give me a visa. Yet we first had to make it to Bordeaux. Though we had worked out a route on side roads which were remarkably free of traffic, it soon became clear that the car was heavily overloaded. It was well down on its springs, and we could move only slowly. More ominously, one tyre kept losing pressure, and we had to stop at intervals to blow it up. Finally at three in the morning, when we were halted by a police barrier on the outskirts of Poitiers, it blew out.

As we worked to change the wheel, I put the issue to Scherb. If she and her sisters wanted to be evacuated to Britain, I would keep going as we were, and get them through somehow to Bordeaux. But if they intended to stay in France once the fighting stopped, there was no point in them going further than Poitiers. They would be as safe there as in Bordeaux – safer, indeed, for the chances of bombing would be less, and they would be closer to Paris when the time came to return. In floods of Russian the sisters debated the question. Only when we reached the centre of Poitiers did Mara Scherbatoff suddenly say, 'We will stop here.' I found them beds in a large hotel in the city centre which had set up a dormitory in its ballroom. We reached it through a surrealist setting. The hotel was being modernised, and the long, glassed-in corridor leading to the ballroom was lined with row upon row of new lavatory pans, fifty or more of them, like parading troops.

Scherb had made a wise decision. She and her family were back in Paris within a month. Their flat was intact, and they spent the war safely there, troubled by food shortages – but no worse than they would have known in Britain – and free from bombing. After Paris was freed Mara Scherbatoff met and married an American general, went to the States with him, and became a journalist in her own right in the New York office of *Paris Match*. My final sight of her was tragically unexpected. In the summer of 1956, she was killed in a road accident whilst driving to report on Arthur Miller's marriage to Marilyn Monroe. A television news cameraman filmed her body by the roadside. Watching rushes in the projection theatre at ITN in Kingsway, I suddenly saw her face on the screen, on the grass verge of an American freeway, with cars moving swiftly in the background, sixteen years on from the early morning on which our working lives had parted in Poitiers.

Millar and I drove on southwards in the grey half light. All along the roadside cars were dotted, with families sleeping in or around them. As dawn came one after another gathered its belongings and started again on this seemingly endless journey. Traffic was as yet light, and the drivers drove at speed, with tired, set faces, racing to the next village to try to get petrol, to try to get food, housing, rest. On and on went this procession. We stopped ourselves to sleep for an hour. We fell asleep and woke to the roar of cars, leaving their stink of petrol over the fresh countryside. It was a nightmare of exhaustion, with people pressing on, on, uncertain where to go, leaderless, without news – for there were no car radios then – without advice, a nation disintegrating into a mass of squabbling, exhausted, desperate individuals at the one time when it needed cohesion in the face of an enemy.

As the sun rose, to bring one more glorious day, we found ourselves in rich, rolling country, lush with grass and trees and old farmhouses. With only ourselves now to fend for, I felt a sudden sense of relief, almost of exaltation, even though we had no certainty that Bordeaux might not prove a trap rather than a way of escape. We got petrol from a roadside pump, served by a woman impressed by Millar's spick and span uniform. When she found that we had no certificates for it she was furious, but we thrust the money into her hand and drove on. By midday we were in Bordeaux.

CHAPTER TWENTY-THREE

An End and a Beginning

Bordeaux was another, larger, more crowded Tours. There were no rooms to be had, not even a sofa in an hotel lounge. On the steps of the Café Bordeaux in the centre of the town stood a familiar figure. It was Colonel Thomas, grey-faced, tragic. He nodded to us stiffly.

A few minutes later a big car drove up outside the Hôtel Splendide near by. Troops on motor cycles who had escorted it rushed to the hotel door to form a cordon. A small figure in uniform strode briskly into the hotel, his lean face set, unworried. A woman cried 'Weygand, Weygand' and the crowd clapped. The Generalissimo had arrived for the last two decisive Cabinet meetings.

Behind a cordon of sloppy, young Senegalese troops, their black faces vacant under their steel helmets, the first Cabinet meeting was held that afternoon. We waited in the Trade Union building, which had been made a press headquarters. Black clouds massed overhead, and suddenly peal after peal of thunder crashed out. An aeroplane flew across the storm towards the airport. It was a setting worthy of a Greek tragedy, worthy of these dying days of this France.

We knew that we must now plan our escape. The British consulate, close to the quayside by the wide River Garonne, was already besieged by people trying to get away from France. Frenchmen, Poles, Belgians, Britons crowded the staircase leading to the consulate offices on the first floor, packed the waiting-rooms and hallways, pleading for visas, for passages on ships, for information. Fear and despair filled the air. The consul could give us little help. A British destroyer, her grey masts and superstructure clear above the waterside warehouses, was in the Gironde, but would have space only for British diplomats and military men. Other ships had been called for, but there was no certainty when or even whether they would arrive.

Meanwhile the Cabinet meeting went on. We thought that this

211

was to decide whether the French should fight on in France, or move to Algeria, which was legally part of Metropolitan France, and continue the battle from there. But events had already raced past that point. Now the argument was whether to fight on at all. Reynaud wanted to continue the struggle from North Africa. Against him now were ranged, we were told, not only the less resolute civilian ministers like Chautemps, but also Pétain and Weygand. Weygand, it was said, had at the start of the Cabinet meeting flung open his hands and stated, 'Gentlemen, the armies are beaten.'

Throughout that afternoon the argument for peace grew steadily. Reynaud, supported by Mandel, hung on, and at seven o'clock the meeting agreed to defer a decision until the next day, when they would have before them a reply from Roosevelt to Reynaud's appeal for American help.

Meanwhile, by one of the extraordinary coincidences of war, George Millar had that afternoon come face to face with his wife in a street in Bordeaux, the first time he had seen her since Paris. Netty was tired, and her MTC uniform dusty and crumpled. The unit she had been with had been overrun by the Germans, and she and another girl had escaped through the German forward posts in a car which they hid by day and drove by night. But by evening, neat and elegant as ever, she was ready to dine with us at the Chapon Fin as if she had just arrived by air from London.

The Chapon Fin was one of the great restaurants not only of France, but of the world, and its tables that evening were thronged by Cabinet Ministers and ambassadors, generals and admirals, and the vivid women who in France never seemed far from the centre of power. A menu the size of a newspaper page offered the *specialités de la région*, and the incomparable red wines of the Garonne valley. Laval was there, swarthy and sinister, wearing his customary white tie, and looking far too pleased for our comfort. At a table in the centre of the room the British Ambassador, Sir Ronald Campbell, and the chief British Liaison Officer, General Spears, dined with their staffs. In another corner a noisy group of expatriate Britons had just arrived by car from the Riviera, where they had been helping the war effort by eating French food rather than returning to eat rationed foods in Britain. Now with Italy in the war, they were making a bolt for home. Gold, diamonds, pearls glowed and glittered against suntanned faces above superb Worth and Molyneux gowns. Arrogant, raucous voices rang out across the room, scorning France in defeat, and proclaiming that she had had this coming to her ever since the Reds got power during the Popular Front.

We slept well that night, underneath the wide stairway leading up to the British consulate. I had noticed a substantial, well-protected area there, in which we spread out our sleeping-bags. It was against the rules, but no one discovered us except a friendly RAMC sergeant who was acting as caretaker, and who rushed downstairs with a rifle when, in the dark, I broke a glass panel in the nearby lavatory door. Reasonably rested, washed and shaved, we came out the next morning into the overcrowded, sleepless city whose nerves were worn bare, almost bleeding.

On the terrace of the Hôtel Splendide deputies and senators, editors, army officers and businessmen, and their wives and mistresses, weary after broken sleep on hotel floors or in the backs of cars, waited still more wearily for coffee and news. Above all, for news. All Paris seemed to be there. Pierre Lazareff, tired, mal-shaven, but still energetic, was talking to Prouvost – '*le patron*' as they termed him on *Paris Soir*. It would be no fun for Lazareff if France surrendered. His name had been on a list of those who were to be the first arrested which had been found on the body of a dead German police officer outside Paris. Tabouis was there, for the first time looking elderly, very pale as she walked along on the arm of her young husband. Pertinax, monocle in eye, was talking tensely to the burly Emil Buré, that staunchest of supporters of Reynaud. Campinchi, Lous Marin, Admiral Darlan came and went. It was the last parade of the Third Republic.

Morning and evening the Cabinet met, while we searched the docks for possible British ships to get to England on, and harried the consulate to make arrangements for us. All sorts of British people were pouring in now. Under the trees outside the consulate waited a detachment of infantry in battle dress, cut off in the south. Half-a-dozen RAF pilots turned up, a group of naval officers, the whole of the MTC, more Riviera-ites.

Steadily but definitely during that day you could feel anti-British feeling grow in Bordeaux. Stunned by their sufferings and the steady realisation of defeat, the French looked round angrily at their Allies and particularly at those Allies preparing to get away. Opposite the consulate a small hostile crowd gathered, staring at the British refugees coming and going. We still had one more chance. Theirs was finished – unless they chose to risk everything and fight on. But the possibility that they would do so diminished with every hour that passed.

Against Reynaud the whole weight of Pétain, Weygand and M Lebrun, the President, was thrown. Pétain, already eighty-four, was physically and nervously worn out by the strain of this journey to Tours and Bordeaux. His mind, full from the days of Verdun with pictures of suffering, recoiled from the horror of the stampede from Paris. He had seen how Verdun brought a mutiny of 700,000 men. This might bring revolution inside France. The businessmen inside the Cabinet – Prouvost, Pomaret and their like – supported him. They wanted their property back, whether under the Germans or not. Weygand said the armies were done. A rigid, aesthetic Catholic who detested democracy at bottom, he believed France must be purified by suffering, that she had been slack and godless since the last war. And he chose the sufferings of defeat rather than the sufferings of continued struggle.

He too believed in the dangers of a Communist revolt if the war continued. I did not see any evidence for this possibility. During the last days in Paris I had made contact with the underground organisation of the banned Communist Party. Though they were strongly against the war they knew that to try to revolt at the moment when the Reichswehr were spreading all over France was a pipe dream. Their main leaders were already in prison, arrested by the Daladier Government in the violent anti-Communist drive carried out in the early days of the war. Most importantly of all, Stalin was at this stage appeasing Hitler, and kept the brakes firmly on the French Party.

Above all Pétain believed that if he became Premier and sued for peace, France would get better treatment and would retain more of her independence. Hitler the soldier would accord respect to Pétain the soldier.

Just before ten o'clock that evening the final vote was taken. Fourteen members of the Cabinet voted for peace, for an immediate armistice. Reynaud and nine others voted to continue the struggle. When the final result was announced, the staunch old Conservative, Louis Marin, in tears, opened his hands and, staring at Pétain, said bitterly: 'Gentlemen, I am ashamed to be a Frenchman.'

A few minutes after ten I was eating supper in the Hôtel Splendide when Charles Gombaux appeared in the doorway. 'Reynaud has resigned. Pétain has taken over,' he said. We rushed round to the Préfecture and asked for Mandel. Cool, inscrutable as a buddha, he confirmed the news. He displayed no emotion, this man who from within the innermost ranks of power had seen one war won and another lost. He had been the trusted aide to Clemenceau, the fiery old man who had held France together, and brought her to victory in 1918. Mandel had stood by Clemenceau's side at the Arc de Triomphe during the victory parade of 1919. On this sultry evening twenty one years later he must have known that, as a Jew, he faced great personal danger in a defeated France – and indeed, four years later, a prisoner of Pétain's Vichy Government, he was murdered by their Milices, their French stormtroopers. Yet at this moment I could detect no trace of fear on his pale, drawn countenance.

Exhausted, I returned to the consulate and settled down to sleep again under the stairs. I was woken an hour or so later by sounds of a row on the stairway. A voice, easily identifiable as that of one of the most assertive of the refugees from the Riviera who had behaved so crudely the night before in the Chapon Fin, was shrieking, 'Your wife called me a drunken whore. Do you hear me? Your wife called me a drunken whore.' I could not see who replied, but his riposte was swift. 'And are you?' he queried.

An hour or two later, I was wakened again by the voices of naval officers seeking the consul. They cursed him heartily for not being on the premises – he had apparently a code they wanted – and for not leaving any official in charge at this moment of crisis. The officers' confident, cheerful voices were like music in this atmosphere of indecision. If the navy was here, and taking over, we should get away before the German army arrived. My guess was right. By nine o'clock the next morning the consulate was functioning like a new concern. We were told to get down to Le Verdon, at the tip of the southern peninsula on the Bordeaux Estuary, and embark there.

De Caux was breakfasting calmly on the terrace of the Hôtel Splendide. We stopped the car to say good-bye to him, and to Eric Sevareid, who was standing by to report to America the speech Pétain was due to make on the radio at noon, the speech in which he was to utter the chilling words '*il faut cesser le combat*'. We drove north through flat country rich with vineyards. Mouton Rothschild and Château Latour, Margaux and St Julien proclaimed themselves on roadside signs. At Le Verdon a naval cutter was waiting close by the memorial commemorating the first landing of American troops in the 1914–18 war. Netty and George and I piled our luggage into it, left the car on the quayside, and were ferried to where the SS *Madura* lay in mid-stream.

The *Madura* was a 7,000-ton P and O liner, a smaller version of the ship on which I had travelled from Sydney eight years earlier. She had been on her way from East Africa with 120 passengers, mostly Empire builders and Empire maintainers coming on leave, when she had been diverted to the Gironde. On to her in the next twenty-four hours were to be crammed a further 1,623 people. Ambassadors, ex-premiers, ex-cabinet ministers from France, Holland, Belgium, Poland crowded in with journalists, the Riviera gang, bank officials, stray Britons from all over France, and French men and women who either feared the Nazis or were, like Eve Curie, determined to continue the resistance. That evening bombs were dropped just to our stern, throwing up great white cascades, in a series of air raids in which, to the north, the Cunard-White Star liner *Lancastria*, with some 6,000 British troops on board, was sunk, with some 4,000 men drowned. There was another attack on the *Madura* the next evening, but it was beaten off by the guns of the cruiser HMS *Arethusa*, which had drawn in alongside us. An hour later we drew out into the Atlantic, followed by another P and O liner on which were Embassy officials, the MTC, a number of British troops, and some star refugees like Madame Tabouis – I could see her thin form leaning on the rail – and Pertinax.

We spread our sleeping-bags on the boat deck. Every yard of deck space was covered with sleeping bodies. We mounted anti-U-boat watches in relays throughout the night, and again throughout the long sunny day which followed. In the intervals of taking our turn, George Millar and I discussed our futures. We were both sure we had to join the army. He would enlist in a Scottish regiment. With no New Zealand unit apparently open to me, I would opt for an English regiment.

'We have to accept that war is a much more normal part of life than we have been taught,' George argued. 'Mahbub the Pathan in Kipling's *Kim* had shot his man and begot his man by the time he was sixteen. Maybe we have to begin to think in those terms.'

At eleven that morning two grey shapes showed on the horizon, white bow waves racing with them. They were British destroyers. Gracefully they slipped into position ahead of us, weaving to and fro, a reassuring presence. The next morning we woke to see the coast of Cornwall, and soon Falmouth, its harbour crammed with ships which had escaped from France.

It was a superb day of high summer, and on the green headland above the harbour they were stacking hay, loading it by pitchfork on to big wagons, as we had so often done in New Zealand. A grey church tower rose above thick green trees. Even the close-packed suburban roofs around Falmouth had a warm beauty. That afternoon England looked very much worth fighting for. Now that we were on our own, the war seemed not only a struggle against an evil creed but also a matter of straightforward patriotism.

We moored alongside in the late afternoon. There was still time for us to get our stories to the papers in time for tomorrow's editions if we got off immediately. The American correspondents, aware of their country's hunger for news about the last hours of France, were particularly anxious to get ashore. But the authorities were not to be hurried. Journalists could wait their turn, and that turn came well below those of the diplomats. First off must be the consul's party – amongst whom, I noted, many of the Riviera gang were now included. Their luggage had to be sorted out from amongst the massed baggage on the deck. 'The little green hat case, and the pigskin suitcase next to it. Yes, that's it, old chap,' the clear, untroubled voice called as the slings were slowly and carefully loaded. Minute by minute our edition times ticked away. I watched H. R. Knickerbocker's face. He was a good friend of Britain. What he had to write could help, at this crucial stage, to win or hold us vital friends in America. Weariness, and a scorn close to disgust showed on it. His edition times were going too.

At last we were ashore. In a Falmouth hotel that night I listened to the BBC News. France was suing for an armistice. Australian and New Zealand troops had disembarked in Britain, and were now stationed to help resist invasion. Here was my opportunity. A month later I was marching along a Surrey road in battle dress and steel helmet, with familiar New Zealand voices around me, a rifle slung on my shoulder, and live ammunition in my webbing pouches. For all the perils ahead, my mind was more at ease than at any time during these years when I had watched us slip into this gulf of danger.

As It Looks Now

The war which in that spring and summer of 1940 had got into its full stride was to last in Europe for five more years. Its aftermath of upheavals, suffering and minor wars was to continue over at least the next decade. Those who were caught up in it were too absorbed by its immediate problems and horrors to think much about how it had come about, and whether it might have been avoided. Yet one great issue of the time continues to tantalise historians. Of all the 'Ifs' of history, one will continue to pose itself to those who lived through the Thirties. If Britain had stood firm in September 1938, and had given the Czechs the support they sought, and given the French Government the backbone which they − but not the French people − lacked, would we have halted Hitler without war, or at least fought him on more favourable terms?

As the dust of events has settled in the intervening fifty years, it is clear that the last chance to have checked Hitler without risk of war occurred in March 1936, when he sent his troops into the demilitarised zone of the Rhineland. The obligation not to fortify the left bank of the Rhine, or to station troops within fifty kilometres of its right bank, had first been imposed upon Germany in the Treaty of Versailles. But it had been freely accepted by an elected German Government in 1925, as part of the Locarno Treaty, designed to avoid a new war breaking out in Europe. Now Hitler had spurned these undertakings. His order to his troops to march into the Rhineland on 7 March 1936 was the first occasion on which he had openly repudiated an international treaty.

The first reaction of the French Government was that they should order the mobilisation of the French army and demand that Hitler withdraw his forces. At the time the French army was overwhelmingly stronger than the Reichswehr, and had it been mobilised Hitler would have had no option but to withdraw, with damaging consequences not only to his prestige but to his confidence. But the British Government, under Stanley Baldwin, urged the French to do nothing more than refer the matter to the League of Nations − a League which was proving itself impotent

218

to halt Mussolini in Abyssinia. The opportunity passed. The French did no more than protest, and Hitler was left with his triumph.

Baldwin's attitude met with widespread public approval in Britain, with Winston Churchill once again as almost a lone voice warning of the dangers of letting the Germans trample on their freely given undertakings. Most British people echoed Lord Lothian's view that 'after all, the Germans are only going into their back yard'. This apathy and readiness to yield was in sharp contrast to the mood the previous autumn, when Britain had strongly endorsed, and indeed advocated, the League of Nations' plan for sanctions against Italy for her invasion of Abyssinia. This had tapped a vein not only of patriotism, but also of idealism in support of a new international order. Those of us who were of fighting age reconciled ourselves to the possibility of being called up. In the news room of the *News Chronicle*, for which I was working at the time, we discussed which branch of the Services we might find ourselves in. Veterans of the Great War, as we then still called it, advised us whether we would have a better chance of survival in the trenches as ordinary riflemen, or as machine gunners. The office wit coined a recruiting slogan. 'Join up and take a pop at a Wop,' he suggested.

But with the revelation of the Hoare-Laval Pact to carve up much of Abyssinia behind the back of the League of Nations, and the rapid failure of the half-hearted sanctions, cynicism spread. If Britain was not prepared to stand up against a blatant war waged against a primitive people, whose country was a member of the League of Nations, there seemed little reason to go to arms against the Germans for asserting themselves within their own borders. The opportunity to take this stand against Hitler whilst all the odds were still in our favour passed almost unnoticed.

But the Anschluss of Germany and Austria two years later was a very different matter. It was clearly the outcome of intimidation and of force, of the ruthless bullying by Hitler of the Austrian Chancellor, Kurt von Schuschnigg, and of the massing of German troops along the Austrian frontiers. Schuschnigg resigned rather than either yield to Hitler's demands for a merger of the two states, or shed German and Austrian blood by resisting them, and a new, pro-Nazi Austrian Government gave way, providing a transparently thin cloak of legality for what Churchill termed 'the rape of Austria'. Once again Britain and France did nothing but protest. We had the excuse that Schuschnigg, hoping to the end to save something of his country's independence, deliberately played down to the outside world the nature of Hitler's threats – until it was too late.

Yet if the Anschluss provided no opportunity for us to intervene, even if we had been so minded, it did provide a striking opportunity for the British Government to warn the British people of the true nature of Nazism, and prepare the country for the dangers which lay ahead. For the incorporation of Austria into the Reich meant that Hitler had broken his word. He had solemnly declared, after he had seized the Rhineland, that 'Germany neither intends . . . to annex Austria, or to conclude an Anschluss'. Here was the clearest proof that his assurances could not be trusted. The spectacle of the German army on the march, even in those pre-television days, had also provided vivid proof of Hitler's readiness to use force to impose his will. But Neville Chamberlain, who had taken over by then as Prime Minister, sounded no such alarm. Though he did something to speed up our limping rearmament programme, his main reaction to the Anschluss was to get ready to appease Hitler by clearing the way for him to secure his next objective, that of bringing the three million people of German stock, who lived in the Sudeten area of Czechoslovakia, within the borders of the Reich. Far from warning the British public of the dangers ahead, Chamberlain – and Beaverbrook – did their utmost to lull them into the belief that what happened in distant Czechoslovakia need not concern them. Only when, at Godesberg, Hitler's demands went beyond what even Chamberlain then felt reasonable (though he was to change his mind, and concede everything at Munich five days later) did the Prime Minister set about preparing the British public, almost overnight, for war.

Should we have stood firm, and refused to yield at Munich, even if that had meant war? At the time I had no doubt that we should have done so. My reasons were not based on any fine calculations of the relative strengths of either side, information available then only to the inner circles of the Military and of the Government, but on an instinctive feeling that Hitler would have to be faced, and it was better to do this sooner than later. An impressive volume of evidence has since emerged to show that this attitude made good sense. Much of this evidence came from the German files seized by the victorious Allies. Other material came from statements at the Nuremberg War Crime trials. Though in the year between Munich and the outbreak of war we improved markedly our armaments and our preparations, the Germans improved theirs even more markedly. In the field of weaponry much play is made by those who seek to justify Chamberlain's policy at Munich of the fact that in those intervening twelve months the Spitfire and the Hurricane fighters came fully into service. At the time of Munich only five RAF squadrons were equipped with Hurricanes: none yet had Spitfires. These were the planes which were to win the Battle of Britain in 1940. But no Battle of Britain could have been fought in 1938, nor any massive bomber raids mounted against English cities, unless the Germans had won airfields in the Low Countries and Northern France. To do that, the German army would have had to overthrow the French army. Yet in 1938 the Germans were not in a position to do this. They did not yet have enough tanks, of sufficient size and armament, to dominate the battlefield. In a war in the autumn of 1938 the French superiority in artillery, resting on the famous 75-mm guns of World War I, would probably have been decisive. Winston Churchill, writing in 1948, with all the experience of World War II to call upon, declared categorically, 'The German armies were not capable of defeating the French in 1938 or 1939.'[1] Another factor in the equation was the shift of Czechoslovak military might from our side to the Germans. By abandoning Czechoslovakia we lost the 35 Czechoslovak divisions, whilst the Germans gained not only the powerful Czech armament industry, based on the Skoda works, but laid their hands on Czechoslovakia's high-grade tanks. A considerable portion of the front-line tanks employed by the Wehrmacht to break through on the Western front in the spring of 1940 were drawn from the disbanded Czech armoured divisions.

The one gain which Chamberlain secured from Munich was that when war came in 1939 the British people, and those of the Commonwealth, entered it fully united, convinced not only of the rightness of their cause, but also of the fact that no other course had been open to them. We had leaned over backwards to meet Hitler's demands, in an effort to avoid war. When, despite all we had conceded, war came, no one could have any doubt that it was not only right, but inescapable. This was of immeasurable value in uniting the country and in sustaining morale throughout the long, dark years of war. Such unanimity did not exist in September 1938. A sustained policy of educating the public in the reality of Hitlerism, in the fact that gathering all people of German race within the Reich was not an end in itself, but a means to domination of Europe,

[1] *The Gathering Storm*. Cassell, 1948, p. 304.

might have done much to convince people, by the time of Munich, that we should fight. But no such campaign was undertaken by the Government, and even Churchill's eloquence was not enough to convince the public that appeasement would not work. It took the Nazi seizure of Prague in the spring of 1939, and the invasion of Poland on September 1 that year, to demonstrate beyond doubt what Hitler and Nazism, truly were. Perhaps it is an inescapable fact that a democracy can only learn such lessons the hard way, by what happens rather than what people are told.

Yet it is the duty of the leaders of a Parliamentary democracy, equipped as they are with a mass of military and diplomatic information, to warn the public of what lies ahead, and to prepare the country to face it. On this count both Baldwin and Chamberlain failed the British people. Understandably reluctant to contemplate the horrors of another European war, and grappling with the problems of the Great Slump, Baldwin averted his gaze from the dangers of Hitlerism as long as he could. Yet the evidence of Hitler's aims was clear. It was set out in *Mein Kampf*. It was contained in his speeches, and in the reports of knowledgeable diplomats. But Chamberlain spurned all this. Confident he could do a deal with Hitler, and relying on the views of the British Ambassador in Berlin, Sir Nevile Henderson, who put a favourable gloss on everything the Nazis said or did, Chamberlain not only failed to alert the British people to what might happen, but refused himself to recognise the ugly possibilities of Hitlerism, possibilities which his own actions were to help transform into probabilities.

This attitude led Neville Chamberlain, in the spring and summer of 1938, to spurn pleas which reached him from senior military men in Germany that he should stand against Hitler's pressure on Czechoslovakia. In 1945, when the long slaughter had ground to its close, and the enemies were free to speak, General von Halder, who had been Chief of the German General Staff in 1939, declared that he and a number of other generals had made plans to arrest Hitler, Goering, Goebbels and Himmler, and set up a military government in their stead, if Hitler persisted with his plan to seize the Sudetenland on October 1. Von Halder argued that they were on the point of acting when Chamberlain set out on his first mission to Berchtesgaden. If Hitler could gain a victory by bluff, without having to resort to war, then their plot had no point.

How valid this claim is can never be established. Sir Winston Churchill, in *The Gathering Storm*, recounts it, and contents himself with describing it as a tale 'which the historians should probe'. The outlines of the plot were known to the British Government in September 1938, for the conspirators sent emissaries to London who were seen not only by Churchill, but by the Foreign Secretary, Lord Halifax. The reports of these messengers were no doubt too insubstantial for British policy to be based upon them, but they were one more argument for a strong rather than a weak line.

In the end the British Government's decisions in September 1938 turned above all on one factor – an estimate of Hitler's true character and aims. Chamberlain misread both. It was to prove one of history's costliest mistakes.

Index